Praise for

Behind the Scenes

"Such a powerful and transparent collection that showcases the strength and resilience of the military community. Each story takes you on a journey through a military spouse's reality showcasing how they have used their personal experiences in a way that empowers others. The information, tips, and insight in "Behind the Scenes" is invaluable for anyone who has ever wondered what it takes to make a difference."
—Judy Davis - The Direction Diva

"I am not a big reader, but I have to tell you that not only did I read this book once, I read it a second time. As I read it both times, I felt as though I was experiencing what each of the writers experienced. Each story gave me the deep feeling they shared and even more appreciation for those serving, their families and their friends. What a blessing to have them share their life in this book. THANK YOU ALL a million times for your spouse's service and sacrifices. Also, your own sacrifices. WOW, that's all I can say! I have a whole new appreciation to say the least. The organizations that are developed by some of the writers to help others is an inspiration. It's a very inspiring read. I hope all the families know there are so many that admire them and support them." —Dawn Lomax

"Whether you are a newlywed at your first duty station or gearing up for retirement, if you are a military spouse you need this book. You'll laugh, you'll cry, but most importantly you will see that you are never alone in this crazy world called the military. Get involved and make a difference, and learn from spouses who have done it before you." —Robin Pruitt, 2017 Armed Forces Insurance Kentucky National Guard Spouse of the Year

"Behind the Scenes" is an amazing compilation of heartfelt stories from military spouses who are leaders amongst their communities. I found this book to be very poignant look into the heart of volunteerism, entrepreneurship, and the desire and success of military spouses to bring positive change while living a life of commitment to their military service member. I am inspired by these spouses' stories. The stories come from a diverse group of military spouses, but I felt a connection to each story in a personal way." —Heather Smith

Behind the Scenes

The Tales of American Military Spouses
Making a Difference

a military spouse legacy project

Behind the Scenes: The Tales of American Military Spouses Making a Difference, a military spouse legacy project
Copyright © 2017 Cara Loken

Book Cover Design by Brian L. Alvarado
Design and Compiled by Cara Loken
Edited by Sheila N. Rupp
Title and Synopsis by Bianca Strzalkowski

Library of Congress Control Number: 2017910469

ISBN-13: 978-1548103804
ISBN: 1548103802

CreateSpace Independent Publishing Platform
North Charleston, NC

All portions of the proceeds benefit nonprofits and charities chosen by each writer.

DEDICATION

This book is dedicated to the many military spouses around the globe that continue to make impactful contributions in their communities from behind the scenes or boldly out in front. We are inspired by the countless stories of women and men who do so much, even when faced with the challenging aspects of our unique way of life.

To Armed Forces Insurance – you have become so much more than a company to us, you have made us a family. Your continuous support of military families through their hopes and dreams, hardships and trials, while cheering us on reaffirms your authentic commitment. Thank you for making it possible to get these behind the scenes stories in front on people.

Table of Contents

Foreword

Military spouses are capable of anything! Over the years, I've had many wonderful opportunities to build friendships and provide support to some of the strongest, bravest and most compassionate military spouses in the nation. As a former military spouse myself, the ability to continue my passion of serving America's armed forces and their families through my career at Armed Forces Insurance is a true blessing. AFI and I share the same mission at heart: "Our mission is you." And every day, I am grateful to live that through my professional and personal life.

When AFI was founded in 1887 by military leaders, they had one goal in mind: to protect the property of those who protect the nation, and they have remained true to their founding message. Not only that, the company has branched out over the years to provide even more support to the military and their families. As the president of the Armed Forces Insurance Foundation, I've worked to advocate for our military families in a variety of ways, including sitting on the board of some esteemed military spouse organizations and providing education on an array of personal financial topics.

When I look at how the landscape has shifted over the years, from my time as a military spouse to now, I realize that a vast majority of advancements for our military families were made by trailblazing military spouses. Military spouses are the greatest advocates for our armed forces and they are truly the support of the nation. In these pages, you will read their stories – their heartbreaks and their triumphs, the quiet moments when they questioned if they could continue, and the "like a phoenix from the ashes" stories in which they push forward, taking not only themselves as they rise up, but their families, their friends, their communities.

My mission is to support these spouses and their families through the challenges and the successes. I am grateful to introduce these incredible spouses to you, the reader, and hope you are as inspired by their courage and truth as I am.

Lori Simmons

Chief Marking Officer and VP, Marketing & Communications,
    Armed Forces Insurance
President, Armed Forces Insurance Foundation

Odd Man Out

Brian L. Alvarado

The military community is full of diverse life stories. Stories of love and compassion, struggle and sacrifice, and stories of friendship and duty. As military spouses, we each have one of those unique stories. None of us are identical but we do have several qualities in common that we learn and cultivate together. Qualities like leadership, empathy, humor and commitment. Those qualities are the backbone of our survival kit. And as a 38-year-old male military spouse in an interracial, same-sex marriage, I especially rely on that survival kit! I mean, could I be any bigger of an odd one out?

When I first got married to an active duty sailor, I was scared and nervous at the thought of integrating myself into the military community. Even though "Don't Ask, Don't Tell" had been repealed in September 2011, it didn't mean that all of a sudden the military community was going to welcome a gay male spouse with open arms. Right? I remember keeping my head down while shopping on base. I remember that lingering sensation that I didn't belong, that people were staring at me, that I wasn't supposed to be there. (What was I putting myself through?)

One day a friend of mine sent me some information about an organization that supports and advocates for LGBT partners and spouses of service members and veterans. Not knowing anything about being a military spouse, I reached out to that organization and from day one the American Military Partner Association (AMPA) became a resource for me and eventually a source of networking and support. After the shock started to wear off that I wasn't the only odd one out, I started to come out of my shell and interact in discussions in that community and I started to feel a little better.

The personal histories of LGBT military families are full of tragic and painful years of hiding, decades of fear, and lifetimes full of facing hatred. The LGBT community fought hard for equality, and that isn't anything new. We are a nation that is built on long-fought battles for progress. It's how we roll. While there are still some policies that need to be updated, the bulk of the Department of Defense's equality

1

initiatives are in full swing. Operation Change Hearts and Minds is peaking at its success.

It has been just under two years since the United States Supreme Court's 2015 ruling on same-sex marriage equality and six years since the repeal of the "Don't Ask, Don't Tell" policy. The Department of Defense should be proud of the progress that has so quickly been made. The military community is full of new stories of acceptance, new stories of command events celebrating diversity, and new stories of individuals, who otherwise would have stayed in the shadows, now stepping out into the light. (Insert clapping and cheering here). More and more LGBT military spouses are volunteering, participating, and being embraced by the military community.

I started to form a bond with several people within the AMPA community and through their experiences, I started to wonder what I was missing by continuing to be a military spouse that didn't participate in the military community. So many LGBT people had worked hard, and been through horrific scenarios of hate and bigotry so that I now have the opportunity and right to be married to my sailor. One day I realized that with all of those rights also come responsibilities, and I needed to step up and get over myself. I could do this!

That year, my husband Matthew and I agreed we would face our fears by taking a chance and attending a command holiday party. This was the first time in 14 years of active duty service that he had taken anyone to a command event. I was sweating bullets in my tuxedo. I was terrified and my imagination was running wild. My head was full of what-ifs like, would we be bullied, or would we be heckled, or even roughed up. I almost didn't go in, but I put on my big boy pants and walked into that room where an entire command awaited. And my life has never been the same.

We were immediately greeted by a shipmate of Matthew's. She walked up to us and obviously knew Matthew. He introduced her to me. I went to shake her hand but she demanded a hug. There it was, first contact. (For you non-Trekkie readers, that means the first contact with an alien species, which is really what it felt like.) Something about that first contact immediately made me start to release some of the fear and doubt. I will always be thankful to that sailor for being my friend and catalyst into military life.

Beyond that first contact was an entire battalion of sailors, both enlisted and officers, and their spouses who without reservation invited me into the military family and I haven't looked back. I jumped in to volunteer with the Family Readiness Group (FRG), and was quickly voted in as board president. We did a lot of good work to support the families of the command. And yes, this 6'5", 38-year-old grown man finally walks into the commissary by myself and goes grocery shopping. WHAT?!

While serving in the FRG, I had the awesome opportunity to get to know hundreds of sailors and a lot of their families. We started to form bonds with people that we wouldn't normally socialize with because of age differences or other social segregations. One of my favorite stories of truly making a difference comes during this time. I met a young spouse at a command event one day and then noticed her at several other events and we eventually started to talk and get to know each other. She told me one day that she was having a really difficult time finding a job. She wanted to do something challenging that would give her professional experience while she continued to work on getting a degree. She was young, unexperienced, and a military spouse, all of which are traits that can be unattractive to employers.

This has become a serious trigger point for me as a military spouse. I didn't marry into the military until my career was well established with a vast professional network. I reached out to that network and landed her a contact at a financial services company. She then landed herself an entry-level job and has since grown to be a full-fledged mortgage lending assistant. This is the very power of having and maintaining networks! To this day, the success of that first spouse I worked with is what drives my passion for helping spouses improve their first impressions and manage their personal brand to best prepare them for entering and surviving the work force. I will forever remember being at that first command and the opportunity I had to help so many people.

Right before a PCS from that duty station, the command leadership met with me for debriefing of my year as the FRG President and to thank me for the work we did. The first and only time that my sexuality was ever brought up happened at that meeting, and it was me who did it. I had to thank them and make sure that they knew how much it was appreciated that they put their faith in me as a volunteer leader and never made me feel like I was different or anything less than a full-fledged member of the command family. I am man enough to admit it took everything in my power not to let the tears flow as I spoke to these naval officers about how their leadership was setting the new standard for diversity and equality in the military.

Towards the end of the meeting, the command master chief (CMC) told me that the secret of my success is that I always made it about the sailors and their families and never about myself. I took that sentiment and continue to hold it in my heart and make sure to remind myself of that on a constant basis. I also pass on that message to other up-and-coming military spouse leaders. We always need to remember why we do what we do and who it's for. The Merriam-Webster Dictionary defines the word volunteer as "one who renders a service or takes part in a transaction while having no legal concern or interest." Interest is the piece that ties into my example. We need to remember always that when we volunteer, we do it for others and not for ourselves. I will always be thankful to that CMC for giving me that insight as I continue my military spouse journey.

The roles that I have taken on since then within the military community have been cherry-picked from an almost dizzying amount of organizations that need solid help. I am serving as the of command ombudsman for my husband's command as well as a chapter lead for In Gear Career, a program of the U.S, Chamber of Commerce and Hiring Our Heroes. This organization works to improve the quality of life, morale, and stability for military families by enabling military spouses to seek professional employment and maintain long-term career paths despite the transient nature and demands of the military lifestyle. You already know how important military spouse employment is to me, so this helps to satisfy my desire to help increase the percentage of military spouses with gainful employment and improve the public perception on the abilities of military spouses. These volunteer positions, on top of my own career, are my main projects. I've spaced these out to even leave me a little time to get involved in less demanding projects.

It can be daunting at times trying to navigate where to spend your available hours. Balancing priorities is a daily ritual for all of us who wake up in the morning with more to do than lounge around, however that is one of the secrets of success. Giving yourself a refresher period every now and then to unplug, decompress, and rejuvenate. I have learned over the years that you can't take care of anyone if you aren't taking care of yourself. I know that some of us are so busy with families and careers and spouses of deployed service member that it sometimes may seem impossible to take any time for ourselves but we must, even if it's a late night meditation session after the kids are tucked into bed. I find more energy and dedication to projects and work when I've had my downtime. That energy then allows me to really find my balance which comes with a few evaluations I always put to the test when taking on projects or activities.

When I am debating on fitting in a volunteer project or taking on a new responsibility, I always ask myself whether or not I am truly going to be able to complete the task successfully. I never want to over-promise and under-deliver; that isn't benefitting anyone. That is the first tool in balancing activities and life priorities. Performing that one simple evaluation and making subsequent decisions on whether or not to take on a particular activity gives me the opportunity to have a higher success rate.

Another part of that evaluation, for me, is deciding whether or not I am the right person for that particular project, or is there someone in my network or maybe casting a bigger net for someone that possibly would be a better fit. I have strengths in some areas, experience in some areas, and abilities in some areas but like anyone else, I don't know it all. If an activity or volunteer opportunity comes up, I very plainly ask myself if I am the right person for the job. And if not, I may pass it on to someone else. Or, if it is something I think I could learn quickly or step in as a placeholder I can do that as well. The sweet spot is when an opportunity arises that is something I know I can do, have the time to do, and will do well.

The remaining evaluation is whether or not an activity is something I even want to do. I put a bigger priority on things in my life that pertain to the United States military community because that is my passion and gets pushed up the front of the list. Deciding whether or not I want to do something always includes the impact it will make on my family. Whether it will make positive impact, a negative impact, or have a neutral effect on the life of my family are the main focuses for my evaluation. It can go without saying that it would be easy to say no to a negatively affecting activity. All of this keeps me as balanced as possible on my journey, because the journey is full of a lot more than volunteering.

The military spouse journey also gives us experiences that for the most part our non-military related friends might not quite be able to relate. The biggest is the lack of control we have over our lives and our marriages. The military is the boss! We go where it tells us to and if the military wants to take my spouse and send him to the middle of nowhere, I don't get a say. If I want to take a vacation but the military doesn't approve my husband's leave, guess what? No vacation. In the beginning, this was the most difficult aspect for me to overcome. As a bonafide Capricorn, I have an incessant need to be in control and I had to let that go faster than a speeding bullet! I've now gotten to the point where I handle it pretty well but I still give a little bit of side-eye when I have a fancy dinner planned and then out of the blue the command gives my husband a night watch duty. But then I feel bad and take back the side-eye because I remember that my husband is serving our country, not serving at a country club.

Getting to this place early on was a factor of success for me. I had to learn to not only take the good with the bad but to learn to appreciate the bad. And now, as a seasoned military spouse, I don't even consider the bad to be bad anymore. Understanding that the inconveniences or the frustrating aspects we may deal with are a result of a bigger picture. I may not get to have that romantic dinner but it's because my husband is at work, training a new crew on a new type of vessel so that the crew can successfully join the fleet and the fight to protect the rest of us. That's the sweet spot. If you can get yourself to that realization, you'll save yourself a lot of heartache. There is one exception to this rule however, and I'll just say one word ... Tricare. Did you roll your eyes yet?

A super fun part of this military spouse journey is dealing with insurance! I haven't met a single military spouse that at one point or another didn't have a unique and sometimes hilarious but sometimes frustrating story about Tricare. I'll let you decide into which category my story fits. I was recently asked to speak at the San Diego Military Family Collaborative's Annual Conference. The conference attendees were a mix of military spouse volunteer leaders and military family resource providers. When I was putting together the outline for my speech, I wanted something to draw them in and be a topic both groups of attendees could follow, so I told them my Tricare OBGYN story. This story has since become quite the humorous conversation piece so I thought I would share.

When I first got married and switched from private insurance to Tricare, I signed up for a primary care physician and went about my business The first time I wanted to see my doctor, I had a terrible sinus infection and just needed to pop in for an exam and a prescription for an antibiotic. When I showed up at the office I was shocked to see that I was assigned to an OBGYN. Obviously that wasn't going to work, so I headed on over to the regular clinic and got treated. I called Tricare and explained what had happened and they said they would assign me to another primary care physician. Fast forward a year or so and the annual winter "man" cold came around and it went on for a day or two too long and I went to see my new doctor. When I arrived at this office my jaw dropped. They had sent me to yet another OBGYN! I finally had to call and as bluntly as possible tell them that I appreciate all they do for military families but I simply do not have those parts! So, what do you say...hilarious or frustrating? I'm sticking with hilarious.

All in all, being a member of this village of warriors, both in uniform and out, is an honor and a privilege. The absolute best part of being in a military family is being surrounded by constant patriotism. I love this country with a passion that I would rival against anyone. I believe in our democracy with such love that even at 38 years old, I still get the chills when I hear The Star-Spangled Banner. We are a nation of fighters. A nation of passionate, diverse, and creative people. A nation that strives for a better tomorrow. While we have different political parties and even some rival ideas as a nation, we still come together in the end and will defend our principles. We will give our only shirt off our back to help a fellow American. We learn from each other, we work hard to be stronger and smarter. In the military community, you find the best of these qualities. Being around that kind of patriotism holds me accountable to participate and give back the best I can.

Brian Alvarado is a Real Estate Executive by day, and a military spouse, gadget geek, and amateur kitchen genius by night. He is also a speaker, a writer, and a Tri-Care comedienne whenever and wherever there is an audience of military families. He is currently serving at Fleet Anti-Submarine Warfare Training Center as a Command Ombudsman aboard Naval Base Point Loma and as the San Diego Chapter Lead for In-Gear Career, a program of the US Chamber of Commerce Foundation and Hiring our Heroes.

Reluctant Military Spouse

Shelley Kimball

I often consider myself a reluctant military spouse. I grew up moving often, so I never wanted to spend my life trailing an active duty service member. But, then love found me, and I was willing to go with him. And I guess you choose the life you know.

I was born into an Air Force family. My dad enlisted long before I was born, and stayed in until I was in middle school. Right around that time, my brother enlisted in the Army, and he stayed in for nearly 30 years. So I felt like I had put a lot of love and effort into military life, and I was not interested in more disruption and uncertainty. My childhood was a series of schools and apartments, passports and boxed-up belongings.

I remember having two distinct life dreams when I was in elementary school: watching American television with commercials, and having my own bedroom that I could paint any color. I wanted to see the commercials because I couldn't understand what they were and why people talked about them so much. I felt like an outsider. I wanted to paint my own room because I wanted a place that was my own – a place I thought I could stay for a while.

I also recognized very early that storytelling brought us together. I would listen to other kids tell me what America was like because I had very little memory of it. We had been stationed overseas for most of my life. I would tell them about the countries I had visited because they might end up there eventually, too. Sharing those experiences broke down the barriers between us, and connecting with others through story was one of the easiest ways to feel like I was not alone – I was part of something greater.

Those same dreams still resonate with the adult me, but now it is a need for stability and being part of a community, and I often find myself building community connections through storytelling.

Becoming a Coast Guard spouse has had more of an effect on my adult life than I originally envisioned. I thought I would float along in support of my husband, but I would be able to live my life my way. Work wouldn't be an issue, and we would make a lovely life wherever we landed. (If you are a military spouse, you are either shaking your head or laughing at me right now.) I was naïve. And I was wrong, but that doesn't mean it was a bad thing.

When I met my husband, I was about halfway through graduate school. I already had a career as a newspaper reporter, and I had decided to go back to school to research and teach journalism. I was just about done with my master's degree, and I was starting my Ph.D. He was stationed about 400 miles away in a neighboring state. Perhaps because we dated and were engaged long distance, and the fact that I did not move in with him until the month before the wedding, I didn't have a realistic idea of what Coast Guard life would be like.

I assumed that I would be able to do my work wherever we moved, that I would find a job writing or teaching anywhere, and we would live happily ever after. (Again, naïve and wrong, but I was learning!) Things actually did flow along pretty nicely for the first 10 years or so. I stopped working full time when I had our two kids, and worked as a freelance writer during those years, telling stories of family dynamics and military life. It wasn't until the 12-year mark that it all came to a screeching halt.

I was working at my dream job – a tenure-track position at a university in which I was teaching classes I loved. My colleagues were phenomenal. I felt like I was home. I had exactly what I wanted: I was part of a community of people who inspired me with their dedication, and I had the stability of a full-time job.

And then my husband got orders to his dream job, which was 700 miles away in another state. I had to decide if I was keeping my dream job and letting him go to his alone, or if I would sacrifice my work and keep our family together as one unit. This is never an easy decision for any family, and the right decision for us was for me to leave my job.

I submitted my resignation. It was so hard for me that my boss had to tell me to let go of the piece of paper and hand it to him. I remember crying so intensely when I drove away that I had to pull over up the road a bit to clear my eyes. It still puts a lump in my throat to think about it.

We moved to an area with a big city, so I assumed that my work experience and my degrees would open doors. This is the part where I realized how very wrong I was. There was a hiring freeze on academic positions when I got there, and in my work, they take a long time to fill. So if you don't get a job right away, it is unlikely you will be chosen to fill the spot. (Who wants to take a year to fill a position with a person who will leave in a year or two?)

So facing unemployment, like the thousands of military spouses before me, I had to come up with a plan. I called everyone I knew. I sent applications for work everywhere. I kept coming up empty. After months and months, I needed a new plan. I really thought about what I needed for myself. In the absence of my dream job, what else did I want to do? I had always felt that working full time left little time to devote to helping the military community. When I was sitting in my office, daydreaming about where else I could be, that is what I imagined.

I scrapped the old plan, and I started from scratch. I literally packed up the files I had been using, cleaned off my desk, and I tried to figure out how to begin again. I stuck a motivational quote on the wall over my computer screen. It says, "Every accomplishment starts with the courage to try," and it still hangs there.

I am not going to lie – I was scared. I love the stability of the familiar. This wasn't it. This was new and different. I felt like I had pulled up my occupational anchor and pushed off from shore. (You had to expect a little ocean metaphor here and there from a Coastie, right?)

I started by looking at what my favorite jobs entailed, and how I could break apart the skills involved and use them in other ways. I write, I research, and I teach. I started looking for ways to share that expertise in another area, and I focused on nonprofit organizations that serve military families. I researched agencies, and I found two that piqued my interest. I got in touch with both of them, explaining what I wanted to do and why I was a potential candidate to do that. Almost every job I have had has come from these kind of cold calls. I send emails to people all the time who are not advertising job openings. It feels embarrassing, but it has worked for me more often than it has not. Many employers may not know they need you until you tell them.

One of the nonprofits was clearly a better fit than the other. I started volunteering for them to see how it all worked internally. I ended up continuing for three more years. I also got in touch with those inside the organization who were in charge of research, and I offered my help. By the time we moved to our next duty station, I had written a book chapter for them about the effects of deployments on families, I lead a team of researchers whose job it was to help make sense of data from a very large survey, I planned and carried out events for military families around our area, and I made inroads to bring Coast Guard families forward in the military support community.

All of that work also led to an offer from the Coast Guard to write regularly about our families and their lives. We recognized that our families needed to connect through their experiences, and that telling their stories was a way to show that we are all in this together. For more than three years, every other week, families so generously share their stories with me and I get to communicate them to our community at large. It is one of the greatest honors of my life.

More than once during these years I thought I was on a road to failure because I couldn't find work in my usual career path. I was shocked at the success of this journey in advocacy. I was selected to represent Coast Guard families as the Armed Forces Insurance 2013 Coast Guard Spouse of the Year. I remember accepting the award, feeling like I was having an out-of-body experience. I had not quite shaken the idea that I was not succeeding because I had stepped off the job track I thought I was supposed to be on. And yet there I was, accepting an award.

As much as I am still so honored by that recognition, that award was never really about me. It was about all of the families who trusted me enough to tell me their stories, to show up for events, to take my hand in assistance. I think that one of the most personal things you can do in military spouse life is to ask for help, and I have felt the deepest bonds with friends who have been willing to help me and let me help in return. I found my stability in that community.

More than once, I have found myself standing in the White House as a result of my advocacy work. Above my desk now, next to that quote, is a picture of me talking to former First Lady Michelle Obama about our Coasties. It is a constant reminder to me that pushing off from shore can be frightening, but there may be something waiting for you on the other side that you never, ever would have foreseen.

If anyone told me that this would happen while I was mourning the loss of my dream teaching job, I would have said they were confusing me with someone else. It took being brave and starting over to get there, just like for so many other spouses like me. I know my story is not that unique. As long as the military moves us, we will need to reinvent ourselves and adjust to new beginnings. I have so much respect for military spouses and their enduring ability to face adversity and disappointment and find a way around it.

I have spoken to many spouses through the years who have struggled with their careers. I am gratified to see that many states have eased the licensing requirements for spouses, though I know it is still difficult. I am grateful that we can get unemployment assistance if we need it, especially because it is a recognition of the effects of our sacrifices for military life. Our unemployment rate is still too high, and I look forward to the day that employers stop worrying about when we might leave and instead applaud the opportunity to hire a talented employee.

As you could have guessed, right when I felt like the ground beneath me was stable, and I had figured it all out, my husband got new orders. This time, it was back to a home we loved in a city I adore. I remember telling my husband that I was excited about the orders, but I was really tired of trying so hard to be useful and relevant in my work. I wanted to apply for a regular job, go to an interview, and get hired. Unfortunately, it wasn't meant to be.

I got to my new city trying to put on a brave face. I still had some of my nonprofit service, but I also needed to get back to my academic work. No jobs were available. Not a one. I was exhausted. I was over it. What happened to that idealized version of my life in which my degree and my work experience would mean employment would be easy? It wasn't reality, and I had to accept that.

So I started cold calling again. I sent emails to every department I could think of to ask them whether they saw any openings on the horizon. I remember writing an email to one department chair at a well-respected university, and my heart was beating out of my chest. "Who do you think you are to write to him?" was on a loop in my head. I stopped, took a deep breath, ignored my fear, and I pressed send.

Within a few days, I got a considerate "we have no openings" response.

And then, within a few months, after revisiting the needs of their department, I got another message asking if I was still available. A few days after that, I got a phone call asking if I wanted to teach. I very calmly said, "Sure, I'm available." I hung up the phone and cried on my husband's shoulder out of pure relief.

It is so hard to look for work over and over again. It is demoralizing, frustrating, and exasperating. I feel like I have pieced together a good situation now. I am doing all of the things I love – teaching, researching, writing, and I still have time for military family support. It turns out the community and stability can come in smaller pieces. When you put them together, they can become a satisfying, if unexpected, whole.

Now, I am on the board of directors for the Military Family Advisory Network, a nonprofit that serves military families of all branches. I am an Arlington Lady. I teach media law at two universities, and I still write regularly about military family life. So I have cobbled together all of the pieces of work life that matter most to me. But my mind is still leaping ahead to the next upheaval, the next round of trying to rebuild. I don't know if that will ever change. I have a list of things I remind myself when I start to worry about what will come next.

If I were sitting talking to you about what I wish you knew, I would tell them to you, too:

- It will not always be easy, but you will be probably be better for overcoming the obstacles.
- Sometimes, the best goal is the most basic one. What do you know that makes you feel your most content? Where can you find that?
- Don't limit yourself in where you look for your work. Your skills may fit into a lot of categories, so be open to where that may take you.
- Ask for help. The strength is in asking – not in pretending you don't need it. We all need it.

I believe strongly that a variety of experiences make us better candidates for jobs. We have seen more work environments, learned from more people, adjusted to more obstacles, and we do it quickly. I have absolute faith in the military spouse community as a work force, and not just because I am one of you. I have seen hard workers who get it done quickly. We are used to running out of time, so we know how to make the most of it.

I don't think I am the best at making this job search thing work. I have met some spouses who are absolutely amazing at it, and they take it in stride. I'm not like that. But I am persistent. I will not stop because I know I am a great employee, and I truly love to work. I want the same for you. I want to be the friend who tells you, "Keep going, you got this!" If you have those messages in a loop in your head like I do, the ones that are not the most supportive, I hope you will drown them out with me. I believe you are exactly the person who can do this.

I have no idea what is coming next for me in my work, but I am more confident that I can figure it out. It took going where I feared most, having no work and no prospects, to learning that I can find my way back out if it happens again.

I can't help but think back to that 10-year-old me coming home from school to find movers packing up my bedroom. That kind of shock, like the world is shaking under my feet, is what I feel at the beginning of a lot of moves. I would tell that version of me that it can be overcome. And that sometimes that kind of shaking will break open a part or us that we never even knew was there.

Though being a military spouse was not what I intended, this life helps me understand what to appreciate. It's not the stuff in the boxes, it's the people around me that make me feel like I am home. I almost said that it wasn't about the paint on the walls, but that's not true. The paint on my walls still matters. I need to feel like I have some roots and I belong. But now I know that it's up to me to make that happen. Just like it's all in you.

Shelley Kimball is a Coast Guard spouse, an Air Force daughter, and an Army sister. She holds a Ph.D. in mass communication, and she teaches media law at two universities. She writes From the Homefront, a column about military family life published by the Coast Guard. She is a member of the board of directors and a researcher for the Military Family Advisory Network, which finds resources and support for military families.

An Unlikely Advocate

Reda Hicks

I was an unlikely candidate to be an advocate for military families, even though I grew up with military influences all around me. I was born and raised in West Texas, a part of the country where military affiliation is pretty common. My grandfather fought in World War II. My uncle is a retired Air Force colonel. My aunt is a Navy veteran, and her son, my cousin, is a Marine Corps veteran. Several of my childhood friends are the children of veterans, and quite a few went into the services themselves. Two of my friends made the ultimate sacrifice in Operation Iraqi Freedom, at a time when we barely qualified as adults. Grieving with their families remains an acute memory of mine.

Yet even with these influences all around me, I was oblivious. I didn't have a clue. It wasn't until the military was living in my home that things finally clicked for me. In all my childhood dreams about one day falling in love and getting married, not once did I ever picture myself marrying a soldier.

I was born and raised in Odessa, Texas. It's not a small town by most states' standards – when I was a child, the population hovered around 90,000 people. But it was small by Texas standards, and reflected the small-town Texas values you'd expect: God, country, and high school football! Yes, if you've heard of the "Friday Night Lights," you know exactly where I'm from. I lived in Odessa until I graduated from high school in 1999. After that, I moved to the much bigger, much more liberal Austin, Texas, to attend The University of Texas (Hook 'em Horns!), where college football is king and has basically no rivals on the priority scale.

In the summer of 2002, after graduating from UT, I moved to the even bigger, even more liberal, Berkeley, California, to attend Boalt Hall School of Law at the University of California, Berkeley. This was perhaps the biggest culture shock of all – little discussion of God, discussion of country only in the context of debate, and far less emphasis on football, unless the Stanford game was coming up.

With an Air Force base just up the road from the Bay Area, you might expect to feel more military influence there, but it's just not the case. In 2002, Berkeley continued to reflect much of the personality that gave Berkeley its reputation in the 1960s – very activist, very left-leaning. Ironically enough, this bastion of liberal thinking was where I got the first taste of what my future was going to be like, in the form of my best friend. She was my law school classmate, married to an Air Force guy, and living in the Bay Area while he continued serving in Southern California. It would be nearly a decade after meeting Cat that I would learn the term "geobaching," but that is what they were doing. I remember watching her miss him on birthdays, weekends, and even just nights when she had to eat alone, and thinking, "Man, that must be so hard!" Little did I know …

After finishing law school in 2005, I moved to Houston, Texas, where I took my first bar exam, then joined a law firm called Diamond McCarthy LLP. I could never have guessed it then, but accepting the job at Diamond McCarthy is where my journey into advocacy began. I graduated from Boalt with not only a *juris doctorate*, but also a specialty in environmental law and policy. And, as luck would have it, within weeks of my joining the firm, one of its partners landed a very large piece of environmental litigation. We would be representing a small island province in the Philippines called Marinduque against a Canadian mining company for environmental damage caused by mining on the island. I quickly learned that "we" included "me," because few other attorneys in the firm had any experience with environmental law.

I was a little apprehensive about the assignment at first. Not the law part; I felt confident there. Rather, it was the experience I wasn't sure I could handle. I'd never traveled anywhere in Asia before, and knew little about the culture in the Philippines. I'd never been to a Third World country before, and so I had no idea what to expect from an island province that many Filipinos actually refer to as "Fourth World." I worried about saying or doing the wrong thing, offending someone, or somehow making an already-terrible situation worse. But the opportunity was simply too big to pass up, and so I went.

And I loved it. I loved the people, and the culture. I loved working with my brilliant colleagues in Manila. And I loved Marinduque. It was, indeed, a highly impoverished place, and the environmental damage on the island was extensive and highly visible. But the people were so resilient and hospitable, and eager to welcome me. In 2006, I wound up weathering a Category V Super-Typhoon on Marinduque (an experience I don't recommend). Even in those dire circumstances, the people were focused on taking care of each other. And the very next day, they were out in the streets rebuilding together.

Representing Marinduque broadened my skillset as an advocate in incredible ways. I traveled to the Philippines several times a year for about a decade. My job involved the usual legal work – witness interviews, briefing, expert reports, and so on. But there was

16

so much more to it than that. The environmental damage on Marinduque affected entire towns of people, entire river systems, and one of the island's largest bays. The national government was involved because the environmental damage involved violation of national laws and permits. Citizens' groups had formed, and were working to voice the concerns of the affected peoples. National and international environmental groups became involved in speaking out about the damage and its impact on local land and populations. Even the Catholic Church – very active on social justice issues in the Philippines, including environmental concerns – was involved.

It was my job to manage the Province's relationship and communications with these various groups, and to coordinate advocacy efforts, as well as efforts related to improving local laws that governed mining. Working for the Province of Marinduque was my first time to do anything of the kind, and frankly, it was nothing but trial and error on my part to begin with. As an attorney, I was trained in "advocacy," defined simply as finding the strongest angle of the strongest argument in order to persuade a decision-maker. But coordinating different groups and individuals with different agendas, navigating the differences to find common ground and reach a common goal – this took an entirely different skillset than what I was used to leveraging. It was driven almost entirely on trust, communication, and the strength of relationships.

I can't say I really knew what I was doing to start with, but I loved it, and I was good at it. Eventually, the mining laws in the Philippines were revised to reflect international best practices, and I had the honor and pleasure of participating in that process. I even got the chance to co-author a paper on the new law with a leading professor of Constitutional Law at Ateneo Law School, and the advisor on Environmental Protection in the Office of the President which was, in a word, awesome. Additionally, the various organizations involved in the advocacy efforts on behalf of Marinduque continue to work on environmental issues all over the Philippines. These efforts over the course of nearly a decade served as my foray into what I now know is called "stakeholder engagement."

Diamond McCarthy is where my work as an advocate began, but the Philippines is where my family, and my journey into military life, really started. You see, on one of my many trips there, I met a guy.

I was out with friends one Wednesday evening at an outdoor tapas bar in Manila. It's an ex-pat city; people come and go pretty frequently, so making friends with newcomers is common. On this night in particular, two American men joined our table for dinner and drinks. Then they joined our group for the remainder of the week.

Several days went by before I even spoke with either of the men. Both of them were very popular with my local girlfriends and were, I presumed, otherwise engaged. But when I finally did strike up a conversation with Jake, I knew immediately he was something special.

We talked the rest of the week until it was time for him to travel to another island, and for me to fly home. From that point, the only thing that changed was the communication medium – we became pen pals, talking over text and email. Eventually we both found ourselves back stateside, and started flying back and forth to see each other. That was 2007. Two years later, in 2009, we were married. The following year we welcomed our son, Howie, the first of our three children.

I didn't know Jake was Army when I met him; Special Forces soldiers keep a low profile in the field. And it was never something Jake felt comfortable talking about over electronic media either – he was too well trained for that. So I didn't really know much about his service until we were both back in the U.S. and talking face to face again. I learned that he was thirteen years into a career, had been a Green Beret for a number those of years, and that he had just put in an application to become a warrant officer and go to flight school. It's funny, but at first Jake didn't know I was an attorney, either. My work on that trip involved a lot of government meetings, and he presumed I must have worked for the U.S. Embassy or something of that nature. Since then, he has made it a point to tell me regularly that if he'd learned I was an attorney sooner, things might have turned out differently. I guess neither of us ever imagined a life quite like the one that we have together.

At first, Jake might as well have been speaking a foreign language for as much as I understood of his life in the military. The alphabet soup of acronyms was downright dizzying! But what was simple enough to understand from the beginning was the geographical challenge. When we met in 2007, I was living in Houston, Texas. I'd built a career in the Space City. I was on track to become the youngest partner my firm had ever made, and the first woman to be named partner in years (and in 2010, I accomplished both feats). My community ties were deep, both in the civic space and in the philanthropic space. Then suddenly I found myself in love with a soldier who was stationed at what is now Joint Base Lewis-McCord in Washington State. He couldn't tell me where he was going to be living in six months, other than it sure as heck wouldn't be anywhere in Texas! I'm the planning type, and this was maddening. I found myself thinking again about law school, about my best friend and her far-away husband. It's funny, although she really loves Jake now, my friend was pretty apprehensive about him at first. I wonder sometimes if part of the reason for that was having first-hand knowledge of the challenges we would face living the military life together.

Jake's packet to flight school was accepted a few months after we met, and in the fall of 2007, he moved to Fort Rucker, Alabama, to begin flight school. Fort Rucker was better for us than Fort Lewis – it was closer, and we were in the same time zone, but getting to see each other still wasn't easy. A couple of times a month, we would meet in Fort Walton Beach to spend a weekend, and those were always wonderful. I will always have a special place in my heart for Eglin Air Force Base, where we'd pass those weekends together. Still, over a two-year period we only spent about 120 days together. Jake finished flight school in 2009, just before we got married. Once we got back from our honeymoon, we loaded up a U-Haul and moved Jake to his next duty station – Fort Polk, Louisiana.

We talked about the prospect of me moving to Louisiana, but ultimately decided I should stay in Houston. For one thing, Fort Polk was only three hours away by car, which meant we were together every weekend. But more importantly, getting licensed to practice law in Louisiana was going to be incredibly difficult.

You see, the tricky thing about being an attorney married to the military is that your license to practice law is good only in the state where you pass the bar. Move to a new place, and you have to either take the bar exam again, or waive in through a reciprocity rule if the new state has one. Either way, it's a very expensive and time-consuming process, and you can't practice law in the interim. For our family, my not working was simply not an option; Berkeley is an amazing school, but it's also expensive. My student loan debt alone meant we needed me working. So we decided that I'd stay a Texan, and Jake would be a Louisianan.

Marrying Jake quickly brought into perspective just how much I didn't know about military life. Sure, I'd been around it all my life, but knowing other people living it is just not the same as living it yourself. I didn't know deployments. I didn't know the heartbreak of packing up and moving away from friends every other year. I didn't know the hardship of inconsistent schools or health care. I didn't know the burden that frequent moves place on a couple in which both people are career-minded, or where a family simply needs two incomes. I didn't know. And I had no idea just how much I didn't know.

From the beginning, the thought of how hard it must be to be a military spouse with a law license crossed my mind. I found it very frustrating, but it didn't immediately occur to me to do anything about it for one simple reason – I thought I was the only one! But in 2012, a friend from Houston reached out to me and asked if I had heard about the bar association for military spouse attorneys. In fact, I had not, but the Military Spouse JD Network was easy to find. It was a relatively new organization, but it had started with three women and had grown rapidly to hundreds – by word of mouth! I was very excited to finally find others who understood the struggle, and I leapt at the opportunity to get involved.

I started out working on MSJDN's newsletter as part of the organization's communications team in 2012. Then I had the opportunity to serve as its governance director, and ultimately on the organization's Governmental Affairs Committee. One of MSJDN's main goals is to ease the burden of maintaining a continuous career across military moves by reducing licensing barriers state-by-state. Since 2011, MSJDN has been successful in obtaining military spouse licensing accommodations in 24 states, and I'm very proud to have contributed to several of those efforts.

For the three years Jake was at Fort Polk, we were a weekend family. It was during this assignment that I learned the term "geobachelor," meaning a soldier living away from his or her family in order to serve. It turns out, something like one in five military families have experience with geobachelorhood, which is a staggering number in my mind. Kind of clever, really, the terminology; but that's the military for you, always coming up with a humorous way to talk about something that is terrible. It actually worked pretty well for us; I'd cram all of my work into weekdays, and spend the weekends in Louisiana with Jake, and later Howie when he came along. We were hoping that we'd be able to spend the remainder of Jake's career that way, but the Army intervened.

In 2012, Jake received orders transferring him to the Big Red One at Fort Riley, Kansas. A move to Kansas was certainly going to put an end to our "weekend family" groove. I couldn't imagine being in Houston with Howie while Jake was in Kansas, going weeks without seeing each other. It was the orders to Kansas that finally made me consider leaving Houston and moving to be with Jake. It was maddening, really. By 2012, I was licensed to practice law in four different jurisdictions, each of which had multiple military installations in-state. But of course, none of them was Kansas. So that summer, I put in my application to be licensed in my fifth jurisdiction.

Then things went from bad to worse. We learned that Jake would be deploying to Afghanistan for nearly a year just a few months after arriving in Kansas. In other words, half a year before I would even receive word about a license in Kansas, my entire reason for obtaining one there would be half a world away. Literally. When we learned about the deployment, we decided that uprooting Howie and me from a place where we have a strong support network was simply not going to work. We were just going to have to – and here comes another one of those military humor-covers – "embrace the suck." So for the few months before Jake's deployment, we were a twice-monthly family. All I can say is thank God for technology, and the most adaptable little boy on the planet.

Deployment is definitely a learning experience, but I think the lessons might have been a little different for my family, having lived remotely for so many years. For one thing, my then-three-year-old went through "Daddy withdraw" on delay, because it took him several weeks for to figure out that he hadn't been getting to see his Dad in person. Eventually he figured it out, and then commenced the daily, "When's Daddy coming home?" interrogation. After a few days of this, to save my own sanity, I constructed a paper chain with a link for each day left of our deployment so that Howie could take a link off each day, and watch the days pass by in a way that a kid not able to count past ten could understand. The thing was huge! It wrapped around our banister from the second story of our house to the ground, but it did the trick.

The thing that deployment taught me is that I handle grief better when I'm busy. Not just busy doing whatever; busy doing something, outside myself, that matters. Sure, the occasional girls' night was nice, whether out with local friends or having a virtual glass of wine with another military spouse. But most of the time, I needed to be as far away from "woe is me" as possible. Jake was on a mission and I needed a mission of my own.

I was already involved in MSJDN by that point, and that's where I started pouring all of my extra time and energy. I jumped in with both feet, and in doing so, was introduced to an amazing network of military spouses, attorneys and otherwise, who were all working to make life better for military families. Engaging with this community gave me the opportunity to help develop programs like "Making the Right Moves," a career intensive for military spouse attorneys working to balance supporting their service member with a career in the practice of law.

I also had the opportunity to champion my friend and fellow military spouse Judge Patricia Millett, the spouse of a Navy veteran and now a judge on the Court of Appeals for the DC Circuit. Through countless Capitol Hill fly-bys, periodicals, interviews, a social media campaign, and a senate press conference, I was one of the voices urging leadership to recognize one incredible military spouse attorney's career accomplishment and #ConfirmPattie.

The connections I made through MSJDN and #ConfirmPattie led me to serve as a policy lead on collaborations like the #KeepYourPromise Coalition, which fought to overturn cuts to veteran retirement benefits that were approved by Congress in 2013, and #Nix296, a campaign to stop California from passing a bill that, as written, would have made it even harder for a military spouse to obtain a license while living in the state with his or her service member. I was also able to help in the development of Homefront Rising, which provides political training for military spouses. Needless to say, I had plenty to keep me busy while Jake was in Afghanistan!

Jake came home from his deployment in April 2014, just a few weeks after Howie's fourth birthday. He finished his assignment at Fort Riley, and retired almost exactly a year later in April 2015. Now Jake spends more of his time here in Houston with us, although he still does some defense contracting work that takes him away for weeks at a time. Once a soldier … But having Jake home more has given us both the chance to focus our attention on the military and veteran community right here in Houston. With over a quarter million veteran families, along with several thousand active duty, guard, and reserve families, there's always more work to be done.

Since Jake's retirement, we've added two more kids to the Hicks family. In 2015, after three and a half long years of waiting, we brought our adopted daughter Josie home from the Philippines. And in 2017, we welcomed a new baby girl, Katie.

My son is a military kid through and through, which of course means he's one of the most resilient people I know. But his sisters won't have to (get to?) experience the same crazy ride he spent the first five years of his life on. It is a strange thing, and a little bittersweet, that my daughters will grow up knowing none of the experiences that Howie has had. At least not directly, anyway. They'll see the work that we do in community but, like I used to be, they'll always be one step removed from the military life.

I'm an attorney, so advocating for my client's position is part and parcel of the trade. But there's something different about advocating for something you care about, for lending a voice to something that matters. That's what I found in the Philippines and now apply in the military family community – I found a place to put my skills to work on something that makes life better for people, and in particular, the people who are defending our freedoms, and their families. It's a tremendous feeling, finding your passion, although I think that in many ways mine actually found me.

People sometimes ask me how they can get involved, and how they can be a voice in their own community. To be honest, I don't really think there's a one-size-fits-all answer to this question. But there are a few lessons I have learned along the way that I think are helpful.

First and foremost: Be Open

Some people know exactly what they are meant to do, but most of us don't. Be open to the new, the different, the unusual, even if it's a little scary. If I hadn't taken that case in the Philippines, I'd never have learned how to be an advocate for change, I'd never have met my husband, and I wouldn't be an advocate for military families now. Opportunity takes many forms, and often those forms don't resemble anything we've imagined for ourselves. We never really know what path is going to lead us where we belong, so be open.

Second: Relationships are Key

Everything in this life is about people. That's the truth of the matter. Change is made by people for people, typically with the help of a lot of people. Invest time in people. Get to know people. Build relationships that last. Place a high value on people who will speak truth to you. Be intentional about ensuring that there's always someone willing to offer you the opposing view. Advocates almost never work alone – they get things done by working with other people and organizations that can amplify their message. And it's really important not to burn bridges. We never really know who we're going to need to help accomplish our goals, so relationships, even (and perhaps especially) with the opposition, are key.

Third: Be authentic

Advocacy is about getting to the heart of the matter – it's getting a decision maker to care about you and *want* to give you what you are asking for. Sure, a good advocate has done their homework, knows the data, and can discuss the issues. That's all very important, yes. No question. But at the end of the day, what makes a decision maker care is that *you* care. Why does this issue matter to you? What makes it personal? In other words, what's your story? A good advocate has thought about these questions, and is ready with answers. If they're articulate answers, that's great. But far more important is that the answers are authentic. They need to be your words telling your story in a way that reflects who you are. Because, again, relationships are key. A decision maker who has never met you before will connect with you if they can connect with what you are saying.

Lastly: Leverage your assets

Advocacy is about the message that you bring – what is the strongest angle, on the strongest argument, you can use to persuade a decision maker? When advocating for an entire community, though,

23

it's almost never just one angle, just one argument, or just one voice. Advocacy also involves knowing when you're the right voice, and when you're not. This means even as you remain true to your own authentic voice, you are strategic about what specific decision makers need to hear in order to *want* to give you what your community wants. That starts with asking, "Am I the right messenger? Is mine the right story to connect with this decision maker?" Sometimes, the answer is "no." But that's what makes relationships so important – the ability to leverage other voices, other stories, toward a common goal. Think strategically about the relationships you've built. Call on people with common goals whose voices differ from your own. Allow other people to amplify your voice. Just don't forget that relationships run both ways – if you want people to help in achieving your goals, it's important to help in achieving theirs as well.

For me, the military life has been a little bit like a track meet – sometimes a sprint, sometimes a marathon, sometimes jumping hurdles, and sometimes a relay. I've navigated it with almost equal parts skill, providence, friends, and flying by the seat of my pants. I think that's true for most people, although sometimes it's a hard thing to admit. I've also learned that embracing this crazy military life cocktail is really the key to finding your voice as an advocate: we can't do it alone; we have to come prepared, but also knowing that curveballs are going to come our way; and we have to put our hearts into it!

Reda Hicks is an attorney and policy advocate based in Houston, Texas. She is the wife of a recently retired Army Special Forces soldier, and mom to three beautiful children. Reda is very active in the Houston community, serving in a number of civic and volunteer capacities; she loves leveraging her network to help military families and veterans. She currently serves as the Chairman of the Board for Leadership Houston, and the Vice President of Civic Engagement for the League of Women Voters of the Houston Area.

The Rookie

Kelli Chappelle

The Rookie is how I have referred to myself in comparison to many of my other military spouse friends. Moving to Okinawa at 28 filled my life with numerous firsts: my first base, my first PCS, my first time living overseas, and my first real introduction to the military culture and lifestyle. I had no idea what I was getting into. I just knew I was in love with a man who was leaving to go to a foreign land and he wanted my daughter and I to go with him. We got married and within two months our little family of three (with one on the way) was headed to the other side of the globe.

Prior to becoming a military spouse, I was deep into the retail business. I had worked at a variety of clothing stores, but was still searching for something more, something I could be passionate about. I was already a mother to an incredibly active little girl, while staying active within our community. Now I was starting from scratch.

Once we arrived in Okinawa, I thought I would be able to easily relocate, quickly put everything in order, and keep moving on with life. I was wrong. I quickly realized everything I needed and everything I did was linked to my husband. All of my appointments, our house and cars, my daughter's school paperwork – everything was listed under my husband. I went from being an independent mom capable of conquering all, to the dependent of my husband and "sponsor." Needless to say, stripping me of my independence was difficult for my mind to adjust to. I struggled to understand all of the new military lingo and their meanings. I made friends with primarily Marine and Army wives who seemed to be speaking in secret code. I did not understand that different branches had different titles, acronyms and protocols. There were so many alien terms to learn and questions to answer such as: what was a FRO? Why don't you know your DEROS? What is your husband's unit? Who is the squadron's first shirt? What rank is your family? I was completely honest with people and simply answered with, "I don't know, let me text my husband."

Gradually, we made connections with other families. These other families were who we celebrated holidays, birthdays and promotions with. We helped each other through deployments, illnesses, pregnancies, ER visits, and days off of school. This small collection of individuals created a new community for our family. My husband and I both come from families who are involved in each other's lives so it was important for us to provide our children a sense of family, belonging, and a safety net to love them here in Okinawa. We made sure they understood this was not to a replacement of the family we left back stateside, but an addition to the love coming from across the ocean and beyond.

One example of our newfound support system was when my daughter fractured her jaw while my husband was scheduled to leave on a short deployment the next day. There I was, alone with a small baby learning to walk, an 8 year old with a fractured jaw who was put on a liquid diet, and we were charging into typhoon season with a full head of steam. A small platoon of moms and wives continuously checked in on us and dropped off soup and shakes for my daughter. Luckily, the dental hygienist who worked with my daughter's oral surgeon also was a family friend who lived close by. She was not only able to regularly check in on my daughter, but was also available to answer any questions or concerns that came to mind. The sense of community and belonging was important to us. This process did not happen overnight; it took concentrated time and effort to cultivate. Each time family friends have relocated, it has created holes and a feeling of starting from scratch to find new friends and has tested our resilience to make new connections. We are still in contact with many of the families who have left the island before us. Distance has not eroded the bond created on this small peninsula.

Becoming a stay-at-home mom was difficult for me. I had to adjust to a different type of work and it became a source of frustration for our family. Honestly, I found it hard to be the available parent and considered a dependent, especially since I had been a very independent adult prior to moving. I started to feel lost as Kelli, as a person separate from my family. Once I expressed my concerns and frustrations to my husband, he suggested I figure out what I wanted to spend the next few years doing. I began finding online personal development seminars and stayed up late to participate in various webinars, listen to speeches, and read up on how to discover my passion. My neighbor informed me that as a spouse, I had an education grant with MYCAA of $4000 to put towards any degree I needed to obtain.

Having already obtained my bachelor's degree prior to moving, I searched for other programs I could use the grant for. My interest in becoming an entrepreneur increased. I wanted a program which aligned with my passion of natural beauty and spa services and my degree in hotel, restaurant and institutional management. I wanted something that would allow me to become an entrepreneur so I could have a flexible work schedule I controlled. I used the education grant to complete a makeup artist certification and began to slowly take on clients. During our first few months here, my family's hair and skin responded differently to the new atmosphere and high humidity. I began to research and experiment with natural remedies for our skin, hair and other health issues. I had grown to depend on my natural remedies, and I looked to support businesses which are natural or vegan products.

I met two other spouses here in Okinawa who were planning a beauty expo for the fall, and I contacted them and volunteered for the planning team. Upon meeting these women, their overall vision became clear: uplifting military spouses who were self-employed within the OCONUS community. I learned valuable lessons from this pair of entrepreneurs to include the everyday struggles spouses were encountering here and many other bases. They also wanted to fill the growing need for business owners to find workable solutions, support and opportunities to learn and engage to become successful. I joined the charter chapter for Milspousepreneur and supported the business community here on base by creating various workshops for business owners. We also focused on developing opportunities for business owners to operate as vendors and network with each other and the community at large. Working with the local community of spouses, veterans and active duty, to assist them in the growth of their businesses has been rewarding so far. I have promoted MYSECO webinars and on-base trainings open to spouses, and attended and participated in a variety of local events and trainings. I have made many new connections, and learned of solutions and a variety of resources, conferences and grants to assist self-employed spouses reach their business goals. I plan on continuing to work with Milspousepreneur and other organizations such as In Gear to assist self-employed military spouses and veterans to discover workable solutions at my next base.

For our next base, we will be located just outside of a mid-sized city. This will certainly be an amazing new adventure for my family, undoubtedly riddled with new hurdles and adventures. I will continue to do my part and positively aid the construction of the bridge between the military and civilian communities.

Prior to joining forces with my airman, my close circle did not regularly encounter military families. I have tried to provide a translated version of our experience the best I can. Like I mentioned earlier, being a member of the military community has changed some of my vocabulary as I have adapted to my new environment. I try to remember they don't speak military, so tailoring the words and acronyms I use with family and friends became imperative to us speaking the same language.

I believe it is my responsibility to continue bridging the gap between military and civilian families. As a military spouse, it is important to remember that you're not just an individual looking to cultivate your passions, but a member of an ever-growing community. I am a part of a group looking for long-lasting and forward-thinking solutions to reduce the anxiety of continuously starting over.

I have found it helpful to share articles or research as it pertains to our lives on various social media platforms. Teaching families military lingo, and promoting military owned and operated businesses, blogs and services have each provided a window into our small but significant piece of the military life experience. Many civilians are unaware of the everyday hurdles and challenges faced by the military family. In a lifestyle where the uncommon becomes routine, it is important to recognize the inner strength necessary for the success of each family unit. I encourage friends who are completing higher degrees to research the military family experience within their individual disciplines. Regardless of the specific area of study, military families have a unique list of stressors and needs. An increase in academic research on military families is needed and, in my opinion, necessary due to the overwhelming amount of families who reside within civilian communities. These families are patrons to civilian businesses, members of various church congregations, and other locally owned and operated organizations.

As military families embark on the transition from active duty service to join the civilian world, it is imperative that families receive assistance and support from systems within their new community. Assisting the transition into civilian life while carrying a military perspective is a difficult task to say the least. Employers who hire military spouses or veterans may need special training to understand the needs of an employee who is also a part of the military community or have various systems in place to ensure this type of employee can not only be successful and valuable, but flourish in their company. This type of training should be facilitated by members of the military community in conjunction with a human resource employee.

Military kids have a unique childhood experience. My own children, like many other military kids, have learned to be flexible with our family schedule and holiday celebrations. Military kids do not always attend DoD-run schools, therefore they will have a different set of needs and types of support during their academic career due to the nature of the military family lifestyle and schedules. Civilian teachers and classmates will not always understand behaviors, temperaments, and concerns of the military child. Training regarding known and potential challenges encountered would be helpful to navigate these issues. As a parent of school-aged children, I hope I would be afforded the opportunity to assist in providing this type of training and facilitate these discussions. It has been my experience that without both sides being open and willing to have honest and regular discourse, as well as open lines of communication, civilians will continue to be unable to adequately meet the needs of military families and will continue to have a lack of knowledge of our community.

In the future I hope to create business opportunities, specifically within the beauty and health industry, for military-owned businesses and civilians to work together and learn from each other's experiences to expand services and clientele. My goal is to work closely with already established organizations and programs to be a bridge to connect the two communities.

So far my adventure of being a military spouse has been a lesson in staying flexible and steadfast, making connections and finding my passions in life. I will take all that I have learned about myself as a wife, a friend, a mother, an entrepreneur, and a neighbor as we head to our next duty station to continue to grow as a military spouse.

Kelli Chappelle is a Penn State Alum who is a mother of three, loves makeup, tattoos, Pinterest and Target. Her motto is "Forget what you feel and go after what you deserve."

A Military Wife's Journey

Kimberly Merritt

Nine years ago I found myself a world away from home, and everything familiar. I left my job, my family, my comfort zone, and my home to begin a brand new life in another country as a brand new military spouse. My husband and I met while I was in high school, were married in our early twenties, then began our Air Force journey after our first year of marriage. He went away to basic training and tech school, and then we received orders to RAF Lakenheath in the United Kingdom. We had no idea what was in store, but I was eager and excited for our new life as a military family.

I'll never forget the night we received our first assignment. I was at work and was anxiously awaiting the call. Looking back, I laugh at my former self. I had romanticized so much about what our new life would look like, beginning with our first duty station. My heart set on California, our hometown of Colorado Springs, Vegas, Arizona ... then the phone rang. We were headed to England six weeks down the road and my mind was blown. I had never lived out of state, let alone in another country. I was loving my job. We had two dogs. I had no idea what was in store ... but I was excited. The next few weeks were filled with more paperwork and visits to the local base than I'd ever done before. It was truly a whole new, very intimidating world. My husband ended up arriving to the UK about a month before I did because of paperwork drama, and within two weeks of my arrival he was off to a 3-week training in Germany. I found myself jobless, friendless, and living in the potato country of England. I was living 45 minutes away from the base, trying to find ways to fill my days. Driving on the opposite side of the road was terrifying, so for a few days, I avoided it at all costs. So I explored our little village of Downham Market, found a grocery store and a tiny, tiny town square, and watched reruns of Friends until the phone rang. It was one of our station Key Spouses, Angela, and she was just the beam of sunshine I needed in the cloudy British sky. She welcomed me with open arms, invited me to the next group gathering and was so unbelievably personable and helpful, I couldn't wait to drive on the itty bitty country road to meet her.

It was a breath of fresh air, and looking back now, the beginning of my military spouse journey. While I had only been there for a month or so at this point, a few things were made clear to me.

Community in the military is important.

There is so much common ground between shop and military spouses.

One person could truly make an impact on someone's life.

I went on to join the local spouse group, and became a Key Spouse myself. We had arrived with initially zero help, and had Angela not called me to connect, our England tour could have been a completely different experience.

Fast forward to April 2011. My husband is away again, and I was due with our first baby girl at "any time now!" said the nice doctor who had no idea that my husband had just left for a 3-week training. Needless to say, I was induced at 42 weeks. Such is life, right? We worry, we stress, we plan, plan, plan again, and things never go as we expect! However, we always survive and thrive throughout the process. Our baby "plan" was 5 years. I mean, who has babies halfway around the world? Turns out, lots of people do! We spent the pregnancy learning and weighing all the pros and cons to having our baby girl so far from family, but in the end, it turned out to be such a blessing and experience for our family.

Being around the world and very much on our own, I had to expand as a person. Get out of my own head, and learn that there were many successful ways to raise a baby and be a great parent. It played such an important part in how I learned to get out of my own head and grow towards the person I was supposed to be. It would have been easy to fall in line with everything that was done before. However being so far, I was challenged to truly educate myself and decide what was best for me and my family. I swear, back home they all thought I was crazy! And while there were many challenges, like learning the ins and outs of cloth diapering, everything I did was my own. Everything was intentional and a part of the puzzle that is my life. Each small decision lead me on the path to the next.

Shortly after our daughter was born, I found myself a bit lost for the first time. I was lucky enough to have had an amazing job that I had loved, managing a studio at the BX with a London-based photographer. However, the base shop closed down and I was once again, jobless. Except this time, I had a baby and new schedule to work around. I loved being a mom, and I loved my daughter! However, I also truly loved having a job. I found my friends beginning to PCS and start new adventures in other locations, and I was just stuck. I wasn't sure of my place anymore, and missed wearing business casual clothes, adult conversations, and having extra cash to spend.

These were all things I craved and missed from my old pre-mommy life.

It then became time for our England adventure to end. We had received orders to Okinawa, Japan, and were counting down the days. I was born for the sunshine and loved the sandy beaches. So while many others refer to Okinawa as "The Rock," I had high hopes it would quickly feel like home. We landed at the Kadena Passenger Terminal, and were warmly welcomed by a fabulous group of people. Spouses, sponsors, even their kids, and the shop mascot greeted us. Our hotel room had some food basics, a welcome card, and one family even went to get milk for our daughter then left us with their personal cell phone so we could connect to the world again after such a long flight. I truly had no idea how magical fresh food could be, until we spent 24 hours eating airplane meals, snacks and sandwiches from vending machines, and Burger King or Taco Bell. The sight and thought of an apple was truly pure joy. The kindness and generosity of those who walked where we just walked was inspiring.

The rotator flight into Okinawa is no joke! It is long. You have one long 10-hour flight, followed by two three-hour flights, with two three-hour stops along the way. The terminals don't even have a convenience store type facility, let alone a food court. It was the longest day of my life! So the warm welcome and the thoughtfulness of complete strangers was beyond noteworthy. It inspired me to do the same for others as they arrive. To aim at setting people up for success as they step into this brand new world, jet lagged, with crying babies, and exhausted souls. We hold such a gift, giving people the opportunity to land with both feet on the ground. These are gestures that are so appreciated and never forgotten. How powerful a positive connection can be for us all.

A few months into our time at Okinawa, I was completely loving island living. The sun, the sand, the ocean, heck, even the typhoons that rolled in one weekend after the next! I loved it all. However, I was missing the community that made RAF Lakenheath home. While I knew a couple from our arrival, I am just naturally an extroverted social butterfly, I am energized by people. And I wanted a job! I missed the extra family funds, and we felt like we were always having to miss out on experiences because we were so broke from the move. Many know that military spouses deal with a lot of employment issues, and overseas it is just as much a hardship. Most positions are held for our host nation's citizens, and the spouses are given what is left. So I decided to take matters into my own hands and give entrepreneurship a shot. I needed something with flexibility, income potential, and honestly, I wanted to find something I enjoyed to fill my time with. Then a company called Lemongrass Spa Products came into my life, and everything changed for the better.

Entrepreneurship became a way to bring in a solid and decent income while treating military spouses to a well-deserved spa treatment. I met some amazing people and heard amazing stories. I felt a newfound purpose, a new piece of my identity, and a passion I never know was there before. As my personal business grew, I did too. I had found a way to fill my cup, and be the best version of who I am; the best mother, friend, and military spouse that I can be. I discovered that I had a love for education and knowledge centered around healthy and natural living. I was refreshed by sharing a cup of coffee over a foot spa with a new mom or deployed spouse. I felt impactful using my business to help others raise funds for programs that were meaningful to them.

Everyone has a sense of self. A personal identity. The person that you were born and destined to be. We each have strengths, passions, and callings in our lives. However, at some point along this military journey, many of us feel that we lost that. It happens at some point between hearing the phrase, "if we wanted you to have a spouse and family, we would've issued you one," being asked your sponsor's last four about a gazillion times last week, or been told you need your spouse in order to drop off or pick up a piece of paperwork. You can't make that appointment, and you can't do task A-Z for your impending move without what feels like your active duty member holding your hand. You leave your home, your job, your friends, time and time again. And at some point, pieces of you drift away. Maybe for a season, a few months, or an entire duty station. A year, or 10. Now this is not to say that we don't take our job on the home front seriously, or that we don't truly love that specific job being a military spouse entails.

Most of us understand the value and importance of what we do, but while we work so hard to keep all the marbles afloat, we yearn for connection with the person and soul that resides in our core. We keep life moving forward, for our kids, for our families, for our spouses, and for our country. But we often miss the person we use to be, and amidst all the what ifs, the ups and downs, the ins and outs, the moves, deployments, TDYs, it's no surprise that this is a regular struggle and common heartache of military spouses around the globe.

Owning my business not only helped me expand as a person, but it has become a vehicle I've used to help many other women find their place again as well. The importance of self-care is often overlooked. Unfortunately, it is sometimes given some not-so-nice labels in the context of military spouses. After just a few months in business, it became apparent to me that these labels, these words, were just that. People give others labels, because it is often much easier that trying to see what is going on underneath. Underneath is a mom who has three kids under four, a spouse who is gone 18 hours a day, and hasn't had a family member visit or a reliable babysitter in two years. Underneath is a brand new military spouse who is a natural home body; timid and shy; overwhelmed by the ins and outs of this new military life; and out of place, and not sure where to start. Underneath is a spouse who homeschools her three children, who she has raised them primarily herself, while her husband has been deployed six months of the year. Underneath is a military spouse who has not had a tribe or community in her corner for a decade, because they have been relocated eight times in 10 years. The gift of my business with Lemongrass Spa was I could now provide the opportunity of self-care, self-confidence, financial freedom, and pure positive community to those who put the mission first on a daily basis. Sharing the business opportunity that could bring their family choices, dreams, new experience, and new ways to impact their local communities. Entrepreneurship gave me my person back. My own mission within the mission. And the one thing more powerful than that is being able to share that empowerment with others.

About two years ago I was introduced to a local private organization called Milspousepreneur. A community, spearheaded by power house and brick and mortar shop owner Lakesha Cole, once again expanded my horizons. Collaborating with other local business owners, networking, and working at influencing base policy to expand support of spouse-owned businesses brought me into another amazing military spouse community; men and women who were working to impact their families' futures and the community around them at the same time. Being overseas, it is easy to feel disconnected. I mean, we are on a completely different time zone schedule! Having that local support, and watching so many others working their businesses for a cause, just like me, was inspirational at least. I had found another way to get involved, and make a difference in the lives of those around me.

We face many challenges as military spouses, many as businesses owners, and many living overseas. However, over these past nine years as a military spouse, five years as a business owner, and two years as a Milspouseprenuer organization board member and volunteer, I have learned many things.

One, is that amidst all the uncertainty, and although we struggle greatly, we hold great power as well. We have learned so well how to try, try, and try again. As a military family, we may live with so many things outside of our control, but our strength and power is born from our struggles. It can emerge and turn into our purpose and path.

Two, sometimes we just have to let go of the person we thought we were going to be, and find the bigger, stronger, more evolved person waiting in our soul.

Three, we must take action and make decisions in our lives. What many of us don't understand, or take too long to realize, is that we hold the power to spend the majority of our military journey not losing a piece of ourselves each step along the way, but finding our true self, our evolved heart. A mission that works alongside our military lives, but operates outside. An influencer, a world changer. Someone who can change the lives of others for the better. We have all heard the great quote of Gandhi, "Be the change you want to see in the world." As military families, we travel the world through our duty stations. Our connections and relationships do the same. We hold such a wonderful opportunity to bring that quote to life, and influence change, one person at a time, on a global scale.

Sometimes we have to lose ourselves, in order to find who, we are truly meant to be. For me, civilian life was comfortable. It was convenient. And it was lovely. But it was predictable. It lacked adventure. And most of all, it lacked the challenging and uncomfortable circumstances that were necessary to push me out of my box and into the bigger room where I belonged.

This is the opportunity that military life grants us. A chance to push back, a chance to expand beyond where and what we knew as possible.

However, like everything else in this life we are given, it is up to us!

Kim Merritt is an Air Force spouse, small business owner, homeschooling mama, and passionate about finding workable solutions for fellow Military Spouse Entrepreneurs. She has spent her military spouse career living overseas, and aims to use her experiences positively impacting those around her. She thrives off of coffee, mascara and sunny days at the beach.

Realities of a Veteran Caregiver

Emily Kaufman

I want to preface this with the fact that I grew up in a non-military household. No one in my family was active military. My grandpa served in WWII but never talked about it. No one in my family had substance abuse issues. I was for the most part sheltered from pain. I had to learn everything through experiences on my own.

I met Ryan one night at a bar. Ironic, isn't it?

I never believed in "love at first sight" and still don't to this day because that first night I really wasn't interested. I had recently been hurt by another guy and was not looking for a relationship. I got stuck on the inside of a booth, and Ryan happened to end up on the other side also stuck, or should I say that he chose to sit there after climbing over booths. Here was this 6'3" guy walking on top of tables. It was quite the sight. I told him to sit down, and we ended up talking all night. I told him I was a teacher. He told me he was from the projects and had a rough childhood. He mentioned being in and out of foster care. I shared with him that we had a group home that sent their kids to the school I worked for, and I thought they could use a mentor with similar.

I told him I would get him their number. The funny part of that was that I actually did go to the counselor's office at school the next day and get the number for him, though I had no intention of seeing him again. He called me seven times that next day. Each time he called, he left a message that said, "Hey this is Ryan, call number one;" "Hey this is Ryan, call number two," etc. The following day I was going back to the same bar we met at and I decided I should probably give him a call and see if he wanted to come, which he did — with another girl! I was disappointed, but he eventually ditched her and that was the night we made our first real connection.

I fell hard and fast. I couldn't pinpoint what it was about him that was so intriguing to me, but I made mention of it to my mom and my best friend. I said things like, "He is nothing like anyone I have ever dated, and for so many reasons I shouldn't be with him. We are opposites." My best friend told me, "Just have fun. It's not like you are going to marry the guy!"

Things went quickly and pretty soon we were spending every day and night together. Looking back, I should have noticed that something wasn't right, but at the time I was young, in love, and blind.

I remember the first time Ryan blacked out in rage. We had been out that evening and when we got back to his place he just flipped a switch. He went into a blind rage, yelling at me about things I had no idea about. It was unprovoked and scary. I remember going upstairs to my best friend at the time, who also somehow became one of Ryan's roommates, and sobbed. I didn't understand what happened, and I had never been spoken to or treated that way by anyone. The next morning Ryan called me from work and asked if I would come pick him up. He said he understood if I didn't want to. I decided to give him the benefit of the doubt and hear what he had to say. I consider myself a positive person who wants to believe the best in everyone. He apologized in a vague way and when I repeated some of the horrible things he had said, he told me he didn't remember them. I didn't know what to believe or think.

As time went on at the beginning of our relationship, the closer I got to him, the more he pulled away. It was as if he didn't want anyone too close to him. He didn't want anyone to know what was going on in his mind and he continued to push me away. I will never forget one night after we had broken up, he told me, "You could have been, should have been, and still are the one for me. I'm just not ready for you yet."

Shortly after that break up, we went out to a bar in Benson where he had grown up. We were about to leave and I went to the restroom. I prayed that night in the bathroom. I prayed for a sign that we were meant to be because if we weren't, I couldn't continue to put myself through the pain. When I exited the bathroom a lady I had never seen in my life walked up to me and told me she was his mom's best friend. She asked me to take care of him. It was the answer to my prayer. I knew that he needed me, but I had no idea the origins of his demons and wouldn't for quite some time.

In 2007, Ryan asked me to marry him, but not in some cute romantic way we can tell our daughter about someday. After we got engaged, he moved in with me. It wasn't until then that I really knew how bad things were. I didn't know that he was blackout drunk three to five nights a week, followed by a period of two to four days of recovery. When I say recovery, I mean too afraid to leave the bedroom even to shower. I had to hide my debit card at night or he would take it and spend hundreds of dollars on alcohol. I hid the keys under the mattress in hopes it would keep him from driving. There were many nights when I had to work the next morning that he would wake me up in a drunken stupor for no reason, sometimes just to pick a fight. Looking back, I think he just didn't like to be alone in the dark.

I started to encourage him to seek treatment, counseling, whatever he needed. I knew that I could not fix it. One month before our wedding he entered a treatment facility in Lincoln. I remember feeling a sense of relief. I was naïve enough to think that it was going to cure everything and our life would be *normal*. After roughly seven days, Ryan was asked to leave treatment because of another incident of rage. When I got the call, my heart sank to the floor. I was terrified. He came home and for a short period of time things were okay. We got married and were on cloud nine after our special day. However, within a few weeks he was back to a depressed state. I told my mom the night before we were to leave on our honeymoon that I was fearful he wouldn't go. Luckily, he showed up, but his demons did too. We had a huge fight on the third night because he wanted to stay up and drink, and I just wanted a romantic night in the hotel room. I didn't even understand at this point that Ryan was avoiding sleep to avoid nightmares.

When we returned home from our honeymoon, things continued to deteriorate. It wasn't newlywed bliss, and I was fearful for my husband. My gut said that this wasn't what marriage was supposed to be. What I didn't know was the worst was yet to come.

One night in May, the exact date I have chosen not to remember, I came home to Ryan arguing with someone on the phone. He came inside and walked into the kitchen. I heard him open a pill bottle full of lithium, prescribed for bipolar disorder, which was the only explanation we had been given for his issues. I don't know why this time, and not the countless other times he had taken his pills, I was scared. I walked in and he was on the ground. He said to me, "You better call 911 or I'm gonna die."

By the time the medics got there he was not conscious. I tried to get him to throw up as many pills as I could by sticking my hand down his throat. I rode to the hospital in the back of a police car, and called his brothers and sister and my parents. It didn't hit me until I reached the waiting room that my husband had attempted suicide. He was almost a statistic.

Following this incident, we started family therapy together once a week. I thought it was helpful, but one day we got home from the grocery store and Ryan opened the fridge and found old peaches. He lost it. He was screaming at me at the top of his lungs because we had bought more peaches. It was ridiculous, but at this point I was so accustomed to being yelled at, living in turmoil, fear, and constant anxiety, instances like this had become my new normal.

Things like that continued to happen. It wasn't until about a year later that Ryan finally opened up about what was really eating him alive, literally. One night we were watching a military movie, and although I knew my husband had served, I didn't know a thing about post-traumatic stress disorder (PTSD), or his experiences overseas. He went blank that night. I have never seen anything like it. He was telling me things, but nothing made sense. They weren't complete thoughts, but for the first time I saw him as a very vulnerable, scared boy. The anger and fight were gone.

Shortly after, we attempted another inpatient treatment stint. His counselor told him that he needed to be honest about what was happening with him. Finally, for the first time in front of me, he described the horrific events that he had witnessed and experienced while overseas. I didn't know what to say. I wish I could say that things got better after this huge step, but they didn't. Even though Ryan had opened up about his trauma, he wasn't treating *it.* Instead, *he was treating alcoholism, which was a direct result of his trauma.*

Over the next three years Ryan was in and out of treatment. We would separate and reconcile. He made and patched up countless holes in the walls, he broke dishes, and he would disappear for days at a time. We had many sleepless nights, he would have nightmares and one night he actually kicked and punched me while we slept. *Nothing was getting better.*

The only thing that was happening was that the strong woman I was when I married him had become a weak, scared, girl with no self-confidence, no hope and no sense of boundaries. I was confused. I knew I loved him so much. I knew I wanted to take his pain away ... fix everything ... but I had realized *I couldn't do that.* I also couldn't continue to live the way I was or I, too, would die.

One Saturday night after another unprovoked fight, Ryan was yelling things about divorce and how things were all my fault ... I left and went to a friend's house down the street. I walked in and looked at her and said, "I'm ready to leave. I need your help." She called my parents, who up to this point were oblivious as to how bad things were. She told them things I didn't have the strength to say. We reserved a U-Haul, called friends and family members to come help, and the plan was in motion. I was moving out of my own house because I had no other options. If I didn't leave my husband would never get help, and I would continue to slowly die.

It was the second worst day of my life. When Ryan woke up, or came to as he says, and saw us moving my things into a U-Haul, the hurt in his eyes was the worst thing I had ever seen. I never wanted to hurt him. He was so angry. I think he felt betrayed and abandoned. I can't imagine how he was feeling that day, but I know I was devastated. Only God gave me the strength I needed.

I moved into an apartment. I cried every night and every day for months. I would have moments of clarity, happiness even, and then in a moment of weakness I would drop to my knees and sob. It wasn't an easy journey that I had begun, but it was necessary. My friends and family rallied around me and helped me get back to the strong woman I was when I got married. After I moved out people wanted me to get a quickie divorce, but I told them over and over that *I didn't want to divorce Ryan*. I told them I didn't know what was going to happen, but right then divorce was never an option for me.

I come from a family where people stayed married. My parents have been together for over 40 years. I have heard marriage described as being a covenant, not a contract. I believed in my vows. In good times and in bad ... in sickness and in heath. I wanted to focus on me, and let Ryan focus on him.

The events that got us to today are not my doing. God played a huge role in our journey. I prayed, and prayed, and prayed. I prayed for strength. I prayed for patience. I prayed for wisdom. I prayed for Ryan. Maybe your God isn't the same as my God, but finding a power greater than yourself could be very helpful in your quest to find answers.

I was lucky that while I got healthy, Ryan was also getting help and finally dealing with his PTSD. However, we didn't speak during this time in our lives. I would text him or he would text me once or twice a month. I remember waiting for my phone to buzz and when it was him, I got butterflies. He would send me song titles and I would listen to them and that is how we communicated. It was like the feeling you get when you started dating a new person.

He sent me letters during his treatment and I still have them today. We slowly built back hope. I started feeling free of stress, pain, and anxiety. I had hope for my future, and even some hope for our future together. No one understood how I could talk to him again, or even entertain the idea of getting back together. The thing I had to remember during all of it was that the only people who understood what we were going through were a select few. My family and friends had never dealt with PTSD. I wasn't lucky enough to have a support group of military wives who could understand me. I had to do it alone.

As our reconciliation progressed, Ryan invited me to go to Idaho on a trip with veterans and their spouses. I was so excited because it was to be the most time we had spent together since our separation, and the first trip we had taken since our honeymoon. This time it was going to be sober, and it was life-changing. I finally met other wives, and I realized that my story was not unique. I wasn't experiencing things that they hadn't. I was normal in their eyes.

After this trip, we attended a PTSD informational session provided by Veterans Affairs. The psychologist described our marriage to a T. I felt empowered to know what we were working with, why Ryan did the things he did, and to finally learn how to be a couple together. I realized that we didn't have to let PTSD define us. We could do it together.

One way that we have gained strength in our marriage is by finding a purpose for what we went through. We get the amazing opportunity to travel the country and share our experiences with other military families. This is part of our healing process, and it is amazing that while we heal we can help others heal as well. I also started a support group in my town for spouses of military members. I got help from a local nonprofit and we meet once a month at a fun little dessert spot in town. These ladies build me up on a regular basis and remind me that I am never alone.

I recognize there is still work to be done. Ryan and I both continue to work at our marriage every single day. Let me rephrase that: every single day both partners need to give 100 percent. This is a common misconception. People often say that marriage is 50/50. This is not true. If you are working at a 50/50 level, you are bound to have problems. Ryan and I live by the principle that we each give 100 percent every day, that way when one of us can't give 100, the other one picks up the slack.

In going through the challenging times, we have also redefined what is important. Are the dirty dishes in the sink really important? Is that a battle worth fighting? No. It is no longer on the list of priorities. What is important to me today is that my family is together. What is important to me today is that we are financially stable. What is important to me today is that my husband and I can laugh together every day, and on days that we can't laugh, we can communicate and find solutions.

This experience has not only been a gift for Ryan and me, but it will be a gift for our two beautiful children. My hope for their future is that they see how important the love between a husband and wife is. I hope that they will take this experience and apply it to their future relationships. That they will work hard for what is important to them, and fight for love. The best gift that we could give our children is the opportunity to hear this story at the dinner table, from both of us, and not have to hear it as a memory from another narrating what broke their family apart.

Our future is bright today. I don't know what tomorrow holds, but I know it will be okay. As Ryan said at our wedding night as he toasted the crowd, "We've been through highs and lows, and things will only get higher and lower, but we can get through it together." Yes we can. Yes we will.

Life will never be perfect for anyone, or any couple, but today we have a marriage that has been tried through faith and action. I wouldn't trade a single second of our story because the experiences we went through made us who we are today. We wouldn't be here without the support of other veterans and other veteran spouses. Shared experiences with others can make trials feel a lot less lonely.

Emily Kaufman is a teacher, caregiver, and advocate for veteran spouses. With degrees in education, and curriculum and instruction, she has taught middle school students for the last 15 years. Through her own experience of caring for her husband in his post-military life, Emily sought to create a spouse trauma support group to help others enduring a similar journey. A resident of Grand Island, Nebraska, she resides there with her husband and two children.

From Military Member to Military Spouse

Lori Bell

I remember the day I became a military spouse. It was quite a transition from what I was used to. There was no ceremony. No oath. No promises. It was me, an airman, and a new ID card.

I walked up to the counter at the Pass and ID office in the building where I worked at the time. I sat in the chair on the wall with the most boring blah background: a plain white wall. I hoped this was not prophetic of the military spouse life that awaited me. There was a camera in front of me. Smile! Click. Boom. The deed was done and apparently it was final.

I handed over my Air Force issued Common Access Card (CAC) that stated I was a military member. There I was, proudly wearing my BDUs with my prominently displayed rank of major. In a flash of memory, I saw my commissioning ceremony on my last day of college graduation. I remembered my first duty station, and meeting this fine chocolate brown lieutenant who later became my husband. I thought of the promotions we both had together and even how he promoted me to Captain by having me recite the oath when we were stationed in Japan. And I saw my last promotion ceremony to major and thought of my baby daughter. Sigh. Yes, it was time to do something different.

It's not that I felt forced to leave or anything. I knew it was time, because I felt the call of other goals and desires from when I was a child rise up within me. Every time I had to go TDY, PCS, or deploy there was another longing to pay attention to something else. And so, I was afraid to leave. The Air Force was one of those "for sure" kinds of commitment. There was no guesswork. I didn't have to go "create something" and hoped it was the right thing. I didn't need an internal compass or any assurance that I could do it; I had trained for this. It was completely comfortable and predictable.

Too comfortable and predictable. I knew what to do in uniform. But what would happen when I took that uniform off for the last time and had to figure things out? Could I really depend on the power of my own dreams?

I looked at my ID card one last time, longingly. Was I sure? Was it too late? Was I crazy?? The airman whisked the card away so quickly I snapped out of my nostalgia. To him, it was a tick of one more responsibility of his day before he moved on to the next customer. But to me ... it was a defining moment. I was now a Military Spouse. Oh. Em. Gee.

My transition from active duty officer to military spouse was a difficult one. I found it hard to let go. Why?

It was the identity of being an active duty airman. Being an active duty member held prominence. I was responsible for stuff, money, and people. I was rewarded for good performance and promoted based on future potential to perform just as well. *I was a leader.* And I was known.

At the gate of any military installation, before entering, I would hand over my ID card and sit up a little straighter. At my own base, I always waited for what was inevitably coming from the civilian gate guard police officer. "Oh, you're an officer? Wow, thank you for your service, ma'am."

Yes, that's right.

I'm an officer.

And I'm a woman.

And I'm a *black woman*. Boo-yah on that.

Yes, I was Somebody!

I had 10 years of experience as an active duty airman, but I was walking into this milspouse life totally naked, vulnerable and biased. There was no template, no pre-made blueprint for what comes next. When I was an airman, I walked into ready-made organizations with a clear chain of command. There was a mission; I knew who I was working for and what I was working with. But this military spouse thing ... WHEW. I didn't know if I could handle it just as well.

At root of this fear is actually what saved me—what gave my life substance, and what generated a genuinely authentic way of living. I was stripped of my self-identity as *Black Female Air Force Officer* and rediscovered myself in a new way, free of labels and definitions so I could truly be Me.

But the journey to this freedom was not an easy one. There were a lot of judgments I had to get over. Lots of ideas and belief systems to dismantle in order to get to the truth of who I was and who I wanted to become. People were recognizing me as a military spouse, but I didn't know what that truly meant, because I didn't know Me. I wanted to discover *her*, learn about her and fall in love with her. I wanted to know who I was before any label decided for me. And that's where my journey into military spouse life began.

Dirty Diapers and Flat Daddy

In 2010, we were stationed in Alaska. It was there I experienced my first deployment as a military spouse.

"Lori, I'm deploying."

Just like that. That's how he broke the news to me. Over the poopy diaper of our naked 9-month-old baby. Looking back on that moment now, I guess there really is no easy way to say you're leaving your family to go to war. War stinks. Maybe telling me while holding a poopy diaper was poetic, if not appropriate?

"You're so funny", I said. "Quit playing and pass me a diaper."

"No, seriously. I was notified today that I'm deploying to Afghanistan."

"How long?"

"Six months."

Ouch. That's a mighty long time. That means he'll miss all the September birthdays, our fun holiday traditions, and our anniversary. Our daughter was going to be 3, our son was turning 1, and me, well I was going to be at my most fabulous at 34.

"Well, when do you leave? Hopefully we'll get to enjoy the Alaskan summer together."

"Weeeeell ... " Long pause.

"Well what? When?"

"In two weeks."

Our baby cooed and laughed and enjoyed the moment of both his parents changing his stink. But I was feeling my heart sink. In my former Air Force life, I had troops that deployed. I had deployed twice, before we had kids. I knew the drill. Take care of the families left behind. Check on the spouse and make sure she's getting along okay. Make sure she knows about Airman and Family Readiness and all the resources available to her during this time. The tables were turned and now I was on the other side of those deployment orders. I was so scared to do this.

Two weeks flew by in a blur of him getting ready to leave: training, medical appointments, briefings, deployment gear, legal appointments for power of attorney documents. Whenever he was home, we held on tight, feeling the moments slowly slip away. That first night he was gone my babies and I were a mess. I remember putting the two of them in the tub and each was taking turns sobbing and screaming, *"But Mommy, that's not how Daddy does it!"* Apparently I was missing some key bath time behavior.

I got creative in many ways. I had an idea to create "Daddy's Deployment Countdown Calendar," which was three or four poster boards hung on the walls with empty squares on them. For everyday Daddy was gone, we'd put a sticker on that day. One lonely pitiful sticker and 179 empty squares. It was a week before I realized that was probably not the best idea.

Then I found out about Flat Daddy. Some company would take a photo of your service member, blow it up to about 3 feet tall and cut it out for you. Flat Daddy was a hit! He ate dinner with us, we took him to church, and we even took him to the state fair! The kids loved him, until about month four when my oldest kicked Flat Daddy and said that she wanted her real daddy now.

By the second month, I knew it was time for some spouse connection. We were doing great at home; our commander's wife sent over her 15-year-old daughter to babysit for me and her 17-year-old son took our trash to the curb and cut the grass every week. I didn't even have to ask. I felt so loved as I experienced the camaraderie of the military spouse. It did make me wonder though—did most spouses have this kind of support? What about Guard or Reserve spouses who were not connected to a military installation? I wondered, what did other people do when their service member was not around for a while, did they know how to reach out for help?

When Military Spouses Deploy

Early one Saturday morning, I tiptoed downstairs after a restless night. I plopped on the couch. I saw my big, hot pink Countdown Calendar on the wall and gave it the side-eye. I wondered what my husband was doing at that moment, and eventually my thoughts led me to the very word "deployment." It really sucked being alone. Deploy. What does it really mean, I thought. I looked up the word deploy and was a little surprised to find that it means, "*to utilize; bring into effective action.*"

I turned that over in my mind and suddenly felt a little more powerful. What could I bring into effective action? All this time I had felt that a deployment was something that was being done to a person. But I never considered that I could deploy. I could utilize my gifts, skills and talents in an extraordinary way right now. I could bring it all together into "effective action." That's when I thought of the questions I had about other spouses and how they cope with military life and the idea hit me in the gut. There were spouses all over the country and on U.S. military installations all over the world dealing with some aspect of military life just like me. What could I offer them?

I went to my computer and searched some key words. Back then Facebook was only five years old, and Twitter was a baby at three years. Social media was still very new to the world, and what exists now in the form of private and secret Facebook groups was unheard of then. I was looking for online support groups for what I called "military moms and spouses." I found nothing, and so, I created one myself.

National Association of Military Moms and Spouses (NAMMAS) is what I named it. It was a social group for spouses of all branches of service who wanted to connect with others like them. I didn't know what I was creating. I just knew I liked bringing people and talent together, and this seemed like a great place to start. I invited seven of my friends to join and we started there. I spread the word everywhere I could, and within a few months there were almost 100 members.

Something strange and quite unexpected was happening. People began to notice NAMMAS, and an unrepresented group of women were joining us on our message boards: military moms of service members. When I named NAMMAS I was thinking of military *stay-at-home moms* (like me), and spouses of all kinds and backgrounds. I didn't even know that moms of service members existed (which was weird because both my husband and I had moms!). But they found NAMMAS, and they came with concerns, compassion, questions and resources. By the end of the first year, NAMMAS had 1000 members.

I had found a niche, I'd found my *thing*. I had "deployed" my ingenuity and created something of value! So many wonderful opportunities came from this little seed of an idea to start an organization like NAMMAS. I earned a national award from *Military Spouse Magazine* and Armed Forces Insurance as *2010 Military Spouse of the Year*. NAMMAS was featured on national news media and my personal story was a highlight on *NBC Nightly News with Brian Williams* in their *Making a Difference* segment. I was on *Good Morning America, CNN,* and my mom and I were interviewed on *Fox News.* I was even one of 30 military spouses selected to be with Oprah for a day in a very private taping of *Oprah's Favorite Things,* as we were showered with hundreds of gifts and love from Oprah and her team and Military Spouse Magazine. I was in the spotlight representing over 1 million military spouses and my little organization, which was now at about 3000 members strong. By the end of 2010, I had been on the news locally and nationally in front of more than 30 million people.

Many accolades, recognitions, and interviews later I remember having that same feeling as when I was "*Black Female Air Force Officer.*"

I've made it.

I am somebody.

I am validated.

But in the stillness, in the places I couldn't ignore when I was alone with my own thoughts and feelings, I knew something was out of alignment. If I felt validated when I was doing well and people patted my ego, what would happen when it all disappeared? Who would I be then?

I was so accustomed to achievement. After all, everyone is rewarded for doing well. But for me, it wasn't just about doing well, it was about defining an identity and having "doing well" be my measure of success. In other words, if I was praised for what I did, I must be amazing. If there was no recognition, I must suck. This small nudge in the direction of self-acceptance, inward knowing, and self-love was another phase in my personal development as a military spouse.

Coming Home to Myself

By 2014, we were on our eleventh PCS move, including my active duty time. I was comfortable in my role as a military spouse. Over the years I had been busy. I survived deployments and TDYs beautifully. I was having babies, connecting more, increasing my own popularity and reputation within the local and national milspouse communities, and growing NAMMAS. I was doing what I know best: hustling, working hard, and making it happen.

I thrived on my ambition and was proud of it. I found value in being busy and productive, being results oriented, and reward driven. I even had the bold audacity to train and compete in my first bodybuilding competition! My ambition had been very good to me over the years. Until the day came when it wasn't.

I found that I was always striving for something, working on the next thing, always bigger and better than something in the past. I surrounded myself with other women who were hard-charging entrepreneurs who knew how to get things done. Their pace was lightning speed because they were fast-action takers. I reveled in that for a while. But I knew, from that knowing place deep inside that cannot be deceived, that I was not in integrity with myself. Something about what I was doing was incongruent with who I wanted to be.

At the end of the 2014, I had what I call a "truth moment." It was one of those divinely intuitive experiences that at the time didn't seem like a really big deal, but over the years since then I have come to know it as the turning point in my own evolution.

It was the day I realized I was done with the doing that only led to more doing. The labels no longer romanced me with the promise of popularity. I could not get satisfaction in the rat race that I had created for myself keeping up with people alongside me. I was ready for more ... but I was ready for *deeper*, something more potent than accolades or accomplishment. There was a calling within me that I could no longer ignore or cover up and I was ready to explore what that looked like for me.

It was the beckoning of what I call my "Great Work." The actual thing I am here to do. Every time I thought of it, I was both excited and very intimidated, which are hallmarks of Great Work callings. I could see clearly what I wanted, but the path to it was a mystery. I was ready to discover what this was all about. But first, I had to clear the clutter.

Although I didn't really know where to start exactly, intuitively I knew if what I was feeling was coming up from the inside that must also be where the answers were.

So I began to ask myself some deeply introspective questions:

What do I really want?

And then what?

What do I want to feel?

What excites me, thrills me, sets me on fire from the inside?

How can I bring more of that into my life?

What do I require?

I didn't stop there. I took a look at what I was doing and made a list of all the things to which I gave my energy. I had known for about a year that NAMMAS no longer felt good to me. What began as fun had turned into a chore. I didn't look forward to the work of growing my organization anymore and it drained me. My passion had waned, and I knew the right thing to do was to lovingly let go, so I officially closed NAMMAS.

I looked at my list of "doings."

- Multi-level marketing business
- Bible study
- Training for another bodybuilding show

My list of engagements was about 13 things long, not including being a mom and wife to my family. It was time to cut ties and be free. I wanted a clean slate to choose what I wanted and where I wanted to be.

The biggest realization I had in this experience was that under all that "doing", there was a Me that I really didn't know yet. When I gave up my active duty ID card, I gave up an *identity*. I picked up another one with my dependent card. I traded one identity for another and spent 7 years trying to prove I was worthy. That was my scarlet letter, I suppose. Trying to prove to myself that I could do *this*, be this, that I could shine just as well as a military spouse as when I was Black Woman, Air Force Officer.

The Yes Process

The most courageous thing a person can do is let go. Think about that. When you let go of things that no longer give you pleasure, tasks that no longer fulfill you, and even beliefs that no longer make sense, you step into a realm of power and authority that fuels your life in unimaginable ways. You become free as you say yes to discover who you really are under all that validation. You let go of trying to prove or defend yourself, and you show up authentically in your world. You say YES to being you.

But ... there is a process to yes. And, as I discovered in my own experience, it requires everything you have.

The entire year of 2015 was a going-deep year. I shut down most things I was doing, including social media. I stopped trying to build a business. I stopped being everywhere all the time and relaxed into being in the here and now. I destroyed my religious box, and opened my heart to spirituality and self-acceptance. It was a growing year.

I welcomed transformation in 2016, but growth did not stop. It was time I to come out of my spiritual closet and live authentically and in integrity of truth as it had been revealed to me through my own experience. This was difficult for me. I had discovered so much about myself and I knew that my spiritual path was not going to agree with current relationships. Some friendships fell completely off as new and beautiful ones were forming. I learned to be at ease with myself, and therefore I was at ease with others. I knew I didn't have to "perform" or find satisfaction in starting new projects, and that all the approval I needed came from within me. I was learning what self-mastery was and how to live in true freedom from public expectation or favor.

I wrote a book titled *The Yes Process: Discover the Journey of Becoming Yourself* based on my awareness and insights of peeling back my own spiritual onion. I cleared out my emotional, spiritual and environmental clutter. I let go of things, people, and ideas that I had clung to and assumed were necessary for my very survival. I no longer needed anything to define me. Finally I knew, *I am enough.*

The best part is that reclaiming all my energy from those projects I was plugged into now freed up my creativity. Writing a book was liberating, I could tell my story and help people all over the world. But I also thought, how cool would it be to do this work one-on-one with a woman who was just like me? I had learned that my value is in whom I am, not what I can do. Who I am is powerful enough and I no longer needed to prove it. I knew that if I had felt these things and walked through the process of overcoming them, there must be others like me.

So, I developed my own transformational coaching practice where I support women who are successful high-achievers, but want the freedom to explore their next big step. They are ready to release the blockages that hold them back. I began attracting women who wanted to overcome their blind spots to make room for their Great

Work so that they can do what makes them feel alive, sets them ablaze, and makes them cry just thinking about it. In 2016, I began enrolling clients in my program, only accepting a select few that inspired and excited me. I wanted to do this my way, so that I didn't feel like I was "working," but creating. After all this time I finally feel that I've found my true place, my for real home. And the center of it is in ME.

Today, it's been ten years since I became a military spouse. It is not at all what I thought it would be, but it was the catalyst for my own personal transformation. If you ask a handful of people what it means to be a military spouse, you'll get a handful of opinions. But my deepest discovery is that I make the role; I fill it with my own descriptions. I can be as big or small as I want to be, and I don't have to apologize for what I choose.

I think a strong misconception within the military spouse community, as well as society is to assume a milspouse looks, acts, and is a certain way. There are negative stereotypes of money-hungry "dependas" or lazy stay-at-home moms. Then there are the super-women who volunteer, organize, champion and overcome. And let's not forget the men who are turning gender roles upside down. All of these are someone else's definitions of what a milspouse looks like.

My questions to you are: Who were you before you became a military spouse? Who are you now? Who would you like to be? Define it. Rearrange it. Tell your OWN story and just let it be. You have nothing to protect and there is nothing to defend. When you discover who you really are without all the labels, you discover a wide open space to explore for yourself what works for you. You can create and design your world exactly as you like it to be. That's your real superpower.

When you look around at the messages you are receiving from the media, from friends, from well-meaning groups, you will notice the roles you are expected to fill. Look at things military spouses are rewarded for DOING. Volunteering, starting something, finishing something, being a no-nonsense, hard-charging, overcoming fighter.

But I want to present a new paradigm to you. What if none of that matters? What if, instead of receiving recognition for the doings, you were rewarded for the beings? Don't get me wrong, there are spouses accomplishing amazing things and overcoming incredible odds, too. But you know what? Being a fun mom to toddlers is noble. Keeping house and creating a warm, loving environment for a family, even if that family is two people, deserves respect. And pursuing a career that you absolutely love is worthy.

My message to all women, but especially military spouses is that it is easy to agree with society and the culture that convince us to go along to get along. But we're all greater than that, and the conditioning that exists in our world today makes us forget who we are. It's safer to fit in, isn't it? It's definitely more convenient and acceptable! But I say fitting into nice, neat labels will be the death of your true creativity. There's magic in you! There is a strength that exists because you are You, not because you are a military spouse. When you follow the path home to Yourself, you will find everything you've ever longed for. My wish for all is that we not only live outside of our boxes, but that we know from deep within that there was never a box from the start.

May you discover this path and hold fast to it no matter where it takes you. Flow with it, and be at ease. It's the best ride you'll ever know!

Lori Bell is a mom, USAF veteran, entrepreneur, and author of The Yes Process: Discover the Journey of Becoming Yourself, a transformational self-help memoir written for women who are ready to step into their fullest expression of authentic living. Lori's work in the military spouse community has been featured in front of more than 30 million people, and highlighted on NBC Nightly News Making A Difference, Lifetime TV, Fox and Friends, Good Morning America, OWN, and many others. She currently resides in Oklahoma City with her active duty husband and three children.

Changing Course

Stacey Benson

To say that I am a U.S. Coast Guard wife is not entirely true; I have also been an Army wife – same husband but two different careers!

I am a mom to my wonderfully witty and handsome 12-year-old son Zachery and married to my best friend, and the love of my life, Larry. Seventeen years ago Larry and I met while I attended Winthrop University. At that time, he was fresh out of boot camp, as well as SERE and jump school, and had just been assigned to the 3/7 Group in the U.S. Army. I received my Bachelor of Science in integrated marketing communication and we married in August of 2002. Two years later we welcomed Zachery into our lives. My husband deployed a month later and was unable to share with me where he was going.

Zachery and I went to stay with my parents in South Carolina until Larry came home four months later. My family's support during that time was instrumental with a newborn baby. Up until then, I had flown solo during past deployments trying to keep myself busy until he came home.

When he returned, Larry made sergeant first class and was up for re-enlistment. At that time, he had completed six major deployments all over the world, in addition to attending many schools and training missions. He wanted to do a job he enjoyed, but most importantly he wanted to be a father to our young son. With those goals in mind, he made the decision to "lateral over" to the Coast Guard. He lost three ranks and pay grades just to be closer to us, but he says the decision, to him, was easy.

I have been part of the U.S. Coast Guard community now for 12 years. We have PCSed and been stationed in the southern Outer Banks of North Carolina, on the Great Lakes of Buffalo, New York, and in East Providence, Rhode Island. We have always enjoyed moving to new locations every four years with the Coast Guard and getting to experience all that these new places have to offer.

Our fourth PCS will happen in the summer of 2017 and we are heading to the West Coast. Larry will be attached to Cutter, which is a boat that deploys for 60 days at a time. It is funny how life comes full circle. Larry started his military career deploying to South America while in the Army and will finish his career in a similar fashion.

My career has taken many twists and turns as a result of being a dedicated and committed military spouse and mother. Over the past several years I have been a wedding coordinator, a wholesale travel package seller, a fundraising solution and support provider, a project manager, a cake baker, a photography prop maker, a photographer, a graphic designer, a secretary, and a website administrator. I have had to be creative and use my wits to help support our family and at the same time fulfill my own personal goals. As a volunteer on the board of the Military Spouses of Newport, I have seen other military spouses feeling the impact of putting their spouses' careers and their families' well-being before their own. This impacts military spouses in many ways such as: limiting mobility, competing for jobs for which they are overqualified and underpaid, and overall being discriminated against for job positions due to future relocations.

It has been tough, but we have made it work and it has made us stronger as a family. Due to military life, we have been lucky enough to live in some amazing places, establish some lasting friendships, and have had some remarkable experiences. Knowing back in 2000 what I know now, would I have selected a different path for my life? I would not want to change a single second, because this life has shaped me into the person I am today.

During my free time I love volunteering at the Rhode Island Food Bank where we help to separate donated food for distribution throughout the state of Rhode Island to help cut down on hunger. When my husband's unit needs volunteers, I am always the first to join in as an extra helping hand.

From 2013-2015, I also volunteered as the hospitality committee chair for Military Spouses of Newport. My role was planning and executing social events for newly arriving spouses to the Newport area, including all branches. I planned three large social events a year including spring, summer, and fall.

Over the past two years, I have filled the roll as president of Military Spouses of Newport. My role was to help oversee and run the board of directors, committee chairs and co-chairs, and network with other military spouses.

I was able to utilize my position with MSoN to help my past employers at the Newport Hospital. I did this by using my connections with the MSoN club to help other military spouses find employment in the local health care system.

My real passion is photography. I love photographing military families and telling their stories through the lens of my camera. This allows me to preserve their special memories for a lifetime.

In 2015, I was hired by the Semper Fi Fund as a graphic designer and photographer. The Fund provides immediate financial assistance and lifetime support to post-9/11 wounded, critically ill and injured members of all branches of the U.S. Armed Forces and their families. We give back to them every day, making sure they have the resources they need during their recovery and transition back to their communities.

In 2003, a group of military spouses sat around a kitchen table trying to decide how the $500 they had collected could be given back to service members returning from Operation Iraqi Freedom. The Fund was officially formed a year later and has since raised more than $150 million in assistance for more than 18,700 service members and families.

Me? I'm part of the Fund's marketing and public relations team. I work with other teams to produce marketing and print pieces, and I support the social media and website efforts with graphics and photography. I love telling our service members' stories through my camera's lens. I want my images to be compelling, to show the hardships that someone has had to endure and overcome.

The Semper Fi Fund provides support in the form of grants and programs, giving back to service members and their families, with staff and volunteers located in major military hospitals in and in between both coasts and abroad. The Fund maintains an extremely low overhead; since the inception in 2004, overhead has averaged only six percent of revenue, and rapid assistance is provided with no red tape.

Almost everyone at the Fund is a military spouse, veteran, or has experienced military life in one form or another. Giving back comes naturally to us, and the basic ideal that drives our efforts is simple: For as much as our heroes have sacrificed, they deserve the best care and support available in their hour of need. The Fund helps qualifying post-9/11 Marines, sailors, soldiers, airmen, Coast Guardsmen, and reservists with amputations, spinal cord injuries, traumatic brain injury (TBI), severe post traumatic stress (PTS), burns, blindness, other physical injuries, or those suffering from life-threatening illnesses. We also help spouses and children of active duty service members who face a life-threatening illness or injury.

Every day I'm excited to go to work with an amazing team of people who spend every waking hour giving back. Our staff and volunteers work tirelessly to make the Fund a success, and everyone works in unison like a well-oiled machine – with the ultimate goal of serving those who have served us all in order to protect our freedom.

In December 2016, the Semper Fi Fund was contacted and offered a free public service announcement in Times Square. I was the lead on the project and submitted 40-50 images from many different photographers, who have covered our multitude of events.

These images tell the story of the fund, our programs, and our service members. I wanted all parts of our story to be told. I knew only 30 images would be chosen to be featured in the PSA. When I got the proof back from the company, I was shocked and completely and totally surprised that several of my images were chosen to be featured, 11 to be exact.

Walking down the streets of NYC, into Times Square and seeing an image that you captured is AMAZING! I was awestruck; jumping up and down, laughing, crying, and yelling all at the same time – HEY THAT'S MY PHOTO – HERE IN TIMES SQUARE!! Holy smokes, talk about an emotional roller-coaster. I am a self-taught photographer and never in my wildest dreams would have ever imagined that I would have my images up in lights, much less in Times Square! But it happened, and it was all because of the Semper Fi Fund.

Stacey Benson grew up in South Carolina on her family's farm riding tractors, fishing, shooting guns, 4-wheeling, and helping out when and where she could. This is where she learned the value of hard work, being loyal, trust worthy, and love. All of this taught her how to be independent and valuable in her own right, to stand up for what she believes in, to work hard for herself, and to help others through her own efforts. Her family shaped her into the person that she is today and she will forever be grateful.

Revealing My Sense of Purpose

Natasha Harth

Natasha Harth, 2016 Armed Forces Insurance Military Spouse of the Year. I still get a little flushed when I hear those words come out of anyone's mouth. One year ago I was picking my jaw up off the ground at the honor of being named Marine Corps Spouse of the Year. Present day, I'm probably even more amazed because I've seen the work other spouses do firsthand, and it simply blows me away. Sometimes I even wonder how I stuck out in a crowd that is full of accomplished, selfless, dedicated, and hard-working spouses just like myself.

I was first aware of the program in 2015 when I was nominated as the Armed Forces Insurance Marine Barracks Washington Spouse of the Year. Seeing what prior year nominees and winners have accomplished, and what the spouses of my year were doing, I thought to myself, "Wow! I don't know if I will ever measure up to them, but I sure will try." Darn that little voice in the back of many women's heads that is always under-valuing. I can praise and encourage another spouse in their endeavors and boost anyone's confidence, but it seems like I'm always convincing myself that I need to do more to make a difference.

Well, thanks to this new title, it gave me a sense of purpose to use that title to actually make a difference at Marine Barracks Washington (MBW). You see, MBW is not like any traditional base that I had been attached to before (Pendleton, Lejeune, Twentynine Palms, etc.). There was not a robust Family Readiness Program, and families just didn't get together to do, well … much of anything. The opportunity to volunteer with the command was not available, and with everyone dispersed among all of the bases and towns between Fredericksburg, Virginia up to southern Maryland, it just wasn't the cohesive environment I was used to at forward operating bases. I missed that, and I wanted to provide some opportunity for people there to work together.

Since my family lived close to the barracks, we would often spend time down on Barracks Row at a new restaurant, or over at Eastern Market just a couple of blocks away. It was impossible to ignore the amount of homeless people in the area. Some would just ask for money, a few were isolated with overt mental challenges, many would just be asleep, and there were some with yellow vests selling a newspaper written by the homeless and published for them to sell to have a way to earn some money. One particular man I would see often, Phillip, was one of these *Street Sense* vendors and quite the conversationalist. I would talk to him when we crossed paths and started asking him what it is I could do to help the situation. "I don't have a lot of money," I said, "but I know there's got to be something I can do."

Phillip and I came up with an idea to pack bags, which I later dubbed as Blessing Bags. "Make sure you put them in plastic bags, double them up. The rats will smell the food inside and you'll wake up feeling one of those big things chewing right through what you have — sometimes they end up biting you by accident," he said. The way he continued to describe some of the challenges of sleeping on the street made my skin crawl. At this point, I was determined to do something to help, despite how small I thought my efforts would be. Phillip and I came up with a list of items that the homeless in the area would find most beneficial, and I took it home to think. How would I get these items? Who would I turn to for help?

My first thought was to go to Marine Barracks Washington. After all, the homeless people I am trying to help are right in their backyard. I reached out to public affairs, family readiness, and a few other people, trying to find someone to help me spread the word, gather volunteers, donate supplies, etc. Disappointedly, I was told that they couldn't help, not even to publish something internally and spread the word. The pushback was so cold that I almost dropped it all together. In the end, I relied on a command wife to grease the wheels with the chaplain to round up a few volunteers to help me distribute bags when it was time to hit the ground. I graciously took what I could get.

While my heart was heavy by the lack of responsiveness from the base I was selected to represent, I carried on but was slightly discouraged. I honestly thought I might have a couple of friends donate items here and there, and I was going to dig into my already slim pockets to make up for the rest. If I could at least get or buy enough to make 30 bags, I was going to leave it at that, and know that I gave it my best try. I was armed with a request of backpacks and a list of items needed to fill them, and set out to spread the word. The emptiness I felt was quickly filled by the hearts and generosity of my friends and coworkers. The words "thank you" just didn't seem like enough to express my gratitude for the amazing support I received.

The Air Force Officers' Spouses' Club, for whom I worked at the time, pitched in like wildfire! I had a bunch of gently used backpacks, and they rallied to buy the supplies on my list. The ladies (and our gentleman) went above and beyond by finding blankets, socks, hats and other warming layers as well. Friends would pull up in the driveway with bags, sometimes trunks full, of supplies. My aunts took to Costco and bought socks, gums, and other things to pitch in. A few special friends were able to secure large donations from other organizations, for which I am eternally grateful, including clothes and shoes. There are too many people to thank to name them all individually! My garage quickly became the donation station, and all hopes of ever parking a car in there quickly vanished.

I had the supplies, now I needed to figure out how to logistically get them to those that need it most. A friend at the Joint Base Anacostia-Bolling police department stepped up and rallied her friends and co-workers to escort us through the lower side of Capitol Hill. It was around this time that the chaplain came through and gathered a few volunteers from the barracks that wanted to get involved. Instrumental to operational success was a dear friend from the base library who already went out twice a month to feed the homeless. Her group has been doing this for so long that the local homeless know the schedule and they definitely show up. There are 30-70 people there every time, so instead of walking all the streets of DC, we figured we would walk a calculated path to end up at her regularly scheduled location. We would come to straight to where we knew people would be, and her group made sure to spread the word a month in advance to maximize the number of people we could reach.

The day before our planned distribution date, I threw a packing party in the library. My husband hauled the large totes that contained all items in through the back door, I ordered lots of pizza and soda, and spread the word. We had friends, kids, library staff, and family members there ready to get to work. It was set up like an assembly line – take a backpack, line it with a bag, pass. Put an item from your bucket in, pass. Next … you get the idea. The kids were eager to be part of the operation, and some drew pictures or made cards to be added to the bags' contents. In about two hours, we had stuffed over 70 backpacks. I put them all in a pile, sat back, and just soaked in the marvelousness that teamwork created. I was quiet, thinking about how I thought I was going to have to buy things out of pocket just to get a few bags together, and humbled by the generosity of my friends. If you know me, you would have wondered what was wrong. I'm seldom quiet when surrounded by friends. We loaded the completed bags in the back of the truck, along with bins and boxes of blankets, clothing, and shoes – mostly excited and a little nervous about the following day.

Sunday morning a couple of car loads of JBAB police officers and friends followed me to the meeting spot for the Marines in the barracks. There were about 20 people in total, including kids and spouses, who were excitedly putting backpacks on their backs, two or three deep, ready to pass them out to any homeless person we would encounter during our four block trek to our destination. Smile on the outside, I was nervous on the inside. People were asking me questions about what we would do when we see a person, how to approach them, what to say ... I was trying my best to lead while not wanting to admit that I had no idea what to expect. I thought to myself, "We will figure it out as we go along, just keep your cool and act like you know what you're doing."

The first person we encountered was in the grassy area close to the Metro stop. She was sitting on the ground, surrounded by a few bags and blankets. My heart fluttered; this was my chance to set the example and get the ball rolling. I ran across the street and took a backpack off of my back – holding it out. "Ma'am, we want to give you this backpack full of food and supplies, just to let you know that someone is thinking about you and loves you!" I said with a smile.

"NO! I DON'T WANT IT!" she yelled. My heart dropped to my feet. My recruited volunteers were watching and listening from both sides of the street. Oh my gosh, what do I do? I gently placed it on the ground near her and said, "It's okay, we don't want to bother you. I'll just leave it here to help." I turned around to walk away and again she shouted, "NO, I DON'T WANT IT. GO AWAY!" My face red, I picked up the backpack from the ground, but determined to do something, I placed it out of her eyesight behind the tree next to her and I walked away. Back on my side of the street, I said, "Sometimes people might not want help, and she might not have all of her mental faculties. Let's keep that in mind going forward, and don't force anyone to take a bag." I'm pretty sure my face was still as red as a tomato while I was trying my best to look cool as a cucumber.

We pushed forward and right in front of the Eastern Market, there were two homeless men asleep on benches. One girl looked at me and asked, "Should we give them one?" I instructed her to quietly tiptoe to the bench and leave one on the ground beside it. We had attached notes to the outside of all bags so I thought it was a safe bet that when they woke up, they'd see it and understand its purpose. As two of the girls tiptoed up to the benches, a third man popped his head over and said, "You messing with my friends?" The girls jumped, startled, and then went on to explain what we were doing. At this point, the two in slumber had awoken and listened in. I was holding my breath, praying that it wouldn't go down like our first encounter. "MAN, that's cool!" I heard. I was finally able to exhale, and enjoy listening to the conversation. Those guys led up to a couple more that we were able to give bags to, and we carried on the journey, asking them to spread the word to others nearby about where we were stopping.

When we arrived at our landing destination, my husband who was parked on the side street opened up the tailgate and we started unloading. There were already about 15 homeless men waiting there, as they had heard what we were doing. As I grabbed one box and turning around to hand it to what I thought was my husband, I found myself handing it to a smiling stranger who said, "Missus, we want to help. We are all so excited you're here." I was humbled by their willingness to jump right in and help, not asking what I have, not looking in the boxes for themselves first, not touching a thing except to place the boxes in the park, and ask what they could do next. Even as a couple of men were taking shoes out of the large tub, matching them and placing them on the ground side-by-side, no one asked if they could take a pair or try them on. They took pride in rolling blankets and setting them out for selection, admiring the woolen army ones that I was lucky enough to get and bring. I felt like I was in one of those feel-good Facebook videos where all a homeless person wants to do is share a sandwich with a stranger, or gives their coat to a younger homeless person – giving the very little they have for the good of another. I hugged them all and told them how much I appreciated their help, and I didn't want to let go.

At this point, all apprehension dissolved, and I was just flooded with joy. THIS is what I had hoped for – to be able to reach a large number of people and do something impactful. I wanted to bring military volunteers outside of their base to make a difference in the community that they lived in. My hopes were for people to see that any ordinary person (in this instance, me) could make the extraordinary happen, with the hopes to inspire others to do the same.

Since that initial event, Be A Blessing has quickly grown into helping service members who are food insecure, facilitating a ball gown giveaway in partnership with United Military Significant Others, donating supplies to schools, and other projects on a case- by-case basis. Many people have asked how they can help or get involved. I love it when people in my area are able to support one of my events and lend a hand, and I've found that the volunteers who do so walk away wanting to do more. I feel that the joy I can bring to others makes me probably just as happy, if not more so. I can see those feelings reflected in my volunteers. It truly is a great feeling to give, even if all one has to give is their time.

I fear that my generation of spouses has been accustomed to the "war tempo" for so long that we are so busy just taking care of our families that we forget to do something for ourselves. There was a point in my marriage where I was struggling to find ownership over something in my life while the rest of it seemed out of my hands. I chose volunteering as a way to connect with other spouses and do something good for others, which ultimately makes me feel good myself. Years ago, I never would have guessed it to evolve in such a way that I am spearheading my own efforts.

Starting in 2015, I wanted to prove a point. That point is that any ordinary person can make an extraordinary difference, and not to underestimate yourself. I'm not asking everyone to go out and feed the homeless; what I'm asking is for everyone to strive to make a positive impact in an area they're enthusiastic about. Everyone is different, and that should be celebrated. Artists can take their skills to children's hospitals and bring joy to the kids through creative art therapy and play. Those handy around the house can offer home repairs for elderly neighbors. Someone who loves kids could start a co-op to give overwhelmed moms a break. The list could go on forever. Find what your passion is and use it for good!

Natasha Harth is passionate about finding ways to bloom where she is planted and has thrived by becoming a champion for military families through volunteering and advocacy; she is recognized for bringing communities together. Natasha is the 2016 Armed Forces Insurance Military Spouse of the Year, loves to laugh and make the best of every situation, and believes in the power of kindness. Natasha resides in Burke, VA with her active duty Marine Corps husband and two daughters.

The Unicorn Milspouse:
Perspective of a Male Spouse

Dave Etter

Welcome to your first Family Readiness Group meeting – this is the FRG.

As you look around the room at all the other military spouses, you see groupings of people. Some are looking at their cellphones, obviously reveling in the latest pictures of their little angels. Another group poised with coffee cups raised, casual in their stance, giggling and chatting about some news that is of obvious importance. And another group is hovering around the snack table, eyeing the fares, darting their glances about as if afraid someone is going to see how much they want that donut that is calling their name: the dieters. But, alas, what is that, over there? It looks like a guy!

That is me, the unicorn in the room, a male military spouse. My wife is active duty, a sergeant in the company, who works with your spouse. And, yes, I am at ease in this scenario!

You see, I am a large guy – I stand an intimidating six foot one inch, hefting a frame of around 350 pounds – I am a big guy. I am also fearless, a submarine veteran who remembers when the military did not care if we had families. Fortunately, that is not the case anymore! So, with my commanding presence and cheerful demeanor, I am probably your FRG leader!

How did I come to be the one heading up the show, you might ask? Ah, there's the rub. I am a softy for dispersing information. I want everyone to know about all the features and programs spouses have available. I know / like to stay informed, so I like to make sure everyone else does, too! So, grab a coffee or tea (or beer, I have one or two around here somewhere) and strap in for a fun ride as I get you involved with helping other military spouses!

Before I plug you in, you should know a little bit more about this unicorn you've found yourself with. I am a larger than life kind of guy – I have been a carnival barker, a biker, a bouncer, a movie and television extra, a cable TV commercial character, a radio broadcaster, a grocery store produce manager, a computer repair geek, a land surveyor apprentice, a newspaper delivery boy, a singer, a submarine sailor, a limo driver, and an entrepreneur, just to name a few.

I've been married a few times, with Stephanie being my third and final marriage; she's my soul mate. Between the two of us, we have six kids who claim us, the youngest being 16 and a junior in high school. He is still with us, experiencing Permanent Change of Station (PCS) moves, and seems to be doing okay with them. The others have moved away, striving to come into their own in this big world. They get to miss out on the military life, dang it. More on that later.

I am an author (you are reading some of my work now), an internet radio host, an FRG mover and shaker, a Boy Scouts of America leader, a mentor, a professional volunteer, and I am the 2016 Armed Forces Insurance Army Spouse of the Year. My wife is an active duty enlisted soldier in the medical field; she is currently working as a respiratory therapist at Landstuhl Regional Medical Center (LRMC) in Landstuhl, Germany. Yes, I am an overseas unicorn! At least at the time of writing, I am. I'm the guy everyone finds and becomes friends with because if you are friends with the biggest, baddest looking guy in the room, your back is covered should things go sideways.

Why do I call myself a unicorn? It is because of the male military spouse demographics. You see, there aren't many of us male milspouses who get involved. We are only 7 to 10 percent of the spouse community, both heterosexual and same-sex marriages. Am I complaining? A bit … imagine yourself in our shoes! So, when you go looking for a male milspouse at a function that isn't a dual military spouse, it's like hunting for unicorns – it feels like we don't exist! But we do, and we have our own needs that are quite different than those of the female persuasion.

First off, we cannot multitask. When conversing with a male military spouse, the conversation HAS to stay on topic, or you lose us. We are trying to be nice, listen and engage, and monitor mini-me over there getting into the cake. So, we tend to not speak much. It's not that I don't want to communicate with you, it's that I know I am responsible for what the little human does and they are really trying my patience right now! So, don't think I'm being snooty. I just cannot multitask well.

Another thing about male milspouses is that we are parents, too. It is very discouraging to try and take the little stomach-monsters to the playground and have the moms there looking at us sideways as if we are dangerous. We are not there to cause discomfort to others, it's so our kids can socialize with your kids! I am harmless, trust me! Come sit with me and let's talk about the best way to get spit-up out of the linens, or the easiest way to make cookies that doesn't burn the kitchen down. Any knowledge that will make me look like a hero to my soldier wife will be hugely appreciated!

And here's one – I do more than change light bulbs, mow the lawn, and tinker with the car. Okay, not that last one; I am pretty lost under the hood of the car. But my neighbor on post at Fort Campbell thought I was mechanically inclined. Nope. Grrrrr …

I am just like you, with different plumbing. I have kids and bills, and I miss my wife terribly when she gets sent somewhere for longer than a week. I try to be a miracle chef in the kitchen: the master of boiling water and the magic nuker-box, also known as the microwave. I clean as best I can, I do laundry just about every day, and I collect tips from the spouses who give me tips to make the home nicer. My wife notices my efforts and it keeps her mission oriented. What more could I want than to have a happy spouse?

How did I get here, you are no doubt pondering? Sit down, I'll try to be as brief as I can. I am a military spouse of only five years as of this writing. I have been with my wife for 18 years, so I remember what it was like to be a civilian couple. I ran a successful taxi business that I owned; my wife was in the customer service industry running a locally owned gas station for a good friend of ours. I was, and still am, active in The American Legion and was a local celebrity due to the popularity of the FM station where I worked. Steph was taking a medical course here and there, nothing truly defined, but still making progress towards an associate degree in something.

One day I couldn't stand breathing, every scent was amplified to the point of pain. Every woman who got into my taxi overwhelmed me with their perfume. I didn't want to leave my car once the painful fragrance went away. So, I did a walk-in appointment with my nurse practitioner. She took one look at me and told me to get to the ER as fast as I could. It turned out I had pneumonia in the upper right lung. When Steph got to my bedside, I was in the middle of a breathing treatment. She looked at me, and instead of concern, she had an epiphany! "Aha! I can do that!" is what she said, and went on to explain that both her parents had COPD and breathing treatments, and that is when she just knew she was supposed to do!

She turned her medical learning focus to the respiratory field, and was making great progress via distance learning, until one semester when she had to take a lab in person, and the closest college that offered the lab was too far to travel to for just the semester. We were either going to have to move or she was going to have to abandon the quest. I suggested joining the military, where she would get the hands-on training she needed, she'd get to see the world, and be able to give back to the wounded warriors. Sure, whichever branch she joined would want to see an ROI (return on investment), and she'd have to do boot camp …

It turned out that she was too old for all but the Army, so off we went! After her initial training at basic training (boot camp) and her advanced instructional training (AIT), she landed … drumroll … 1STB 1BCT 101st Air Assault (Special Troops Battalion of the 1st Battle Combat Team of the Screaming Eagles) in Fort Campbell, Kentucky. Yup. High speed first-in, last-out, also known as the Spartans of Bastogne, just where a 40-year-old E-4 wants to go as a combat medic. Just where a newly-minted, now-unemployed male spouse, wants to be. HooAhh.

Now what? I'll wait for help, because I watched "Army Wives" on TV while she was training, just to know what to expect! Right?

After waiting for what seemed like a million years for the FRG ladies to come knocking on my door with a basket of wine, cheese, flowers and such, I came to the conclusion that they knew I was a guy and they didn't want anything to do with a guy spouse. Heck with that, I'll go to them! So I marched my happy butt into the Family Readiness office and announced my arrival. The super bubbly, nice lady behind the desk cringed as she told me I wasn't being ignored, it was that the FRG for my wife's company didn't exactly exist due to a big meltdown of gossiping minds. It had self-destructed. Hmmm, that isn't good, seems I'm not the only one left out in the cold – so, I volunteered to become the FRG leader. Mrs. Brown jumped out of her chair, did a little happy dance, and ran next door to the medic's station to kiss my wife on the cheek! I had made her day; someone had actually volunteered to run the FRG instead of be volun-told to do so! That scene will be forever etched in my mind, it was so cool!

You see, the Family Readiness Group is a program of the commanding officer, where the CO can make sure the families of the unit are officially informed of events and other programs designed to assist in all manner of ways. Normally, it is the CO's spouse that would be the FRG leader – what better access to the CO and what's happening in the unit than at the dinner table, the living room, or the bed. Of course, the spouse of the CO should *want* to be the FRG leader, right? But our CO wasn't married; he was fresh and new to the company. Plus, the Special Troops Battalion was different than most line units – think of the overflow tank for your car's radiator, extra water gets stored there until the radiator needs it. STB is the overflow tank to the BCT as the radiator. Simple way to explain it, but it gets the point across; the CO had to interface with all the other companies in the brigade/BCT and hadn't had time to develop a new FRG. This E-4's husband, though, just volunteered, and made him happy, too!

By redeveloping the FRG, I discovered Army Community Services (ACS) and Mobilization/Deployment (MO/DEP) training programs. I took every training that ACS and MO/DEP offered, and became an Army Family Team Building (AFTB) instructor, helping other spouses become proficient in this new and somewhat bizarre military world. I also found myself with unique opportunities that just fell into my lap. The commanding general for the 101st's wife wanted to expand the Comprehensive Soldier's and Families Fitness (CSF2) Resiliency Training program to spouses - that is to say, she had a vision of training dynamic spouses to become Level 1 Master Resilience Trainers alongside the E-7s in each battalion. I got to be in the pilot program, and am a Spouse Master Resilience Trainer (an 8R designator to you Army folk) because of her. Way cool!

That was Fort Campbell. We PCSed to Fort Sam Houston when Steph re-enlisted for respiratory school (remember that? Why we were in the Army, to learn respiratory skills!) and discovered what a headache doing a self-move is. You want a piece of advice? DO NOT DO SELF-MOVES! The military pays for movers, and they cover it all if you stay within the weight constraints. So what if something gets broken in the move – you can get a brand new item with the money they reimburse you with for breaking it, and you can actually replace up in value and quality at the same time! Do not bring family heirlooms with you during this military adventure, put those into long-term storage and insure them. They can't get broken or lost in transit that way. Anyway, back to the odyssey.

Texas. Yup, almost like home to this Arizona native, complete with taco stands, desert, and diversity. I loved being in San Antonio, where my buddy Chris Pape lives! Chris is the founder of MachoSpouse.com, a repository of all things male military spouse – videos, blogs, columns, links, a whole lot of cool macho things. He is also the 2014 Armed Forces Insurance Air Force Spouse of the Year. Steph and I are only going to be here in San Antonio for just under a year, but, maybe I can learn about video arts from Chris …

Chris and I were sitting in this pub, enjoying a beer and just talking guy stuff. I posed the idea of him adding an internet podcast section to the site, and he and I could start recording audio podcasts. Chris informs me that he's not interested in doing that, he's a video guy, and maybe I should do the podcast thing myself. And that is how Male Military Spouse Radio Show got started. Go check it out sometime, it's on BlogTalkRadio.com, on iTunes in the podcast section, and on Stitcher. It's been going since 2014, has some great content, and some true duds, but it's all unscripted, raw, and rated R for language. You'll like it! Anyway …

After she graduated from the Army's RT school with an Associate of Science degree in respiratory science, she got her orders for … drumroll again … Landstuhl, Germany! WooHoo! Overseas, at the largest American hospital in Europe, Landstuhl Regional Medical

Center (LRMC) is where all injured service members pass through on their way back to the U.S. She gets to ply her new skills on the wounded warriors just like I envisioned! And we get to tour Europe without it costing a small fortune! Win-win-win! We get here, and, surprise! The FRG was non-functioning as well. So, I asked if I could be of some help, and I became the FRG Leader of Charlie Company LRMC for a year.

During that year, I was nominated for U.S. Army Garrison Rheinland-Pfalz Spouse of the Year at Military Spouse Magazine. Chris nominated me and a few other male spouses to maybe become the winner of AFI Military Spouse of the Year. Only one other guy has done so since the award has been out, and that was Jeremy Hilton in 2012. Chris got close in 2014, representing the Air Force, and he does his part nominating a few of us each January. Low and behold, I won for the garrison, and moved up to top three for Army. Talk about pressure! The other two spouses who were nominated were powerhouses in their own rights, one of which is a friend of mine from Fort Campbell. I am honored and humbled to be ranked up there with them, and fortunate to be able to represent the male military spouses.

The day came, the best of the three was announced ... and I was selected as the 2016 Armed Forces Insurance Army Spouse of the Year, to go to Washington, DC in May 2016 and meet all the Joint Chiefs of Staff and the other amazing top spouses. I was overwhelmed and confused and bewildered – why me? I have been told repeatedly that I deserve the honor, but I don't think I will ever truly believe I do. But, it is this honor that brings me to you now, to tell you this story.

I have done more with my podcasting, I've expanded to include "Spouse Spouts" as co-host with the amazing Susan Reynolds, and a weekday short podcast called "Spouseworld 1to1". There may be others, time will tell; my story will continue. We are caught up for now, and you have a feel for who I am.

The life of a male military spouse is not far removed from what the female military spouse feels. What is different is how we get help, handle the fears, and embrace the perceptions of us. We cannot find a BFF that we can cry on the shoulder of, we cannot plop down on the couch with a fellow spouse and a bottle wine in our jammies. That would cause A LOT of gossip! We have been raised, for the most part, to be problem solvers. To be the rock the family builds itself on. We are not the natural nurturers the kids need, even though they do not know this yet. We guys are expected to be strong, like all military spouses, to chin up and not cry, to be unbending when the winds of doubt pour over us when the soldier-wife is deployed. Our worst nightmares about infidelity are unfounded, and we know it, but we still cannot stop thinking it may be happening. Is she thinking the same thing of me as she sits in that Forward Operating Base (FOB) on communication lockdown, unable to call me with stories of her day? She relies on me to be able to be her sounding board when she's home, she tries ways of commanding her troops on me to see how they sound and how they are received - who is she sounding off to over there? Am I scared? You bet I am! But I am a resilience trainer. I understand what my head is doing. I know how to combat it. I will be strong, I am supposed to be. And if I can't handle it? I'll just fire up the computer and do another podcast of Male Military Spouse Radio Show!

Dave Etter is an Arizona native, a submarine veteran, a broadcaster by trade. He was the Program Director of the ABC Real Country affiliate KFMM is Safford, AZ for close to 10 years, and is now an Army spouse to his beautiful wife SGT Stephanie Etter. Dave is the producer of three popular podcasts supporting military spouses and families, Male Military Spouse Radio Show, Spouse Spouts, and SpouseWorld 1to1. On most evenings you can find Dave grilling something while enjoying a cold dunkel or scotch.

Making Military Life Work

Sheila Rupp

I will never forget the moment the phone rang and how I felt when I heard his voice catch. He couldn't hide the dread in his voice as he said, "I got my assignment." I don't remember saying anything, but just waiting, holding my breath.

"Albuquerque," he said slowly.

I didn't say a word; I cried.

That might sound dramatic, and I admit that it was probably over-the-top. At that point, while everyone was waiting for their assignments to follow commissioning, for whatever reason, Kirtland was one of the bases that everyone seemed to have less-than-positive things to say about. My reaction surprised me; I was so excited for all that lay ahead of us – his commissioning, our upcoming wedding, moving to a new state. Being together rather than the two and a half hours apart during much of our dating life and throughout our engagement was all that mattered to me. Wasn't it?

I am a perpetual planner. I often joke that I will eventually learn to plan some spontaneity into my life. We had made our plans, and none of that included Albuquerque. Or did it? Looking back, I'm not even sure where we wanted to move, or where we had hoped to be stationed for that very first assignment. All I remember is that everything that we had heard made Kirtland Air Force Base sound like the pits of hell and the most horrific base the Air Force could ever send anyone.

Fast forward three and a half years, I cried a really good ugly cry as we pulled out of our driveway at Kirtland, leaving my beloved Albuquerque in the rearview mirror.

After that initial conversation where I learned we'd be moving to New Mexico, I did what any good military spouse does – research. I got tour books, brochures, saved websites, and read anything I could get my hands on. Then I began my list.

We now call it our Base Bucket List and it begins every single time we get orders. Now, Pinterest is heavily involved, but other than that the process hasn't changed much over the last 13 years. As soon as we get orders, we still make our Base Bucket List of all of the things that we would be disappointed missing out on if we didn't see or do before we leave that duty station. Some of the items are obvious: Disneyland and the La Brea Tar Pits while in Los Angeles, the Balloon

Fiesta in Albuquerque, and the Cog Railway in Colorado Springs, but also on the list are the not-so-obvious like the Emma Crawford Coffin Races in Colorado, and the longest aerial tramway in Albuquerque. Our Base Bucket List has helped us in more ways that I could have ever have thought possible. We get excited about what the new place has to offer by focusing on the positives and things that appeal to us, even if it hasn't been at the top of his dream sheet. There are fewer occasions of, "I'm bored," or, "There's nothing to do." When we have an empty weekend or a day off, we find something on our Base Bucket List to remedy that situation.

It's become even more important having a child as a means of easing the transition when schools, friends, and activities are left behind. In the earlier years of my husband's career, it was just us and we always made it our mission to see the best in every assignment by finding the hidden gems along the way. But adding a child into the mix definitely changes things; they don't choose this lifestyle and we make it our mission to help her embrace and enjoy the lifestyle, while also understanding that every transition would be difficult. Leaving friends and changing schools isn't easy. Earning spots with dance companies or math teams is exciting, and then disappointing when it's time to move on. Our Base Bucket List has given her some ownership of our moves; she becomes excited about new adventures and helps shape what our assignment will hold. She takes pride in her highlighters and list of must-do activities as she peruses tour guides and talks with other milkids. One of her favorite resources has become RoadsideAmerica.com, a website that features awesome, and sometimes odd and often kitschy things to see and do, like the Corner in Winslow, Arizona, and the Concrete Cowboy in Albuquerque, New Mexico. It's been fun for not only each PCS destination, but also our road trips during our travels.

Perhaps it's because it was our very first assignment, embarking on a new life together and starting his Air Force career, but when I close my eyes and think of my favorite places, Albuquerque always comes to mind. This past Christmas, my best friend and our daughter's godmother, whom we met at Kirtland sent us piñon coffee. We are avid coffee drinkers and just one sip of that coffee transports me back to Albuquerque: my front porch on base with a view of the Sandia Mountains, visiting one of the Pueblos to shop and indulge in fry bread, or strolling downtown to see luminarias and having a bowl of green chile stew afterward to warm up.

During our first year of marriage, my shiny new lieutenant was rarely home. Between training and TDYs, I felt like I was by myself in a strange new place. I had to find something more to fill my time, and I needed friends. In the beginning of life as a new military spouse, I wasn't sure how to make friends. We were fresh out of college and newly married with no children, which ruled out playgroups. I was working full time, which made daytime functions more difficult. I joined the spouses' club right away and I vividly remember walking in the first time and when asked to introduce myself and say a little something about why I'd joined, I stammered, "I'm Sheila Rupp and I need friends," which drew laughs, but it was true.

Thankfully, I found an awesome support group there and some of those women are still my best and closest friends today. I had found my tribe. We had a book club, we drank wine, we lunched, we worked, we crafted, and we supported each other through deployments, TDYs, and all of the ups and downs of military life. We were there for new babies, new neighbors, and even some losses. We are scattered across the country now, but those women were the first ones who welcomed me with open arms into their military family.

I was extremely satisfied in my career, I was thoroughly enjoying our new duty station, I'd made wonderful new friends, but I needed more. Volunteering with my new friends became a satisfying way to fill my spare time. First, it was mostly through the spouses' club – making cards for local hospitals, baking cookies for dorm residents, and decorating the base club for the holidays. In the beginning, I didn't think much of it; it was just something to pass the time and visit with my friends.

Though fortunate to not be forced to deal with long deployments, I found it difficult to adjust to my husband's frequent travel. While he was away, I got into a rhythm of working, hitting the gym for yoga classes, and then I said, "yes," to any and every volunteer opportunity that popped up. I volunteered at the local school reading with kids, I sat on committees to plan base events, and I helped in the base thrift shop. I began filling extra time with helping out wherever I could help.

When my husband would get home, sometimes for just days, we would be inseparable for the first day or so, happy to find time together. Then I would find myself getting upset because I was thrown off my routine. I craved normal routines and made lists of things I was supposed to be doing. I wasn't always good at being spontaneous and just *being* and living in the moment, enjoying it for what it was. It's funny, I've always prided myself in going with the flow of military life and understanding that the mission comes first, but I still held onto my roots as a planner.

Had I not decided from the get-go to look for the good and embrace the experience, I would be having a much different life as a military spouse. Our Base Bucket List has helped me not only learn to see the silver lining much more often, but to see the value of not only the military spouse community, but the local community as well. I have had a great deal of friends who rarely leave the base, and then there are those who never step foot on base. I made it my mission to immerse myself in both worlds, and I did that by volunteering.

As wonderful as our first duty station was, my world for those first three years was pretty much the confines of the base, aside from church and our quick trips around the state. We lived on base, we both worked on base, our friends were on base; Kirtland was our home. As we moved along through several more assignments, moving from state to state, most of my experiences were on base. We lived on base, we worked on base, we socialized on base. It wasn't until we went to Los Angeles Air Force Base that things really started to change.

My husband's travel continued in frequency and as my daughter started school full time, I found myself in another transition period. Playdates no longer guided my friendships and I had longer stretches of time during the day with which I had more flexibility to fill my time. I had given up working full time when I found out I was expecting our daughter, and decided to focus on freelance opportunities so that I could be a stay-at-home mom. I took on smaller projects at first helping a local nonprofit dance company. I loved every moment of writing press releases for them and interfacing with the media, something I hadn't done regularly in several years and often missed. Those projects became bigger and I was constantly finding more things I wanted to help with or initiate. I coordinated hundreds of volunteers for the company's annual performances and organized charity auctions. For the first time, I spent more than half my time volunteering with a non-military oriented organization and built amazing relationships with civilians.

Previously, I had shied away from making friends with civilians; I had found it to be difficult as they often, try as they may, don't understand our lifestyle and the challenges we faced with separations and every-day military life, not to mention the constant moving. We experienced parents suggesting their kids not be friends with military kids because, "They're just going to move," which broke my heart. But here, these civilian friends loved me for me, in spite of being a military spouse who could leave them at any time. The dance company took us in and loved us fiercely. By volunteering for the company, I was not only able to use my background to help and serve, but I built some of the most lasting friendships I will probably ever have and for that I am eternally grateful.

My husband was sometimes gone for a few weeks, only to return for a couple of days – sometimes not even weekends, which was a challenge for my daughter. She is a trooper, and aside from a few tears, she rarely shows signs of hardship. Dance has always been her outlet, and the studio and company always nurtured her when she needed it most. Ever the military spouse, I tried to suck it up and keep my head down and keep moving on because life doesn't stop during a mission. I know the amount of volunteering with different groups working on charity auctions, including base programs, sometimes baffled my husband. He has always supported me in whatever endeavor I set out for, which has made all the difference.

Each time he is gone, regardless of how long, I try to focus on all the things he misses out *on*, instead of the things he had missed. It is difficult being away for him, too. He may not be able to be at every parent-teacher conference, but he is there to listen to her talk about school, her dance classes, and anything else that is going on in our lives. We make lists of things that she wants to tell him so that when she gets a chance, she doesn't forget to tell him anything. We take lots of pictures and make plans for when he is home. On my end, I focus on not snapping at him when he can't find drinking glasses because I've rearranged the cabinets, or making sure that I finished up projects before he came home so that I could spend quality time with him instead of making him help me clean out the linen closet for the umpteenth time.

That doesn't mean that life revolves around him and that everything stops when he is home. For us, I've found that the biggest thing was staying in our normal routines was important, but that we needed to be flexible and sometimes plan ahead more with the regular stuff so that we could make room for spontaneous trips and family time. I learned to find a way to play to be more spontaneous. Those trips are still semi-planned; once a planner, always a planner. We always made sure to make our family a priority.

Also important for me was to pre-plan so that my civilian friendships and volunteer positions didn't suffer when I needed to pull back to spend more time with my family. One of the things that makes military friendships great is that you can spend night and day together while your service member is gone, but no one expects to see you when they get home on an R and R or get back into town for a couple of days, and everything picks up right where you left off. With my civilian friends, they so wanted to help and support me when I was flying solo, but oftentimes they weren't sure what was helpful. I sometimes referred to myself as their token milspouse because despite living near the base, many of them had never been close friends with a military family.

As is often said, communication is one of the keys to life. I had to really hone in on communication skills and be open and honest with them. I hadn't always been good at saying when I needed help

74

because I wanted to be strong and keep it together. The freeing thing about relationships with this particular group of civilians was that I could be vulnerable with them. I learned to really talk with them about what I needed and how I was feeling, and they helped in more ways than I could imagine. If I was having a bad day or having a hard time getting something done while my husband was away, they were more than willing to step in and lend an ear for me to vent, or help me figure out a solution.

I have reigned in on my volunteering. I still love working within the community, both within the military community and the civilian side. Helping out at various nonprofits has become my passion, but I am more selective now about saying, "yes." There are some many wonderful organizations out there, and they all need help, and as much as I would love to spend all of my time contributing and serving, I need to take care of my family and myself, too. That philosophy includes everything from being a room mom at our daughter's school to spouses' clubs and local charities.

I've also learned that saying, "no," is often in the best interest of the organization; I can't give my all if I am overcommitted or not truly vested. I'm still a planner and planning volunteer time and projects has become my saving grace. I never say, "yes," outright. Now I say, "I'll check my calendar and see if it'll work out. I wouldn't want to not being able to give enough time." This is twofold: it lets me see if I truly do have time and it still lets the other person know that if I were to say no, it's because I wouldn't want to do a poor job due to time management, or at least that's what I hope it conveys. Without any of us sacrificing our own identity and passions, I always want our family to be a priority.

It is such a wonderful thing to have your service member home, but that transition can be difficult, too. To go from co-parenting from afar to co-parenting together again isn't always easy. Remembering to meal plan became important again because baguette pizzas are not everyone's idea of an appetizing dinner. (My daughter and I could practically live on them even though we're both foodies, but come to find out, the husband doesn't much care for them.) There are things that I surrender back to him with such glee that I can barely describe it: picking up dog poop, trimming the hedges, shoveling the walk, remembering to take the trash cans out to the street. I've learned to take comfort in silly little things when he is home instead of nitpicking on the not-so-great thing like the smell of the bathroom after he showers, filled with woodsy soap and shaving cream, instead of the toothpaste on the towel, and focusing on the lovely new cutting board he made me and not noticing the sawdust boot prints tracked into the living room.

We are coming up on a school assignment this next year, which will mean that my husband is in one place with no travel for an entire school year. We are very excited that although he will have a great deal of study time and work to put in, he will be home with us and his suitcases will stay in our garage. For that year, I will revel in seeing his boots in our closet next to my pumps. I will slow down and enjoy fighting over the covers.

It is inevitable that he will begin traveling again or deploy, and I sometimes worry about how we will feel once that becomes part of our routine again. I will once again take up the snow shoveling, hedge trimming, and remembering to take-out-the- trash-can duties. The poop duties have been relegated to our 8-year-old daughter, much to my delight. I will do those duties because I want to, and not just because I need to do them. I want him to know that we are okay while he is gone, because we are.

It isn't always the easiest life, but it's the only one I can imagine. As we have now gone over that 10-year hump and inch our way to the 20-year mark and his eventual retirement, I wonder what life after the military will be like. Will I like staying in one place? Will I miss the boots in my closet? Where will we settle? Being a military spouse and the experiences I've had during this journey have shaped me into who I am today, and I wouldn't change it for anything. It has made me resilient and strong, but I have learned that it's also okay to be vulnerable. I have learned to think outside the box. It introduced me to the world of volunteering and nonprofits, which I'm not sure I would have found otherwise. It has given me the sister I never had, and amazing friends who are now family. I have traveled the world and seen things that many only dream about. I have met people from all walks of life that have broadened my views and taught me new things.

Thirteen years later, I am still the same girl who said, "I do," to a brand-new second lieutenant, but I know a lot more now. I know that the assignments you aren't sure you'll like are the ones that you will fall in love with the most. I know that there are friends who are meant to be in your life a season (or a duty station) because you need each other then, but there are others who will be by your side forever, regardless of miles. I know that sometimes a day in pajamas is in everyone's best interest. I know to never visit the commissary on pay day. I know that flights get canceled, exercises get extended, launches get pushed, and the mission always comes first. I know that it is okay to ask for help, and more importantly to reach out and offer help; sometimes we don't know when we need it. I know there is good in every duty station, you just need to find it. I know there will be dark days, but they will pass; without them it is harder to appreciate the sunshine. I know that reintegration is hard, but nothing compares to that first kiss when they walk in the door. I know to love fiercely and to cherish every minute; it all goes too fast, and you never know which moment will be your last, so make it a good one. I know that military spouses are the beating heart of the military. We do not stand by and idly wait; we are the movers and the shakers, and we get things done.

Sheila Rupp is a freelance writer and copy editor, as well as a proud stay-at-home mom to her awesome daughter Emily. Sheila is married to her high school sweetheart Michael, and enjoys (most) of the nomadic lifestyle the military brings. In her not-so-spare time, she enjoys reading, traveling, watching Detroit Red Wings hockey, and volunteering, especially with nonprofit organizations and other military spouses.

Eyes Wide Open

Laura Russoniello

My journey on this road began at age five. I am the daughter of a Navy sailor and the wife of Marine. I am a mother of four, three boys and one girl. I have volunteered for the Family Readiness Group for a number of years and I have worked for Family Readiness in Recruiting and Retention. Additionally, I have a background in the legal field and I am a certified divorce and custody mediator. I am the president of a wonderful group of entrepreneurs at Milspouseprenuer at our current duty station, Okinawa. This is my story.

As a child I moved from state to state; I went through over ten deployments and four permanent changes of duty stations. I attended seven different schools and had to make new friends each time. I got to experience several different cultures, adventures, and sites. I attended military balls and military fun days. At a young age I knew how to stand for the national anthem and place my hand over my heart; I also knew the familiar sound of "Taps" and the meaning behind it.

I often thought that I would never marry into the military lifestyle. I saw firsthand how deployments and separations wore on our family and the stress of moving every few years. However, I always felt a sense of pride when standing next to the uniformed women and men of our nation. I was grateful to have explored several ships, many obstacle courses, and the fine dining of a galley. In a nutshell, everything I had experienced as a child would come to benefit me later.

As an adult I jumped into the Marine Corps lifestyle with eyes wide open. I understood that I was marrying a warrior, someone who was called to serve and someone who saw it as his duty to protect our freedom. For that I was proud and determined to stand beside him. Though my identity was not wholly embedded in the military community I knew that there would be the possibility of deployments and most definitely PCS moves, but I was willing to take on new adventures and become a Marine wife.

I was working at Gibbon's law firm in Florida while I was dating my Marine soon-to-be husband. I had started at this firm as a simple receptionist; I answered calls and transferred calls, that was the large extent of it. As time moved on I was given additional duties. I became close with several of my colleagues. These ladies not only took me under their wing and mentored me but they became my friends, my rocks. The lawyers in the firm were amazing as well. They poured their knowledge into us, they helped us grow and become better at our jobs, and they gave us opportunities to shine.

After a year of working with the firm I was asked to take on the additional role of legal assistant to one of the firm's partners. I was asked to start working on guardian ad litem cases for him. In this capacity I would be drafting documents, e-filing, reaching out to people in the community, working with two other firms, and submitting the attorney's answer to the court. I grew exponentially in the following year. In 2013, I had received word that we would be moving from Florida to New Jersey for a PCS. I had mixed emotions as I gave my two weeks' notice to the firm. They completely understood and were very supportive. At the end of my tenure there I had worked on over 200 GAL cases. I am still friends with many of them to date.

Working in the legal field was always my dream. After working at Gibbon's Law Firm I decided to finally finish my undergraduate degree in Legal Studies. We moved to New Jersey and I dedicated the following year to my studies. In December 2014, I walked across the stage at seven months pregnant with our fourth child to receive my diploma. It was a moment of intense joy.

In addition to working through school, I was also volunteering with Toys for Tots Philadelphia. Toys for Tots is an organization which helps the local communities by spreading a little Christmas joy through the donation of toys and gifts. My husband was the coordinator in Philadelphia for the fiscal year 2014 and I worked as the media and marketing coordinator for fiscal years 2014 and 2015. It was an amazing opportunity to give back to our community.

We spent many days donating toys to local shelters, collecting toys from several venues, and collecting funds to purchase toys. We were part of parades, media interviews, and events around town. Our children even became involved and helped when they could. One night was spent at the Ronald McDonald house where we were closely engaged with children suffering from health alignments. My daughter befriended a young girl with spina bifida, who taught her how to play the piano. I talked to her parents at length regarding their struggles. This was most memorable because of the impact it had on the children. They were able to spend one night full of fun, happiness and joy without thinking about all the medical concerns. Their parents were able to enjoy their smiles.

During the course of the Toys for Tots events we met many leaders within the Philadelphia area, including members of the Philadelphia Bar Association. Being in connection with a drive to help the kids of Philly, as well as in a legal setting, was almost too good to be true. I was excited by the possibility of new opportunities.

My husband and I had talked at length about law school. This was obviously the next step for me. However, most law schools maintain a three year track to a juris doctorate. This means that we would have to be at our current duty station for three more years, and we were only slotted for two more. In light of this I began volunteering at the JAG office on McGuire Air Force Base. It was there that I met an attorney who opened my eyes to the legal issues within the military community.

One of the biggest concerns is the high rate of divorce and the complicated custodial issues that follow. It was during this time that I became aware of the benefits of the ADR (alternative dispute resolution process) and the mediation process. I decided to take a divorce and custody course through Good Shepherd Mediation in Philadelphia, Pennsylvania.

The course was an intense overview of all aspects of the divorce proceedings, including the emotional, financial, and custodial earmarks. The class was composed primarily of acting attorneys, one magistrate, a dean and myself. To say I was the one with the least amount of experience would be an understatement. I looked at this as an opportunity to dive into greater minds and gain a better perspective of family law and how mediation was a key player in that role.

I finished the class in August 2015, and began looking for opportunities to mediate. At the time there was a local program at our district courthouse in Burlington County, New Jersey, that took volunteer mediators. In most stateside courthouses they are now requiring couples to attend mediation as well as parenting education, in lieu of heavy dockets that cannot litigate every single divorce case. I met with Diane Talty, who was the head of the program. She introduced me to several of the other mediators and I began volunteering. I saw a number of cases that dealt with military families, because McGuire Air Force Base is located within the same district.

In most cases it is more advantageous for the parties to mediate their cases. It costs less, it requires less time, and it is less adversarial than a trial. Many of the issues facing military families that go through divorce are in sharp contrast to the local civilian community. Military members must think about things like impeding PCS moves, TDYs, deployments, overseas communication clauses, etc. Civilian mediators do not have a lot of these at the forefront of their agreements because they are not familiar with the ins and outs of the military.

In light of this I saw an opportunity to help within the military community. I believe that being a military spouse helps me better relate to my clients currents struggles and issues. They can speak openly and frankly about their lives, without having to explain certain acronyms, or how stressful the last move was, or how they are going to maintain a relationship with their children while they are deployed.

I decided to open my own business, Military Family Alliance Mediation Service, and continued to help families on the JAG side and at the local courthouse. In early 2016, I attended a class at the Superior Courthouse in Trenton, New Jersey. I was given the opportunity to speak to the class of mediators regarding parenting time agreements for military families. I was able to share my knowledge about key issues to look for and how to identify the service member's status (active duty, Guard, etc.) and how that might influence an agreement.

I was inspired to bridge a gap between our local courthouse and our base commanders. My thought was to bring them together and create clear lines of communication to better help our military community. I knocked on several doors and spoke with several commanders, some of whom were not too enthused to chat about anything related to divorce and custody. These are often issues that are pushed to the civilian community; and although some of the civilian sector is prepared to handle military cases, many are not.

We held a meeting with Diane Talty; our family court Judge Tarantino, who had served in the Army; a group of about 20 commanders and judge advocate general attorneys; and myself. I was pleased with the knowledge that was shared and the bridge that was built that day. After the meeting, the judge personally asked me if we could continue these meetings and relations with the base. I politely relayed that my husband had received his orders and we would be leaving for Okinawa, Japan, in about a month.

After moving overseas, I began volunteering with Milspousepreneur, Okinawa. I brought my mediation business with me and knew that this group would be the one to help me get a fresh start in Okinawa. Milspousepreneur was started by Lakesha Cole to help the number of entrepreneurs and home-based businesses build their brand within the community. I attended meetings and started helping when and where I could. I became the interim treasurer in September 2016, and that December I was elected to serve as the president of the organization. It has since been my goal to help other business owners develop their skills while on island.

I have worked incredibly hard to try and bring mediation to Okinawa. I believe that having a mediation program on island could help couples create solid parenting time agreements to file stateside. Couples find it hard to have balanced agreements because they are not allowed to be seen in the same legal office; it is considered a conflict of interest. This often means that the separation agreements that are created are one-sided. Both parties don't have the opportunity to sit down and have a joint voice in that agreement. Conjointly, I developed a co-parenting program for divorcing couples, separating couples, or couples who would like to re-evaluate their past agreements. I would love for this program to take shape and be launched in coordination with a mediation program.

Mediation has been a huge part of my journey thus far and it will continue when we head back stateside. My hope is that I can make an impact on the military community in a very real way. We need to take a closer look at how we are serving our community in some of the darkest hours. Divorce is not a topic that can be overlooked. Both the service member and the dependent need to have an active role in creating their agreements.

When you are a military spouse you live this lifestyle every day. You face it side by side with help from your fellow spouses. You become the phone call away for deployments, the box giver for PCSing, the mechanic when someone is broken down, and the place to call home on holidays when family is too far away. I would like to say that I am the mediator in the storm of divorce, the one with sound reason, who will help you create a plan for your future. A plan that is fair and balanced, that will consider our lifestyle. This has become a passion of mine and I am hopeful it will come to fruition.

Laura Russoniello is a Marine wife, Navy daughter, and mother of four, currently stationed in Okinawa, Japan. She is a divorce and custody mediator and has over five years of experience working with family programs. She is a member of the New Jersey Association of Professional Mediators and a member of the Pennsylvania Council of Mediators.

Right Place, Right Time

Julia Kysela

I was honored to be named the 2015 Armed Forces Insurance National Guard Spouse of the Year for my work with various veterans' organizations with the most significant work being the creation of the I've Got Your Six 6k Run, Walk, and Ruck. Going into our sixth year, it is a great time to reflect on how far the event has come.

As with many things in life, there is something to be said about being in the right place at the right time. I got the privilege of meeting the co-founder of the VALOR Clinic Foundation at a charity event in 2012. After being medically retired, he had begun helping homeless veterans while volunteering in a soup kitchen in 2008. That would grow into his concept for VALOR, which in 2012 was starting to get off the ground but still seeking support.

I knew from that moment that I wanted to help with his mission and offered to develop their first organized fundraiser. Which, after offering my support, meant I had to figure out exactly what to do! My husband and I began to think about the ways in which we could help and it was only natural that we would plan a race. My husband is an avid runner and has been a member of the National Guard's All-Guard Marathon Team. While I wouldn't consider myself a runner, I have moved myself from the start to finish line of races somewhat often. We decided that we both knew enough about races that we could do it on our own as a fundraiser for this charity that we both cared so much about.

Having attended many such events in the past, it didn't seem like it would be too difficult, but planning and executing this event turned out to be a much bigger undertaking than I ever imagined. Fundraising, advertising, ordering supplies, and finding volunteers are just a portion of all the tasks that contribute to success on race day. Not to mention all the coordination that must take place over the course on race day to make sure all participants successfully complete the event safely. It is a long day when you have over eight hours of work in by noon!

Within a few months, we successfully conducted the first I've Got Your Six 6k and Memorial Mile on a small trail outside of Pittsburgh, PA. Race day was especially stressful: we were on a very specific timeline and had over 100 participants relying on us. We had around 20 volunteers to support us as well, most of whom were not runners or in on the event planning. We also had a lot of rain. Thankfully, the event itself was sunny, but tell that to us and our volunteers who were getting soaked making last minute preparations at 5 a.m.! Overall, it cost us around $2,000 to make approximately $6,000 for VALOR. The I've Got Your Six 6k fundraising brand was a success.

It was such a unique experience to be able to build a brand from the ground up. We conceptualized the name, logo, and the distance we wanted the race to be. To gain inspiration, we were looking at some of my husband's photos from his first tour in Iraq. We came across a picture my husband took of his squad leader outside of Habbaniyah, Iraq; he was standing in front of an ornate gate providing a perfect modern soldier silhouette. A simple black and white image of that picture formed our logo, which we felt symbolizes the struggles that some veterans face upon returning home. Given that VALOR's focus is on helping veterans –specifically those affected by homelessness, PTSD, or many of life's other struggles – we felt that it was particularly fitting. The name for our race came from the military phrase "I've Got Your Six" that means "I've Got Your Back." It was born out of a desire to remind veterans of all generations that we on the home front have their backs both while they are serving abroad as well as when they come home. We chose the 6k distance as something unique to set our race apart from others.

As with any event, the first time is not always perfect, and each year we strive to learn from any hiccups we have encountered. Even a good event, where nothing goes wrong, has a lot of room to grow. As with the military, after each event we make note of what we did right, what went wrong, and what can we do better. With success came new challenges though. Like a request to plan another race on the other side of the state, or in a neighboring state. It is one thing to plan something within your own community but harder to apply those same principles to satellite locations. So, what did we do to improve our event and combat some of those new challenges?

1. The Distance. Many of you may not be runners and think this would be a big deal. Part of the draw of a 5K (or any other standard event) is the ability to compare times easily to other races. Sometimes being different is good. Sometimes it is not. We've struggled with altering the distances at a variety of locations to best serve our audience. They are, after all, the ones whose money is going to the charity!
2. What originally started as two races (a 6k and 1 mile) has developed into one. But we didn't lose our memorial mile (a

part of the event to draw walkers –specifically friends/family of the runners who were not running). Instead, we now line the last mile of every course (no matter the distance) with hundreds of flags so that every participant can take part.

3. The ruck. It's a military-themed event, so adding a ruck option is something we didn't originally plan but obviously it was a "duh" idea.

4. Costs ... sometimes spending more money means making more money. But there is a fine line and our biggest fundraising year was also our biggest cost year and therefore, not our biggest net fundraising year. While you can't be too cheap, every financial decision needs to be handled with care, or else.

5. The Community. Our Pittsburgh event never required many volunteers. But the year we decided to bring the course into the community more (while still ending in an old quarry pond off the trail – think: WAY more logistical planning), the race grew significantly. Reaching out to other veterans' organizations, such as Team RWB, has continued to help grow the events.

6. Delegation. This one is hard and we're still learning. The concept and brand are ours but we are not the ones that know the other communities/markets the best. Letting others take the lead and guiding them to completing our vision has led to better results at our satellite events.

So, what can you learn from all this? Obviously, if you are organizing a running event, this may be great! But what if you aren't organizing any events? There are lessons that I have learned from this experience that I think can be applied on a broader scale.

First, find a cause you care about and start to make a difference! Every organization needs support, however large or small your contribution. And you never know where things may lead; my introduction to VALOR was simply a chance meeting where I was basically donating money to another charity during one of their events, and it turned into all of this. Help in whatever way you can, whether it is one hour a month or even simply small acts of kindness. It all can have a huge impact. Not to mention that it can lead to something that excites you and opens new doors like it did for me. If planning an event, make it what YOU want it to be. How else are you going to get excited about it? These things take a lot of time and a lot of passion so if you aren't feeling it – others will notice.

To me you can never be over prepared (that might be why I am a horrible over packer when traveling). Always prepare for a variety of things to go to wrong because something inevitably will. But things going wrong are part of every plan; sometimes people won't even notice and other times, they'll be watching your reaction. Those backup plans can really save the day!

No matter how exhausted you are after your event, make sure to do an after-action report and identify what you can improve upon and what went well; it can only help you in the future. We had a great concept and a great plan going into our first year. To be honest, six years later there have been more changes than aspects of the event that have stayed the same. Constantly learning and reevaluating can only make everything stronger.

Most importantly, you are only as great as your team, so find a solid one! Any event is only as strong as its volunteers, and to have the most successful event, you need to find solid volunteers for the major tasks. You can't be everywhere at once and you will need a few reliable people to make decisions when you are otherwise occupied. Additionally, it helps if these people are heavily involved in the planning process, but that is not always possible. Clear, concise instructions and direction are necessary for everything to flow without you.

Besides learning from each race, I have personally learned that I can accomplish more than I ever thought possible, especially after this year, when my husband was deployed and unable to assist. I was forced to understand the roles that he normally filled and delegate those responsibilities, clearly, to new volunteers. In the past I focused more on the planning and preparation, while he focused on the inevitable problems that arose last minute on race day, I had to adapt to fill the role of quick thinker and dispatcher to ensure all those tasks were taken care of. While the previous years' experience was very helpful, I still had to rely heavily on my volunteers, many of whom were new themselves, to fill these roles.

Overall what this has done is give me leadership experience. I didn't know that is what this was at first. I just knew that there was something I believed in and I needed to make sure the event was a success and to make an impact. What started out as a simple idea has, through some hard work and a lot of lessons learned, become an amazing aspect of my life. Knowing that it is in some small way making a difference in the lives of others is fulfilling.

About the Charity

The Veterans Assisted Living Out-Reach (VALOR) Clinic Foundation was established in 2010 in Pennsylvania by a retired

Special Forces Sergeant Major to provide support to homeless veterans and veterans suffering from PTSD. It began informally in 2008, by helping veterans in need file VA Paperwork and has expanded significantly since it was officially recognized as a 501(c)3.

The long term goal is to improve access to and the quality of Health Care for our nations Veterans by providing integrated health care, life coaching, and shelter to Veterans in need of assistance. VALOR Clinic has a unique approach to address both the visible and invisible wounds of war and their secondary effects, to include homelessness and substance abuse.

Currently, they focus on the following programs for Veterans in Pennsylvania:

- Hope for the Homeless: Providing clothing, food, and other necessities to homeless during stand downs, where they hope to identify homeless veterans within the homeless population.
- Holiday Meal Program: Providing holiday meals to struggling housed veteran families.
- Veterans Unstoppable Program: Provide veteran led counseling to address readjustment, PTSD, and building life skills.
- Pauls House: A 13-bedroom veterans' sanctuary to provide temporary housing to homeless veterans while rebuilding life skills and working towards permanent housing solutions.

Until 2014, VALOR had an all-volunteer staff. With the opening of their first Veterans sanctuary, there is now 1 full time employee who is a live-in caretaker for the homeless guests during their time in the home. However, all fundraising and events are volunteer led, and the charity has been recognized with 92 percent of every dollar received going towards these programs.

Julia Kysela was honored to be named the 2015 Armed Forces Insurance National Guard Spouse of the Year. She currently works in the finance industry and enjoys volunteering her time with local organizations that benefit veterans and military families.

Seeds of Service

Robin Turner

Being a military spouse can expose you to a myriad of issues in the world which seems bigger than yourself. Our spouses are front and center in events that will one day be read about in history books. They have the most dangerous and stressful jobs that can be overwhelming, and our job as a military spouse is to support them in their passion to serve this great nation. We are moved from one community to another with different sets of issues and needs which look like a mountain insurmountable. This can be overwhelming until we realize that we are already prepared for what comes before us, and it is not up to us to change everything. The impact we leave can be small and incremental or large. However great or small, it is necessary. Everything we've been through and seen in our lives has prepared us for this journey. All of our experiences help us make the necessary impact for whatever community we are in at the capacity it needs to be. My journey as a military spouse started as a kid in Lynchburg, Virginia.

Like Langston Hughes, "Life for me ain't been no crystal stair." While I grew up with some challenges, I've had some people placed in my life who influenced me greatly. A retired teacher named Mrs. Lena Williams was like a grandmother to me. She lived this lifestyle of service to other people. I guess she felt sorry for my situation. My mother couldn't take care of me, and my grandmother took my brother and I in. She would come get us and we would spend the weekend at her house. We got to be kids, eat cake, and not have to worry about anything. Her house was like heaven and peaceful. Later, my brother and I were no longer living in the same home, but Mrs. Williams still let me come to her house. I felt safe there. Sometimes I would accompany her to volunteer for Meals on Wheels. After church, she would go to see the "sick and shut in" (what church folks used to call those who couldn't leave their house because of their health), and the elderly. In her old age, she was like a superhero in my eyes, and I was her sidekick. We would sit with them, feed them, have conversation, and I was the source of entertainment. Her 95-year-old mother was still living in South Carolina, and she would go down to see her in the summer. I would go with her, and I watched her mother bring crack-addicted people into her home and feed them. I didn't make the correlation then, but now that I'm an adult, Mrs. Williams' lifestyle of service came from her mother.

My senior year came, and I was eager to leave Lynchburg. The first chance I got to get out of there, I took it. The first thing smoking was an acceptance to Virginia Tech. It was a great school, a state college, which meant it was the least expensive (back then), and it had the major I wanted, education. It was only an hour and a half away, but it was good enough for me. I didn't have anything and I could get there with no problem. Teaching was the only thing I thought I was good at. I had my life planned out; I was going to teach in a school, work my way up to a principal, then go into politics and be a champion for education. Now, I have no desire to be in a classroom, and absolutely NO desire for politics.

It was there that I met this very handsome and cocky guy. With all nervousness and awkwardness, the first thing I said to him was, "You want to see my tattoo?" I had a fresh tattoo with a Japanese character that says "Teach". He wasn't feeling me at the moment. After I began talking about my passion, he began looking at me more seriously than the awkward girl asking him to look at her tattoo. He was a Marine at Virginia Tech as an MCEP to become an officer. We became an item, went through a crazy relationship where I was unsure of myself and clingy, we broke up, got back together, and got married; that's the condensed version. After we got married, that's when things changed. He was told by an advisor that he would not be able to graduate in time because of one class. After he told the Marine Corps, we thought it would be a minor thing because this meant he would get his degree only six weeks later. It turned out to be a really big deal. They kicked him out of the MCEP program and demoted him from a sergeant to a lance corporal. We didn't get paid for two and a half months, and we just had a baby. After all of the damage was done, the advisor came back and told my husband, "Oh, you can graduate on time because you took this class," but he still wasn't able to commission. Talk about frustration. We were devastated. While our marriage didn't really start off on the right foot, we were young, dumb, and determined that we were not going to let these circumstances affect us and our future. There are times when ignorance really is bliss. We were ignorant and happy despite what was going on in our lives!

The first duty station we went to was in Beaufort, South Carolina. As I drove to Beaufort, I came off of the freeway and drove down this very long highway. The closer I got to Beaufort, the more I could smell the marsh. It smelled like rotting death. "What kind of hell hole this man has me going?" I thought to myself. I married into the Marine Corps, so I had to suck it up. The stench was HORRIBLE and I was already ready to leave that place. When we moved into our base housing, I was in the kitchen and this HUGE four-inch roach crawled on the counter! I was ready to leave immediately. When I called housing to complain, the lady on the other end said to me, "Oh, that's a Palmetto bug. Welcome to Beaufort!" I was flaming hot and wanted my husband to hurry up and commission so we could get out of there! This was a very humbling experience for my husband and I. He was a lance corporal with a slash mark, and everyone was looking at him like, "What did YOU do?" I was a young woman with a baby, already pregnant again, and living in a house with rat-sized roaches with the ability to fly! This wasn't the plan I had.

As we got settled, we joined a church, Love House Ministries, and began serving. My husband and I did youth ministry where we mentored middle and high school children. I ran David's Table food pantry and did a lot of work with other food organizations for the needy. Families in the community who needed extra food could come and receive groceries. There were food drives that I coordinated where hundreds of families would come by to get groceries or snacks for their children. We would coordinate the giveaways with holidays and school letting out.

During this time, my children, who were three and four at the time, would accompany me to give out food. Their "special job" was to play with children who came with their parents to get food assistance. If there were no children, they would help me bag the groceries. As I watched them bag groceries or clean up, I saw them as my younger self helping Mrs. Williams serve. WOW! The seeds of service she planted in me as a little girl grew into me making an impact on the community. I had to call her and tell her what I was doing in Beaufort; she was delighted to hear what I was up to and is still volunteering at 90 years old. Through this program, we served hundreds of families and encouraged lots of people and single moms to go back to school. My husband and I hosted youth lock-ins for the area teenagers. These were a fun and safe environment for them to be entertained and inspired.

While in Beaufort, Theresa Roberts was my mentor and her husband, Randy Roberts, mentored my husband. Theresa was helping me as I helped those in need at the food pantry and mentoring the teenagers. As one mentors, it is important that they have someone mentoring them. Her husband was a retired Marine. I looked to her for advice in marriage, parenting, being a woman – everything. She had her own challenges she had to overcome, and she shared with me her experiences and obstacles, and how she conquered them. She had a wonderful marriage where she and her husband were making a huge impact in Beaufort, and she has three beautiful children. Being mentored by Theresa in turn helped me to be a better mentor to others. She entrusted me to mentor her teenage girls, and in return, she helped me navigate through parenting. While doing service for others, especially in the military culture, it is very easy to become self-reliant and not seek out counsel, advice, and mentorship for yourself. You move often and don't get to establish deep lasting relationships with people as they are moving around like you.

However, mentorship is most critical because we have to be able to give from our "overflow." What I mean by that is imagine a tea cup resting on a saucer. As my cup fills, I am able to fill someone else from a place of healing and restoration, or what flows into the saucer. We can't help someone from a depleted state; our own cup also needs to be full because we can't encourage another if we are empty. Strength, encouragement, and mentorship has to come in, so that strength, encouragement, and mentorship can come out. So mentorship is necessary on both ends. To this day, Theresa Roberts is my mentor, and like a mother to me.

From all of the relationships built in Beaufort, I was sad to leave. The smell that once made me gag, was now home to me. When I drove into Beaufort in the past, I would make sure all of the windows were up and no outside air was coming in. Now I roll down the windows and smell the smell of home. When I would be disgusted at the sight of a palmetto bug I now just step on it if it's in the house or walk around it if it's outside. I used to be confused when I heard the Beaufortonians talk. Now I almost sound like them. Beaufort is like a fungus; it really grows on you. The place that I dragged my feet coming to became the place I want be planted and retire in.

Our next stop was Fredericksburg, Virginia, for recruiting duty. Fredericksburg is where I really learned my purpose. I did mentorship here and there, but Fredericksburg was where I met a young lady who was having a hard time. My husband was trying to get her into the Marine Corps. He realized that she was hurting, unsure of herself, and needed help. It was important that he maintain professionalism, but he couldn't have this girl feeling like this. He knew my story, and felt like I could help her. He called me to tell me that he was driving her to the house just for me to give her a hug. We exchanged numbers, but as I began to talk to her, I realized that some of the issues I had growing up, she also had. The insecurities she was going through, I went through. This is when I realized that everything I went through and overcame was for purpose. Every woman who impacted my life brought me to this place, and I needed to be that for this young lady. To this day, we maintain a relationship where I encourage her to be great: to do what she is passionate about and walk with purpose.

After lots of turmoil and persistence, my husband was finally commissioned and became an officer. He worked so hard for this accomplishment and endured so much; I know because I was right there with him.

Our next stop was Okinawa, Japan. We were so excited about this new adventure out of the country. By now, it was expected that we were going to serve somewhere or help someone out. To my surprise, there wasn't much for us to actually do. I taught preschool kids English, and that was fun. We fed the homeless at a park and helped out here and there with other community events, but nothing significant like before, or at least that's what we thought at the time. Japan was very different for me. This was the first time I didn't really have "new" people to mentor.

It was in Japan that my husband and I learned the purpose of us being together. We were able to help young marriages navigate through hard times and rough spots in their own marriages. We were able to share some of the challenges we went through and teach communication skills. Randy and Theresa Roberts mentored us when we were younger and helped us in hard times.

Now, we got to be the Randy and Theresa Roberts to other people. This was a very different season for the kids. This was the first time they weren't really serving on a consistent basis. They helped out at Yogi Park, but that wasn't as significant as what they'd done. They started to get spoiled and have an entitled mindset and I was not going to have that. They started businesses while over there, like dog-sitting and making desserts, and began helping other military children start their own businesses by sharing their business plans and recipes. It still wasn't enough.

Later, we were given the opportunity to go on a mission trip to Cambodia. My angle for this was to make the kids go so they could learn to appreciate what they have. They helped raise the money to go, and we went to Cambodia to save the world and for the kids to get their act together. We went with an organization called "LightBridge International." They established themselves in a small village in Poi Pet, Cambodia, to assist young women in business mentoring. The women in these poor villages of Cambodia are vulnerable to human trafficking and the sex industry.

This was the first time we had seen poverty on that level. LightBridge International established a job creation program where the women make jewelry out of paper beads while teaching them to start their own businesses. One young lady we met while out there went through the program and was on her way out. She had a thriving noodle business generating money that could sustain her. A trip that was meant to teach my children a lesson ended up teaching me a lesson. I saw women who were so grateful for the little money they were able to generate from an honest living. These young women were able to generate money with dignity and not rely on the sex industry. I met Leakena Ten who worked with LightBridge International who lived there. Her only purpose was to mentor these young women, and help them realize their dreams. This was mentorship on another level that I had never seen before, and it was very inspiring. This made me look at Beaufort differently and how I could empower those women.

What made me the most happy was to see my daughter realize her purpose. As she learned about the history of Cambodia and the plight of the Cambodian young women, her heart began to bleed for these young women. The seed of service Mrs. Williams' mother planted in her was planted in me and now that seed had been transferred to my daughter. After living in Okinawa for four years, we unfortunately had to leave; that place was like paradise.

Our next adventure was San Diego, where we currently reside. We've been in San Diego for about nine months, and already my daughter is trying to get to Mexico to help those in need. Homelessness is rampant, and we keep baggies to pass out to those we come in contact with. We are still trying to figure out why we are here, but we know that service is going to be a major part of our existence while we are here. Like everywhere else, we are somehow going to stumble on it.

The older I get while married in the Marine Corps, the more I become like Theresa Roberts in mentoring other young ladies who are bold enough to carry the burden of supporting their service member and being a military spouse. I'm now one of the seasoned wives and it's up to me to drop nuggets about parenting and marriage. It's up to me to be the shoulder to cry on after a husband said something crazy or has been gone on deployment that has been extended. It's up to me to encourage a young girl to figure out her purpose and appreciate her trials which brought her to where she is now.

Some of those who I helped with a bag of groceries and encouragement are now out of poverty. Teens I have mentored over ten years ago have finished college, have families of their own, and are mentoring other teens. Some are doing activism work to help those who have been trafficked in America. LightBridge and LandMine Design, the company who sells the jewelry, continues to grow and help women establish themselves. Some of the ministries that we were a part of grew and are impacting their communities greatly.

All of these accomplishments in these various places and organizations we have contributed to have absolutely nothing to do with me. The accomplishments are because of something bigger that

God is doing in those communities. There are things I have started in various places. There are things I came in to try to improve. They are all doing well and continuing to make an impact in the community with someone else with a fire and desire to make an impact. Everywhere I go, I try to find someone else with the same passion and drive to keep the work going. The reality is, the work is not about me. If I didn't do it, God would put someone else there to do the work. Each place I have left, God has put someone else there to continue the work. I'm just a vessel God uses to get something done, because I said, "yes." Sometimes I am just a placeholder until another person is placed to come and make an impact on the community. Military spouses have a unique opportunity to spread seeds of hope all over the world through service. With our influence, we can create a legacy in one of the towns we were blessed to live in and leave a lasting impression on individual lives and in communities.

As retirement is coming near, I would love to go back to Beaufort, and help out in the process of continuing to improve that community. I also realize that my journey may not bring me to Beaufort but another community who needs my specific help. I'm ok with that. Military wives realize that the uncertainty of the future is what makes life exciting. Everything I've been through brought me to this place where I am now. Where I was once insecure, I walk with confidence. I've done things I never thought I would be able to do. All of these experiences have helped me to mentor women who are going through what I've been through; this fuels my passion. When I got that tattoo as a freshman in college, I always thought I would be teaching the three Rs in a classroom. Never did I think I would be teaching people how to navigate through the landmines of life.

Now, my goal in life is to be the Mrs. Williams and the Theresa Roberts to other people as they were to me, as I grow in wisdom. We can be upset at trials we've had to go through and ask, "Why me?" My questions is, "Why not you?" We can shake our fist to God in anger and frustration at injustice, poverty, and the evil in this world and ask God, "Why don't you do something?" The thing is He already did something about it when He made YOU and me! Let's walk our purpose so we can make an impact on this world by serving in the communities we are planted in.

"Everybody can be great, because everybody can serve. You don't have to have a college degree to serve. You don't have to have to make your subject and your verb agree to serve. You don't have to know about Plato and Aristotle to serve. You don't have to know Einstein's "Theory of Relativity" to serve. You don't have to know the

Second Theory of Thermal Dynamics in Physics to serve. You only need a heart full of grace, a soul generated by love."

-Martin Luther King, Jr.

Robin Turner is a woman who loves to mentor young women to help them realize their purpose. She is married to Capt. Tywan Turner, and homeschools her two children ages 14 and 15. She currently lives in San Diego, California.

Helping Veterans Heal Through Art

Cara Loken

My husband John has gone on several deployments during our 18 years of marriage. This seems pretty routine in our lives – short deployments here and there, with a couple of longer deployments.

My son Tyler's first deployment was different, though. That's *my* son, my baby. As a parent, your first instinct is to protect them from harm. My heart sank when I learned they would both deploy during the same timeframe. I kept thinking, "Why us"? Could my heart and nerves handle both of them deployed to different combat zones? I know they were ready to go and protect their country, but was I ready for them to go? It was hard to say goodbye to John, but even harder to say goodbye to Tyler. Days were getting closer to their departure date and it grew harder knowing it might our last goodbye. Tears welled up just thinking about it all.

I remember Tyler making me a promise when he was 5 years old that he would never leave home and would always stay with me. I wished we could back in time to when he was 5 and he would listen to what I said. When he was little, he never really talked about being in the military. He really never even played pretend military when he was little. I never thought he wanted to join. I always thought he would be a doctor or lawyer, because he always liked to argue his case with anyone. I remember him coming and telling John and me that he was joining the Army. I tried really hard to talk him out of it, and as you know, it didn't work out in my favor.

I really can't say I knew what I was getting into by being "married" to the military. Although my husband is in the Air National Guard, he is gone quite often. Even when my husband is home, he spends most of his morning hours working on military duties before going to work at his civilian job. This was and is still an adjustment for myself and my youngest son, Conner. But, we have to understand, it's his duty. This is the norm.

When Tyler joined, I didn't know anything about serving on active duty, other than the fact he would not live in his hometown for the next four years. Out of those four years, I would only see him 4-5 times, and as his mother, that is not enough. It was hard enough when he moved out of our house and into town, 10 miles away. But, from Lincoln, Nebraska, to Fort Bragg, North Carolina, was so far away. I would only hear about what he was doing, I couldn't go to his base and see, or even volunteer. That was hard. I know we want our kids to grow and be on their own. But, I was never ready. Being a military mom was much different than being a military spouse. It's hard to explain what the difference is, and unless you have lived it, you might not ever know or understand.

After John and Tyler's deployment, there was a lot more talk of post-traumatic stress disorder among the VA system and the media. So, I did what any wife and mother would do: research the crap out of it. I knew there was a possibly with the things they had both experienced overseas that it could happen to them. I wanted to know all the signs and symptoms. I would watch how my husband acted when he came home. But, I remember seeing changes in Tyler a couple of weeks after the newness wore off after he came home. His actions were different than my husband's. He just wasn't the same boy that left for war. He stopped being around people, he told me he was numb to his feelings for anyone besides his daughter. He wouldn't sleep, then would sleep for 24 hours. He was quick to temper, jumpy, couldn't concentrate, and was drinking. He didn't think anything was wrong with him, and kept telling me over and over again he hadn't changed— it was everyone else. He became more withdrawn. I could tell by his large, dark circles under his eyes and not sleeping made his symptoms worse.

It was breaking my heart into a million pieces. He went to fight a war to protect his family and his country, only to come home, broken. Just the same as my husband, I think part of him is still in Iraq and Afghanistan. I am not sure if they will ever be the same as before they left. I know they both have talked about wanting to go back. Because, sometimes it's easier for them to adjust to *that* world instead of the realities at home. That's one of the hardest parts to swallow.

I was not a military kid growing up. I really knew nothing of the military. My grandfather was in World War II and I could barely get him to talk about what he did during the war. That was all I knew. It was never at the forefront of my thoughts until two of my brothers served in the Navy, both stationed out of California. But, still the military was not at the forefront of my thoughts, except for the fact they were away from home.

Then I met my knight dressed in camo. I never thought I would marry, let alone a military man. I remember seeing him for the first time in his uniform and thought, "I am going to marry that man"! Six months later, we said "I do" in a courthouse with a very tiny reception. Three weeks later, he left for training for three months. Four months after that, we welcomed our son, early. My oldest son, Tyler, was 13 years old when we married. We struggled like others do, but we find ways to soldier on. Our marriage wasn't, and still isn't perfect, but we love each other and our sons unconditionally.

For the first 12 years of marriage, my husband was gone for either training, schooling, or deploying at least once a year. But, the longest deployment was yet to come. He came home and said, "I volunteered to go to Iraq for six months." He was excited that he was going to protect his country and his family. Of course, I was absolutely not excited. I had to realize that it is his duty. He has been serving his country for over 26 years and will be in until they make him retire.

For 13 years, it was just me and Tyler. We built a bond that only mother and son could understand. He signed up for the active duty Army in 2010. I was hesitant in wanting him to join, even though he was 24 years old. I didn't want him away from home. His ASVAB score was through the roof; he could have done anything he wanted. Out of everything he could have chosen, he chose infantry. Huh? I know what infantry is and as a mom, I wasn't going to like this. When I asked him why, he said, "I have always lived a warrior lifestyle and this was a way to serve my country the only way I know I could the best." Here's what it meant to me from a mother's perspective: he would be going overseas, on the frontline, he would be shot at, and he could be away from home for a long time. Don't get me wrong, I was proud of him, but scared of the unknown as well. Off he went to boot camp, training, and then his duty station with the 82nd Airborne at Fort Bragg, North Carolina

Here it is 2011: John's first long deployment (since being married) and Tyler's first-ever deployment, and I know what this means, ulcers. We all know how hard goodbyes are to our loved ones. Have you ever noticed that your spouse seems tough as nails when they first learn they are leaving – all pumped? Then as the weeks get closer, their attitude changes and so does yours. I remember trying to stay away from him. I didn't want to see him because he was excited to go. I wanted him to be as sad as I was that he was leaving for a long period of time. He started getting distant as well. I was doing the same, even though I didn't recognize it. He was getting worried, not about serving his country, but for his family. I remember him always wanting to have "the talk," as I call it, in the car, at home, etc. I really tried to stay away and avoided conversations after that. I told him to do what he needed to do, that I know what his wishes are if something happened to him overseas. I never wanted to have those thoughts. I don't want to plan my husband's funeral. But, to have the talk with your son, is just as hard. Have you ever had to do both? I hope you never do.

My youngest son, Conner, had a very hard time during both of his dad's deployments. During his dad's first deployment, he made himself physically sick every day for two weeks. His best friend had just left him to move away to another country. He knew his dad would miss his birthday, Thanksgiving, winning a gold medal in the Cornhusker State Games, and winning scholarships for bowling tournaments for placing first place. He couldn't call his dad right away to tell him all of these amazing things; we had to wait for John to call. Other military spouses will understand how hard it is to leave for them and their children. The second deployment was a little better, but we still were sad and upset. Conner cried and it made me sad watching and holding him. I couldn't make his sadness go away. Conner is talking about joining the military. I don't think I can let him go.

Now, it's *that* time. The morning John leaves and I just can't get out of bed and say goodbye. But, I do with tears in my eyes. But, to watch my youngest son devastated because his best friend and dad is leaving him for six months is so hard. I never knew how hard it was for my husband to leave until he told me. He would love to break down and cry during that goodbye, but he knows he can't because he has to be strong for his family.

Two months later, it was Tyler's turn to leave. He got to come home on leave for two weeks. I was so happy we got to see him before he deployed. He got to spend time with his friends and family with a barbecue to send him off. The day has come for him to leave to go back to Fort Bragg. I didn't want him to leave because that could be the last time I see him. That's still my baby, no matter how old he is. To make matters worse, I am a worrier. He wouldn't let me take him to the airport because it makes it harder for him to leave. He left as the same person he always was.

Conner and I kept ourselves very busy while they were away. Volunteering at our base and anywhere they needed us. When were weren't Skyping or talking to them, we were waiting too. I remember Skyping with John one time and all of a sudden he jumped to the floor. This was odd. In the background I could faintly hear gun shots and loud booms. He would tell me it was nothing. I believed him, I didn't know any better. But, when he came home, the truth came out.

I will always remember the first phone call I received from my son's Family Readiness Group (FRG) leader two weeks after he left and she said, "Don't worry, it wasn't your son that died." I almost passed out. I asked her to not call me again and told her why. I know she was doing her job, but I have two loved ones fighting overseas and my heart couldn't take these phone calls. I stopped watching any news until they both came home. There was a time when I was talking to my son at least every other day, and then it went to not speaking to him for five days. None of his Facebook friend's would answer me or tell me what was going on. Come to find out, he had gotten mountain sickness during a mission and was hospitalized for five days. He didn't tell me, because he knew I would worry, but instead I was worried sick and thought the worst. I later learned that his best friend thought he had died.

Homecoming: John came home first, right before Christmas. His time was shortened because the military was pulling out of Iraq. Homecoming was amazing; we couldn't wait to see him. I wanted to hug him, kiss him, and hold him and not let him go. Christmas was really quiet, just like we wanted. I felt guilty for having any fun during Christmas because Tyler was still deployed. How could I have fun when he looked tired and skinny, plus he was a million miles from home? I told my husband not to talk about overseas until my son came home. It would just make me worry.

We made it through the holidays, but no one told us how "we" would change during deployment. I know I changed; I was the boss again, like when it was just my oldest and I. John was different. Little sounds made him jump, he wasn't sleeping very well or at all. He never wanting to go out in crowds, sitting with his eyes on all exits, and he was quick to temper. Deep down, I think he wanted to go back where it was familiar. We weren't getting along. I wasn't sure we were going to make it. No one told us that what we were going through is common. We figured it out on our own. Our love conquered our shortcomings. Let's just say we were better prepared for the next long deployment.

Six months later Tyler came back to the States. It broke my heart that I couldn't be there to greet him when he got off the plane. No one was there to hug him and shake his hand and tell him thank you. I didn't see him for another couple of months. I didn't see him because he had gotten married on his leave during his deployment. She cheated on him from day one, and spent every cent he had while deployed on herself and her boyfriend. This started his struggles, causing us not to talk during his deployment for months. They are now divorced. He hurt his knee jumping out of helicopters during training and his deployment overseas. He came home on leave after he had knee surgery and was home for three weeks. He would tell stories about being overseas, show pictures. He seemed okay. While home, he met a girl and she was good to him, for a while. It was time for him to go back to Fort Bragg and finish out his time. When his service commitment time ended four months later, he moved back home. This is when I noticed things were not the same with him. Reintegration back into the civilian world is difficult and resources are lacking, more needs to be done. It is a huge difference between military and civilian life.

When Tyler came home, he started school right away. He had a newer relationship and was going to be a daddy in less than four months. It was a lot to take on right away, and he really didn't ease into the civilian world. Because of that, it made it hard to focus, among other things. It was hard to watch the change that happened to him. Things that bothered him before didn't anymore. Seeing so much death caused him to become numb. He started showing signs of Post-Traumatic Stress Disorder within a couple of months. Watching this broke my heart. No mother wants their child to go through this. I kept trying to figure out ways how to fix this, fix him. I wanted my son back to the way he was. He never thought there was anything different about him.

I made sure I was there for him every day; that's all I could do. There were nights, I would cry myself to sleep knowing I couldn't fix him or my husband. It was hard to watch the change in them. After a year and a half his fiancé, his daughter's mom, decided she had had enough and cheated on him with a person from her workplace. Tyler pushed her into this job and he had a hard time getting over her. Blaming himself for pushing her to get this job. In order to leave him, she had lied and taken their daughter away with her. This devastated him. His daughter and ex-fiancé were his world. And like that, it was gone ... This just added to his stress.

We had, and still have, two dogs at the time of John's homecoming. One of the dogs, Daisee, became his "therapy" dog. When John came home from deployment Daisee was immediately by his side. It has been about six years that she has been doing this, and she is the only one that can bring him out of a dark place. Daisee is always by his side and she needs to know where he is at all times. Daisee has never been trained as a therapy dog; she must just have the instinct to know he needed her. I am glad she is there for him, but sometimes I get jealous that she can make him feel better and I can't. I am becoming more understanding the more I learn about therapy dogs and how they help.

I would watch Tyler and would start to notice what made him stressed and what didn't. What helped him make it through his rough times? It is his daughter, and making things with his hands like drawing and painting. These things seemed to take his mind off of everything bad in his life. His face when he sees his daughter takes his mind off of everything. I watched him build his daughter a toy box. Everything was beautifully hand-painted artwork on the toy box. He has sewn Christmas stockings by hand – one for him, his fiancé at the time, and his daughter. He is working on a wall mural for his daughter's bedroom wall.

Over time, seeing how his mood changed while drawing, building, and painting, I thought about how it could help others going through the same issues. Most, who are suffering like my son, don't think they need therapy or counseling. I wanted a safe place where they could come and do something to ease symptoms: art.

I started a nonprofit that teaches different mediums of art to veterans, military members, and retirees who have suffered from PTSD and other mental issues related to military service. It's called Nebraska Arts for Vets. I thought, if it can help my son, it could help others. As an artist myself, I paint or create to make myself happy or take my mind off of stressors. I have been very lucky that some classes are being taught by other veterans with the same diagnoses or issues as my son. This means that the learning environment is more relaxed. Our first class was to learn photography. I gave them a 30-day challenge that was a suggestion from another military spouse. It is always great to see what they see through the lens; telling their story with pictures and how they see the world. Not only do they get to tell their story, but they are up and moving and getting out. They don't have to be in crowds or places that may trigger them. These classes help tell their stories when it's hard to talk about what they have experienced, and they can help them manage their symptoms. We are beginning to get larger classes. Knowing that my nonprofit can help at least one person has made a difference. I continue to educate myself about PTSD. I will continue to find ways to help our veterans who suffer, and little by little we can help ease symptoms through our art program.

I have teamed up with another military spouse, Dr. Ingrid Yee, to make PTSD cards. These cards are intended for a service member to give the people around them when they feel that they are being triggered in any situation without having to give a reason or feel bad for leaving. The cards can be found at www.AFI.org under the Resources and Tools tab.

Just remember, you are not alone watching someone you love suffer from PTSD. There are many resources out there that will help you and those who are suffering from PTSD. Understanding and continually learning is key for me.

Cara Loken is the Executive Director of Nebraska Arts for Vets and Caregivers - a nonprofit organization connecting members of the local military community to art. She has been a National Guard wife for 18 years volunteering her time to assist fellow families. In addition, Cara owns her craft shop that sells handcrafted items. She lives with her husband and youngest son in Bennet, Nebraska. Her oldest son and granddaughter reside close to them in Lincoln, Nebraska.

Sewing Together Success

Monica Brenoskie

Every business begins with a desire, a passion of or about something. To create, provide, offer, and learn. An idea of "I wonder if ..." or "I should ..." begins to toss around in your mind. Maybe you leave it alone and think on it for a few days. Maybe you even forget about it and then come back to it later. Or just maybe, you take it and immediately catapult yourself into the great unknown.

Like me.

My husband is in the military. That sentence alone could be its own paragraph and should tell you about our semi-nomadic lifestyle. Every few years we pack up every little thing we own, whatever survives our pre PCS decluttering ritual, and we move somewhere else on the planet. Unpack, set up our home for a few years, purchase new things we need, declutter, pack it up, move, and repeat. It's a lifestyle that isn't for everyone but is one that I feel very blessed to have. And now included in our moves is my home studio. My very large cutting table, a sewing table, my two sewing machines, an undisclosed amount of fabric, stuffing, yarn, and many, many other supplies and such. In short, I'm a doll maker and textile artist.

The beginning of what I made was initially just for myself and was "self-serving." I had a passion for being artistic and for creating. We had moved to Okinawa, Japan, when I was about four months pregnant with our second daughter. After a lot of searching and disappointment, my desire was to create an heirloom doll that would represent the country in which she was born and that she would know was lovingly made with her mother's own two hands. Especially since we were only there for a few short years, I knew she wouldn't really remember much as she got older. How could I possibly stitch memories, culture, and emotion into a physical object? *Quite the ponderance, right?*

Other than a short-lived business venture in elementary school in which my mom was the one sewing tiny pillows I sold to classmates for about ten cents each, I had never sewn in my life. But that didn't stop me from purchasing a few materials and hand sewing my first doll. I chose a Shisa, because it was both adorable and a guardian. These mythological creatures are found in a few Asian cultures and look like a cross between a lion and a dog. It was the perfect symbol for Okinawa and my love for my unborn child. After seven hours of tedious work, I was loving my creation but swearing I would never spend that much time sewing anything again. The present me is now laughing ironically at that complaint. I had no idea how new ways of making things and an addiction to all things hand detailed would soon consume my days, nights, and dreams. I had no idea that I would spend sleepless nights after my girls were asleep, hand embroidering cherry blossoms and mejiro bird scenery onto kokeshi doll buns, completing a 14-hour project. I had no idea what I'd started.

As a military spouse, the lives of my family and I are broken up into chapters that are most easily remembered by where we were living at the time. For someone like me, who can easily forget what I had to eat the previous day (which is the norm if you have small children ... or maybe because you didn't have time to eat at all) being able to remember times in my life by the place in which I was living is very helpful. I love having special keepsakes of each place we've lived. I even try to make sure I get little keepsakes for my girls as well. I know that they are too young to remember much at this point in their lives, so I take it upon myself to try to capture that time in a tangible object. Maybe they'll remember something when they hold it. It was this wish, that I as a mother had for my children, that really started my wheels spinning. I wondered how many other military moms wanted the same for their own children but maybe weren't super crafty. How many of them were sentimental and wanted that special reminder for their children, represented in a doll or piece of art? What if this desire extended to other adults and not just for parents?

I decided right then that I wanted to be someone who could provide that special keepsake. No matter where someone moved over the years, they would be able to look back and remember that doll being in their memories. When they held my work, they would remember how they felt about where they had lived, or it would stir up a memory. If it was for a young child, I wanted the doll to be timeless enough to never be outgrown. To know that it was given to them with love and that they'd be happy to pass it on to their own children, along with the stories. It wasn't just about providing a doll, it was about providing a service that I felt passionately about.

But how did I even begin to accomplish any of this? I didn't know the first thing about starting a business or being out in the big world. Didn't you have to go to school for it or grow up being a business genius? Talk about a full circle moment and God working in mysterious ways ...

I had just recently attended an event with my husband; I believe it was also to recognize Key Spouses, the Key Spouse of the year, and the Military Spouse of the Year. We were still very new to island but I was already sporting my round belly. It was time for everyone to make their way to the buffet line.

I know a lot of people hang back and politely wait to let others go first. Maybe it's my love for a good buffet or me "selflessly" taking one for the team to break the ice, but I made a beeline to grab a plate. Being pregnant, either I was also constantly hungry or my sugar levels dropped like a stone if I went too long without at least a snack.

I wasn't the only pregnant spouse there either. On this particular occasion, I happened to be on the opposite side of the buffet line of an adorably pregnant woman with extremely short hair, a green dress, and flat shoes. She had also been congratulated on being named 2014 Armed Forces Insurance Military Spouse of the Year. I feel like that no matter your background, when two pregnant woman get around each other, you already have this instant bond. You understand each other's suffering – I'm joking! – But seriously, by the third trimester, I can't think of any pregnant woman who wasn't ready to be done.

Anyway, I made small talk by congratulating her on her pregnancy, asking when she was due, and if she knew what she was having.

I then finished filling my plate and went back to my seat.

(Keep this story in the back of your mind for a minute or two.) When I first got my sewing machine, I had problems right off the bat. When I sewed, I had a huge jumbled mess on the underside my fabric. Nothing I did would fix whatever I was doing wrong. In a lot of frustration, I posted in one of the local craft pages to see if someone knew what I was doing wrong. A very kind lady by the name of Keena offered to come to my house and help me out. She lived on Kadena too and was just a few streets over. I was elated!

Turns out I didn't even know how to thread the machine correctly. Word to the sewing novice, if something isn't sewing right and you have a nest of thread under your fabric or it's not wanting to sew your stitch right, simply rethread your machine completely, take out and put back in the bobbin. I don't know what it is, but you probably unknowingly threaded your machine wrong in some way.

Anyway, Keena was beyond patient in getting me started on my machine. She had her own sewing business and made beautiful dresses for children. I explained to her what I was wanting to do and she was very encouraging. When I asked her how to get started with registering and becoming a legal on-base business, she recommended a lady by the name of Lakesha Cole. Keena told me that Lakesha had a very successful business and would be exactly who I would want to meet.

Now, remember the story about the adorable pregnant lady, 2014 Armed Forces Insurance Military Spouse of the Year, across from me in the buffet line? Yup, that had been Lakesha Cole. I'd been so preoccupied with blind pregnant hunger that I'd missed her name during the formal presentation. I would also like to briefly add in that I am now also good friends with Julia Poole, who I came to meet later through Lakesha at a small business owner's luncheon and who had also been congratulated at the same event for being Key Spouse of the Year. Talk about a full circle and a half, right?

And you can bet that my opening line in my email to her started with something like:

"Hi Lakesha, I'm not sure if you remember me, but I was the preggo across from you in the buffet line the other day …"

We had our first meeting at Chili's Too, while she ate a small lunch of chips and salsa, and I bombarded her with a million questions with my pen and notepad at the ready. I was grateful for her time and wisdom then, but I feel even more grateful now for her generosity, looking back. When she was already beyond busy, she fit me into her hectic schedule. She allowed me to take away from the only time she was able to get a moment for herself to eat something – AND while she was in her third trimester. Throw that cherry on top!

I'm not exaggerating when I say that within 24 hours of our meeting, I owned my own domain, I had set up my Facebook business page, registered my business with my state of residency, set up PayPal, and picked up the form to request approval for being an on-base business. I couldn't have been more excited to get started and I only had a few months left before I'd already need to take time off for my baby. So there was no time to waste.

For weeks, I ate, slept, and breathed sewing. I was working on a Shisa design, watching YouTube videos whenever I had sewing questions, and connecting with fellow military spouses with home-based sewing businesses. The support and knowledge shared was invaluable and I continue to be friends with several of these ladies to this day.

And then there's my husband, Steve. We may have joked that he was my investor and I was expected to turn into a huge success, but in all seriousness, he made it possible for me to purchase whatever I needed and make my dream a reality. He never said of word of complaint when our home routine was completely turned on its head and the house stopped being spotless. I was trying to figure out how to balance being a homemaker, a mommy, a business owner, and teaching myself to design and sew. It's taken years to figure out that there is no such thing as an equal balance. And though sewing wasn't something he had the slightest bit of interest in, he would still listen and be supportive. If he hadn't been in my corner, I really don't know how things would have panned out.

My very first customer was a friend and fellow business owner. She wanted a few pairs of my Shisa dogs to send back to her family. She loved that they represented the culture and she was always looking to send gifts that would give them a small taste of Okinawa. I clearly remember asking if she minded taking a selfie with me, to document my very first sale. She gave me a dollar bill as an added momento. I keep it in my jewelry box but someday I'll get it framed and hang it on my wall.

I ended up taking an online branding class taught by Lela Barker. A friend praised it highly and I finally took the leap. I feel like this class really helped me hone in on my brand voice and really get to the core of it. It helped me sift through all the wording and descriptions of why I do what I do, until I was able to clearly define it. It was like I had been stumbling through the tall grass and all of a sudden I found my path. I thought I already knew the reason 'why,' but this just peeled back the layers and made me dig even deeper. This led to me being able to better articulate what my mission was. When I would write my "thank you" notes to each of my customers, I was able to be genuine but efficient in what I was trying to say. Together with Lakesha's continued support and mentoring, I grew in leaps and bounds.

One of the most validating moments for me was this one mom who had purchased one of my Cuddle Kokeshi for her daughter. They were going to be moving very soon and she really wanted one as a keepsake before they left. I had wrapped up the doll as I always do, with hand-pressed paper, simple brown twine tied in a bow, a dried flower gently tucked under the bow, and a handwritten note. On that note I wrote that I hoped this doll would serve as a keepsake for decades to come and bring a smile to her daughter's face whenever she held it. That in many – many – years later, she could pass it on to her own daughter and tell them about her time on this beautiful island. After I met up with the lady and gave her the doll, we both drove our separate ways. It wasn't long after that I received a text message from her saying that my note brought tears to her eyes when she read it and she thanked me so much for the doll. She was like me in that she saw into a glimpse of years down the road and how this nomadic military lifestyle is filled with stories and memories that need to be remembered. In that note, I had written what I would want for my own children, if that doll had been for them. I had written the very soul of why I make what I do and had put my passion into words. That mother's text was the "aha!" moment that I had succeeded and was really making a difference. I felt so blessed that she had shared her feelings with me and my heart was filled with joy.

Pretty early on, I took a break from my Shisa pattern and found myself drawn toward kokeshi dolls. Traditionally, kokeshi are made from wood and are limbless. Not very warm or soft, but they are beautiful collectibles with a fascinating history and progression in their design. I dabbled a bit in making other items but I always came back to the kokeshi. I created my own cloth doll/art doll versions, completely different from any traditional design. Both adults and children were attracted to my work and it was perfect as a keepsake and heirloom to military families. They were popular as baby shower gifts and when families were leaving the island. For my adult clients and customers, I designed a kokeshi doll that served as functional art. Not everyone wants to hang an entire kimono on their wall or feels like Asian style items go with their home decor. So for them I made a doll that would be a functional art piece, featuring vintage kimono silks and cottons; treasured for generations to come. My favorite materials to search for are hand-dyed indigo cottons. Some of my finds are around 100 years old or more. The older the piece, the more excited I get. Many of the silk pieces are hand-painted. Interestingly, it was common for me to first be told the age of a piece as being pre- or post-WWII. I would then ask for a more specific age range. Kimonos are rich with culture, rooted in tradition, and come with their own personal history. Most of my customers are military spouses who purchase these dolls for themselves and usually right before they PCS. I wanted to make a difference by allowing my collectors to still be able to possess an authentic piece of the culture in which they lived, in the form of functional art.

I've been very blessed to find that my work has caught attention in the civilian world, too. The desire for culturally-inspired dolls isn't limited to those who have lived abroad. Social media has made all the difference, when it comes to networking with other doll makers and getting more exposure for my brand. I did find, however, that kokeshi dolls are a very specific niche. For those who are not in the military community or have never travelled, I wanted my dolls to make a difference by inspiring a curiosity of the world around us. I hoped that someone who received my doll would see the cherry blossoms and wonder more about where they come from. Maybe touching the kimono silk would somehow lead to an interest in Japan or other faraway lands. I wanted to find a way to bring the world a little closer.

I recently also started a whimsical doll collection, called Snapdragon Meadow. My first design in the collection has been unicorns. They're definitely a favorite of mine and I have a personal history and love of horses. Unicorns just add that touch of magic, which is appealing to both adults and children. Again, I wanted to have a purpose with what I was creating, make a difference with my designs, and keep true to why I make these dolls. Again, the conclusion I came to was that I wanted heirloom keepsake dolls that both inspired and were associated with a memory or emotion.

My whimsical collection differs in that it brings the *imaginative* world a little bit closer. Where my kokeshi dolls were intended as reminders of where someone in the military community had moved from, my whimsical dolls were reminders of one's childhood or phases of one's life. They make you look into your own mind and discover what's there. When a grown child thinks of what their room looked like and what creatures they always had interest in, I want them to be able to hold my doll and immediately smile in remembrance. Or maybe they're like me and they're a parent who is wanting to give their child that tiny extra bit of fairytale-type magic, that isn't associated with major brand names. Something timeless and classic. I love to make their dresses a bit more country vintage. No matter the age, your imagination is very powerful and can lead to creative new worlds.

There's a simplicity to cloth dolls that is refreshing and organic feeling. My dolls aren't big brand and are not really associated with a certain time period. That's the way I designed them to be. I don't want them to be in a style that is the current fad. I want to keep that clean innocence that takes you back to a time not ruled over by mainstream marketing and big corporations. I want them to be loved 100 years from now, continue to inspire, and be passed along to loved ones.

When you feel passionately about what you're doing, you believe in yourself and what you're doing. You're more willing to stand by your work and not give up when things get tough. Sure, I get frustrated and burn out on work. But after a short break, I come back with a smile on my face and a million ideas in my mind. Honestly, it's all about what really drives you, in your heart, to do what you do. Do the hard work and figure out what you can so that you are knowledgeable and sure about it. But don't be afraid to ask questions if you need help. That's what your support system is there for and it can be beneficial for both sides. Whatever you get, be openhearted to give back in return. Giving is good for the soul. Personally, I've discovered a self-esteem and purpose that I have never felt before. Putting yourself out there for others to judge is a very scary thing to do. But I believe that when you're doing it because you truly love what you're doing, you want to make a difference, or solve a problem, your business or passion gives back to you in ways you could never predict.

Monica Brenoskie is a doll maker, artist, Air Force wife, and mother of three who embraces the gypsy lifestyle of the military. She is a creative spirit, painting walls and constantly drafting new designs while making the 30 hour day cram into a mere 24. Through her work, she seeks to enrich lives and homes with timeless functional art that both inspires and be passed on.

Military Spouse Identity Crisis

Tammy Meyer

Are you a cat person or a dog person? Some of us are distinctly in one camp or the other, admittedly or not. It can be a polarizing question similar to white wine or red wine, pop music or country, beach vacation or mountains, Hillary or Donald.

When it comes to our four-legged, furry family members, many of us also have plenty of friends that are simply and wholeheartedly animal lovers whom could never bring themselves to choose cat over dog, dog over cat. This is my sister. She has always been a lover of all animals. I remember growing up in the cold, long, dark winters of Wisconsin, on our way to school in the mornings driving over the rolling hills and past the fields where the cows would roam and my sister would ask my mom, "Can we please bring them home because surely they are cold and need to be inside." She is and always has been a tried and true animal lover at heart.

Fast forward a number of years later when we were well out of school after I had just purchased my first home ... with three diplomas under my belt, educated, accomplished, single and financially independent. I was so excited! I was working a lot and traveling a lot. As a first-time homeowner, and for the first time in a long time, I had no landlord to answer to, one of the things I was most excited about was getting a dog. I wanted the companionship and was also looking forward to having a running partner. After all, the long work hours often brought me home after the sun had set. The safety and partner in having man's (or woman's) best friend by my side was something I was so eager to enjoy.

My animal-loving sister, however, had an entirely different idea in mind. She arrived unannounced to my new home for a visit and dropped off my first pet as a new homeowner: a beautiful, longhaired, calico, diva, princess, sassy cat. "A stray", she said. "One that needed a good home," she said. "Besides you travel and work too much as it is. A dog would be neglected," she said. "You need a cat. Her name is Sasha," she said. And just like that, before I could resist, argue or debate, my animal-loving sister turned and left.

As usual, she was right. I adopted Sasha as my own. Sasha quickly settled into her role of wearing the pants and running the house. Although we never did go running together, even with the pink rhinestone collar and leash I got for her, she became my companion, confidant, and the one living, breathing partner that hung out with me hour after hour, day after day, month in, month out, and brought me great joy. She would eventually be there for me, not as a running partner, but as a source of support during the time, as a military spouse, when I would lose my identity.

Like many married couples, pets are often inherited and brought into the relationship, as was the case with Sasha. When I met my husband, Sasha was a package deal. She made my first PCS from Wisconsin to Maryland where my Navy fiancé and I bought our first home together.

With much excitement, Sasha kitty, and dream job in tow, I moved cross-country.

Education? Check!

Established Career? Check! Check!

Financial Independence? Check, check and check!

And just like that it was all completely gone. Within a year of that first PCS, and three days before our wedding, I promptly found myself out of work after 11 years and 5 promotions of climbing the corporate ladder with the same company and absolutely loving what I did. My department was getting restructured and I was offered a big, fat, sizable demotion, both in scope and in compensation. Even though I had no backup plan and no idea what I was going to do, I proudly said, "No, thank you," to the demotion. Although this was my choice (and I still believe it was a significant moment and the right choice), I was unprepared for the loss. Plummeting from just shy of six figures to a paycheck of a whooping zero dollars and becoming unemployed within a year was a blow. But it was about much more than losing my income. I was bitter, angry, lost, confused, and at the time I didn't fully understand why. At the time, I had no idea my identity was completely wrapped up in my career.

Feeling lost but with a strong need to pass the hours of the day, I begrudgingly found myself outdoors in the middle of the afternoon tending to the overgrown landscaping of our new home with Sasha loyally by my side. She was happy as a bug to be basking in the sun and enjoying the outdoors. I wanted to be doing anything else. I wanted to be putting my education and professional experience to good use. I wanted to be making a difference. I wanted to be employed.

It honestly wasn't until much later, after trying to fill the empty void with other hobbies, activities, volunteer work, and "jobs" that I realized I needed my career back. I needed to have something just for me; a little something to call my own. What I truly needed was to apply my education and professional experience to contribute to my family's future and our financial goals. I needed to make a difference. I needed my identity back. I also felt it was unquestionably reasonable to want to be compensated and earn a fair and appropriate income for the education, professional experience, skills, work ethic and drive that I had spent years cultivating. I had no idea how humbling it would be that my new "full-time job" had actually become the job of searching for a full-time job only to lead me nowhere. It was devastating to search and search for months with no success.

It's been ten years since that chapter of my military spouse journey. We've moved five times in those 10 years (and counting) with one of those moves being an international move. I've learned an immeasurable amount about myself, about my potential, and about so many other military spouses who have navigated the same unique challenges of this crazy lifestyle.

With 20 plus years and counting in the fitness industry I set out on a mission to add a life coach certification to my credentials. I felt a strong responsibility to not only coach others on pursuing their personal best in health and fitness, but also redefine their identity and enjoy a thriving career. When I became certified as a life coach, I embarked on a journey to interview as many military spouses that would let me ask them questions about their experience as a military spouse. I started with five spouses that I knew and those five spouses recommended other spouses they felt I should also interview. I have spent hundreds of hours interviewing other spouses. It was crucial to me to hear from others. I didn't want to assume, simply because I was a military spouse, that I knew everything there was to know about this life and the challenges that come with it.

The most surprising and significant takeaway that I learned is that we, as military spouses, more times than not, have attached our identity to all of the wrong factors. I did this myself when I attached my identity to my career. How would you define your identity? A question that pulls the answer out easier for most is "Tell me about you". Often times we answer this with I'm a mom, I'm a military spouse, or we talk about our profession, or all three of these areas. These are not our identity. These are roles. Don't misinterpret.

Stay with me.

These are all important, rewarding, fulfilling, challenging, and life-changing roles. They are not our identity. Our identity is *who* we are, not *what* we do. How would you define who you are? What qualities make you uniquely you? This is your identity.

I am persistent, driven, accomplished, compassionate, modest, fun, genuine, and empathetic. I am a good listener. I have a strong work ethic. I am a Christian. I am an introvert. This is what makes me uniquely me. These are characteristics that I bring to any of my many roles: military spouse, professional, entrepreneur, yoga instructor, personal trainer, life coach, Beautycounter consultant, friend, sister, daughter, niece, etc.

If I had been more grounded in these characteristics and acknowledged these traits as my identity instead of attaching my career solely to my identity, I believe I wouldn't have been quite as lost, broken, and devastated when my career journey took an abrupt turn. Of course, it's still a loss and certainly still challenging to navigate. I believe I would have bounced back quicker, and quite possibly more easily see the beauty in having time to enjoy the outdoors and landscape the backyard with my cat companion by my side. I quite possibly would have been more open to other career options to move forward. I know I would have been more content, assured, easier to live with, and hopeful about my path ahead.

My wish for you is that you take some quiet time reflecting on what makes you uniquely you. Redefine your identity. I took the long, hard route to realize this for myself. I navigated my way back through a number of different strategies. At the time, I wasn't doing anything conscious to dig my way out of a disgruntled state. I stumbled along and eventually, through volunteerism, many jobs that weren't a good fit, becoming educated and credentialed as a life coach and Purpose Clarity Coach, interviewing many other spouses and coaching them to success, I eventually found my way to what my identity truly is. It is who I am regardless of the unique challenges I face; it is not what I do.

The work I do as a mentor to spouses seeking employment or volunteerism is to be a good listener. I listen. I ask questions and then I listen some more. The top employment challenges I see spouses face are the challenges they identified for themselves from the interview I've done with them. More times than not they identified themselves as the one obstacle getting in their own way. We want a little something for ourselves. We need a little something to call our own. Many times, this takes the shape of career however we define career for ourselves. We might be the commanding officer of our household, an employee, and entrepreneur, a consultant, a volunteer, or in search of what's next.

The best recommendation I can give about any of us finding the right fit regardless of role is to first redefine your identity. Identity and connect with who you are first and what makes you uniquely you, instead of attaching your identity to a role. You will naturally bring the characteristics that make up your identity to any role you fulfill. We often already hold the answers to what's next, what's my purpose, what will I be doing when I'm thriving. Connecting with your true identity is the first step in being okay with whatever comes next.

Enjoying the journey with the support of other military spouses (and a four-legged furry family member) makes the experience all that much more enjoyable.

Tammy Meyer helps women carve out a little slice of this crazy military life to call their own by helping them keep their own identity, enjoy a thriving career, and pursue their personal best in health and wellness. Tammy is a Certified Life Coach & Purpose Clarity Career Coach, she has a BA in Exercise Science, BS in Organizational Leadership, is certified in six different fitness & nutrition specialties, and is an educator and consultant for Beautycounter ~ passionate about the safety & quality of our personal care products.

The September 11th Effect

Danielle Medolla

September 10th, 2001

Rob and I are both native New Yorkers and have been dating three years. It is my last semester at St. John's and I'm preparing myself for life after college – applying for federal jobs and agent exams. Rob is working on the ramp for United Airlines and going to school to complete his FAA A&P license with hopes of working full-time in their aircraft maintenance department. We were on track, so we thought. We had our lives figured out. In fact, a recent trip to San Francisco left us with dreams of moving out there and starting our life together. The next day I was taking my first federal agents exam in lower Manhattan.

September 11th, 2001

It's a beautiful morning. I drove into Manhattan and parked my car a few blocks from the Federal Building so I could meet my cousins across the street for lunch when the test was over. Rob was in class across the river in Queens. The proctor interrupted the test to explain all the noise and sirens we were hearing outside and I remember Dee (Rob's stepmom, an airline pilot) was flying that day. They said a small plane had clipped the top of the World Trade Center. Having flown into LaGuardia Airport, I remember seeing the Trade Center from the air and didn't think much of it. "Sure, I guess that's possible," I thought. All I knew at that moment was that we were being told to remain inside of the building. So, we did as we were told. When the evacuation order was given, I don't know why but I got into an elevator. Instinct, I guess. This is where I found out that one of the towers had come down. It was surreal. When I got out onto the street, all I saw were streams of people walking uptown covered in white/gray soot. I checked my phone – no service. I turned to two of the people who had just came out of the test with me and asked them if they wanted to come with me. I knew where I was going.

My cousin works in a high school (across the street), so once inside we were on lockdown, spending much of the day. Once inside I tried Rob on his cell phone with no luck. Next, I called my grandfather landline to landline and he filled me in on the details. I let him know I was safe in case my parents called. Then I called Rob's aunt for no particular reason. I guess I instinctively knew that Rob would reach out to her. She became our middleman. I would check in and relay messages to Rob and vice versa. Our plan was to meet at her house as soon as we could and wait for each other. We weren't allowed to leave the school until late in the afternoon; by that time much of lower Manhattan had already evacuated. We walked through empty streets towards the Brooklyn Bridge. It was open and we were told it was the only way off the island. So, we walked. The whole time I wondered, "Where are the aircraft parts – planes are big, why aren't there pieces all over the city?" The loud, crowded city now silent should have made me feel uneasy, but it didn't; I remember feeling safe. At this point, I still hadn't seen the destruction and devastation. Once to the bridge, my cousin and I got onto the next bus we saw that said "BROOKLYN BOUND." It didn't matter where in Brooklyn, once we were there we would figure that out. Once to the bridge, there was a sense of organized chaos, a calm despite all the fear. I knew that getting to Brooklyn was the first step to getting closer home, closer to my family.

Present Day
That day changed our lives; it changed the direction my life would take forever. Shortly after 9/11, the economic temperature of our country shifted. United started laying off employees, or cutting hours to part-time, and jobs (especially) in New York were hard to come by. As a recent college graduate, I was lucky to find a job. Our dream and plan of moving out west wasn't going to happen, and I never did get those test results. Rob stayed the course and finished his A&P license, while I took a job as a legal secretary for a mid-sized law firm downtown. Each year, each anniversary, I remember the Danielle and Rob of 2001 and think about where they would be today had that not happened.

Knowing that a full-time position working maintenance for United wasn't realistic, Rob started looking for other opportunities. Since aircraft and flight are his passion, he first started searching locally. The NYPD has an aviation department, so he took the exam and started his paperwork. At the same time, a few Coasties stationed at Fort Wadsworth moved in next door to my parents. After a few conversations, Rob's interest was piqued and as luck would have it, the Coast Guard recruiting station was across the street from my office.

In March 2003, Rob enlisted in the USCG. By June, he was scheduled to leave for boot camp and asked me to marry him. This is where our Coast Guard journey began. During the next eight weeks I poured myself into research, trying to find out everything there was to know about the Coast Guard and what my life was going to be like going forward. In my search, I found a chart of what he would be doing each of the eight weeks in boot camp and each week I would cross one off. I also learned that we would move (A LOT) and that Rob could deploy (A LOT). I had gone into it thinking that it was a 9-5 type of job where the reservist filled in on the weekends and that the Coast Guard, well, guarded our coast from land. I was wrong.

The next year was full of movement and upheavals. He spent four months at a small boat station, six months at Air Station Atlantic City for the Airmen Program and then five months in North Carolina for another school. Because of all of this transition, I stayed put. I didn't move, I kept my job, and we made it work partly because before leaving for A-School we found out we were expecting our first child. Two days and one year after Rob's graduation from boot camp, August 4, 2004, on Coast Guard Day, our son Robert Joseph was born.

During this year, we relocated to Air Station Atlantic City. It was there that I realized how isolated and alone I felt as a Coast Guard spouse. This is a present-day challenge our spouses face, too. I was a young new spouse and mother. I didn't know anyone in my new community and the station was 40 minutes away. Even if we lived closer to the station, the chances of living near another Coastie family were slim to none. Still, like everything in military life, this situation was not my forever.

Our next PCS was a ray of sunshine, literally. In fact, included in our "Welcome to Miami" package was a newsletter from the station's ombudsman. Now that was something new, I had never heard of an ombudsman. I learned that she was my link to my husband's command and to the station. She was a reliable, creditable source to get information from and to whom I could express my hardships. WOW! What an incredible resource, I remember thinking, I am going take advantage of all the information she can provide me. Immediately, I reached out and was added to her email distribution list. She did a great job of providing support and information to the families in South Florida. When the time came for her to move, the solicitation came out looking for a replacement. After the second email, I casually replied, "Any takers?" to which she responded, "Nope, interested?"

And that's how my ombudsman journey began. She had done so much for me, without even knowing it, that I promised myself that I would pay it forward and continue the work that she had done so well. The first command I worked with set the stage for me. I always felt important, listened to, and appreciated. I never felt like the issues I brought to them were bothersome, and they gave me a comfort level that I came to expect from subsequent commands. I feel that is what has made me successful. I am forever indebted to those commanding officers and their spouses for guiding me, mentoring me, and supporting me in my role as an ombudsman.

Our most recent move has brought another perspective into my life as we are not directly connected to the Coast Guard community, but rather we are co-located with the Air Force and Navy. We miss our CG family terribly. I know as a military spouse we are all part of one BIG family, but the CG is unique. We are small, in fact we are tiny which makes us CLOSE. Because of this we cross paths with the same families repeatedly. So much so that they become our extended families, our kids begin to call them aunt and uncle, and sometimes are closer to their CG family then they are to their extended biological families. It makes my heart smile when I see that my kids have the same comfort level with our CG family that they do with our real family. We think nothing of taking day long drives to reconnect with friends we were stationed with. Not only that, the unique structure of our service forces us to be a tightknit community. I feel an immediate bond when I run into a Coastie at our current station. It's an internal sigh of relief like, "You get me! You understand," in the mix of tilted heads and strange looks when you explain duty schedules, deployments, and the like.

Our jobs are multi-tiered, for example my husband as a AMT, he repairs and maintenances aircraft in addition to flying and deploying with them. I learned that the other services are more specialized. The CG utilizes one member to do the job of two or three. It's not bad or good, it's just different.

Twenty years ago, I sat across from my college advisor. I remember her asking me what I foresaw in my future. At the time she was just trying to get me to narrow down my major in college in order to put my freshman schedule together. I remember answering, "I'm interested in the law and education." Those two couldn't be more different – I was making her work for her money that day. So I dabbled in both and graduated with a degree in legal studies. Shortly after Rob graduated boot camp and our marriage, I went back to school to earn a master's degree in education. Now 20 years later, I have my teaching license in special education with the intention of becoming a board certified behavior analysis (BCBA).

I have come full circle. I am the same, yet different then the Danielle of September 10, 2001. Rob and I are always reminding ourselves of how blessed we are to have lived this life. Especially when we are sad. We remind each other that if it wasn't for this job, we would not have had these experiences. We would not have met the wonderful people we have. This job gives and it takes; sometimes it hurts, but most of the time it overfills you with joy and happiness. If you let it.

Danielle Medolla is the proud mother of three boys (Robert, Christopher and Paul) and wife of USCG Chief Petty Officer Robert Medolla. Danielle volunteered to serve as an Ombudsman for six years at two seperate duty station and became an Ombudsman trainer in 2016. She has a passion for assisting her CG family and connecting them to reliable and useful resources. Her hobbies include, snorkeling, fishing and reading with her toes in the WARM sand.

A Happy Accident

Ingrid Yee

Be All That You Can Be

My journey into military spousehood (is that even a term?) was not at all the one that I had envisioned. I came into this military life by happy accident. I had some knowledge as the sister of an Army veteran who served during the first Gulf War. But, most of that knowledge was in the form of sending care packages for him and his buddies, or even the occasional visit as he was not combat deployed and stationed in Italy. I truly did not appreciate, at that time, how much of an impact military life could have on a spouse and family. I had zero clue. None. Zilch. Nada. I was a military sister. The only real context I had were those old Army commercials. You know the ones, "Be all that you can be, in the Army." Bet you were singing it too while you read this. You see, that slogan stuck with me.

Army Strong?

Fast forward, nearly a decade later, and I found myself wanting to make a difference, wanting to be all that I could be. You see, I too was watching as the twin towers fell and our country changed forever. I followed the research and the news stories that reported on service members' suicides. I actually remember the exact moment it happened. I was in the waiting area of the doctor's office. CNN was playing on the TV. And there it was, in big bold print on the screen: "U.S. Military Suicide Exceeds Combat Deaths." I froze. I felt sick, my face got hot. I was devastated. How could that be? How can I help? It was immediately after that thought that I made up my mind. I was going to enlist in the Army as a military psychologist, just like my brother had enlisted in the military a decade before me. The thing is, I was already well on my way towards finishing up my doctorate degree in psychology, yet I felt a deep calling to help the military community. I knew I wanted to help. That much was crystal clear. What wasn't clear was just how to do it. So I talked to a recruiter, and was ready to apply for pre- and post-doctoral internships in the military. I would be able to work directly with service members to help reduce the rate of suicides within the community. I was going to make a difference. I was ready. Fate, however, had other plans for me. Just as I was going to sign on the dotted line to become a military psychologist, a kind, and brutally honest, Army recruiter came into the picture.

That Army recruiter, my then-future husband, laid out all the ways that enlisting in the military would negatively impact my career and my family. Secretly, I think he just wanted to marry me. But he won me over, and instead of joining the military, I took the leap, and married him. No big church wedding. City Hall and just us. After all, he had to go away for training. And with that, I married into the military. My baptism by fire consisted of getting married, shortly thereafter having our baby, and then moving across the country, all within the span of a little over one year. I was not ready. Not by a long shot.

Newly Married Life

My life as a newlywed had its ups and downs. It was an incredible high to be living on a military base with fellow military spouses who were going through the exact same things that I was. I put my Blue Star Banner in the window of my new home, as he left on deployment– exactly four days after our arrival on base. I felt lost, alone, worried about him, heck worried about our family. But before those feelings of dread could take hold, my doorbell rang. Again, and again, and again. Fellow spouses, women I didn't know, showed up wanting to help and support us. That right there was the beginning of my love affair with our military community. As I settled into life on base, with my husband deployed and kids to raise, I started to feel the financial and emotional pinch of not having my career on track. You see, I had put it on the back burner. We had a new community, a new life. I had my doctorate and just needed my license and a job. What could possibly go wrong?

My Career – or Lack Thereof

That deployment was my first view of the very real hit to my career this military life was going to bring. I felt uneasy as I went online and searched ... and searched ... and searched for a job. I had the degree, but no license. In my field, that is a death sentence for your career. I had the title, I was Dr. Ingrid Herrera-Yee. But, it took me literally six months to find employment. Six months of cold-calling, trying to leverage my network, searching online, and even the more traditional newspaper want ads. I was desperate. One day, I decided to just walk in to the psychology department of the local university. I offered to volunteer my services to mentor students there. I was desperate to keep my skills fresh and to keep my mind from going into atrophy. I *needed* to work. The department chair spoke to me for a few minutes and came back with an offer for me to teach Research

Methods, Statistics, Testing and Measurement. These were courses that nobody in the department wanted to teach. I jumped at the offer. The upside, I got to teach and mentor students. The downside, I would make about as much money as I would working at a fast-food joint. Do you want fries with that paper? Ugh. The pay was low, lower than I expected. But, I took the chance, and despite the poverty wages, I was happy to be doing something in my field of study. So, this was the start of my career. My underemployed career.

Underemployment – My New Normal

Many moves later, I found myself in more volunteer positions than paid and more jobs that I was overqualified for, but I persisted. My dreams of becoming a well-paid and working clinical psychologist were within my grasp. I could see it. But the gaps in my résumé and explaining to civilian employers that I was a great choice despite the fact that I was going to move in a couple of years was taking its toll on my career. I felt like I was never going to work to my true potential. A doctor in name only. The upside was that all the moving and the variety of job opportunities it brought with it were blessings in disguise. I gained experience in so many different areas – grant writing, online teaching, social media marketing, curriculum design, research, speaking, and writing. Had it not been for my many moves and the amazing military community along the way, I would have just quit. It was hard, I'm not saying it for pity, but stitching together a career has been one of the hardest experiences. Yet, I wouldn't change it for the world. I learned. I learned how to stretch myself, challenge myself, and I grew as a professional. Underemployment was my new normal, and it was a great teacher.

Finding My Village

Throughout my times of struggle there was one thing that always kept me going. My peeps, my tribe, my village. I had managed to make and maintain friendships with some of the most amazing, kick-ass women and men on the planet. They had my back. I had theirs. We knew what the struggles were, we faced them, and supported each other through thick and thin. Heck, they weren't friends, they were family. As I went through this life, there were people, online and in real life, who had my back. I can't describe what an incredible experience that is. But, here's the thing: I started looking around me and though I had an amazing village, I had trouble finding others like me. I had great supportive military spouse friends, and I had great supportive friends in the mental health field. But, I didn't know any military spouses at the time who were in the field. I felt alone. I knew right then and there that I needed to find my village. I needed to find fellow military spouse clinicians.

Making a Difference

Finding my village meant creating an organization so I could find them and support them. This is how Military Spouse Behavioral Health Clinicians (MSBHC) was born. I knew there were other spouses out there like me, but I had no idea how many. Since the inception of MSHBC in 2012, I've been able to connect with spouses, girlfriends and fiancés that are in, or looking to be in, the mental health field. We went from a handful of members to over 1,000 today. I knew that the problems I experienced with licensure and employment were not unique to me. I also knew finding the right school, with the right accreditation, that is portable, is a struggle for many. So, I poured my heart and soul into MSBHC. I lobbied on Capitol Hill for licensure portability, for more employment opportunities, and for harsher penalties for predatory schools. I hosted networking events with fellow spouses, wrote about our plight in national news publications, and made my voice heard. I wanted our leaders to know that we are here. We have needs, but more than that, we have so much potential. We are an asset, not a liability.

With the mental health issues plaguing society as a whole and our military community in particular, who better to meet those needs than military spouse clinicians who don't need to be trained in military culture. We live it. We breathe it. We are it. We can help! We can make a difference.

Clinical Work

Through all the ups and downs, clinical work with our military community was at the core of what I wanted to do. Being a spouse, being a psychologist and living in our community was a privilege. The intersections in my life and work made me a better clinician and I was able to take from the experiences I'd had to help military families cope with loss, mental health issues, domestic violence, child abuse, substance abuse, and issues like deployments and transitions. To this day, my work within my community is the most rewarding work I've ever had. I know that so many other spouses out there feel exactly the way I do. I carry their voices with me always.

Challenges Our Military Spouses Face and How to Beat Them

Like the experiences I detailed before, many military spouses share the same frustrations and road blocks that I've experienced. Unemployment, licensure portability, and finding the right schools are serious challenges that many have to face as they navigate this crazy military life. My advice is simple. If you're facing having to choose a school to get your degree, make sure that the school you decide to attend is accredited in your field of study. Is licensure getting you down? Look up potential states you might live in, research their licensure requirements, and meet or beat them. Find one of the harder licensure states and meet their requirements. In this way, you are more likely to meet their requirements and get that license. It helps with moving, too, because you'll be prepared to meet those requirements much more easily. Educate yourself; find out what the laws are that regulate your profession. As for employment, the best advice I received was to network. Don't be afraid to reach out to someone to connect you to a potential future employer. I've been able to secure employment simply by knowing somebody who knows somebody. Last, but not least, make sure that you are able to take care of your own needs, and reach out to your village to help you with that next hurdle.

Military Spouse of the Year

In the midst of all the work I was doing to help our military spouses obtain and maintain employment in the mental health field, and to ensure that we could help mitigate the shortage of mental health providers in the military community, I was nominated by several friends and colleagues for Armed Forces Insurance Military Spouse of the Year. Truth be told, I was not very familiar with the award. I was moved by the words that others spoke about me. Not wanting the attention, I almost didn't respond. I'm so glad I did, because, in all honesty, winning Armed Forces Insurance National Guard Spouse of the Year changed my life in ways I could not have imagined. Not only did I gain a community of rock stars as friends, I gained the ability to open doors – doors that that were closed to me before.

I made connections in government, military, and business circles. To those audiences I brought the face, the voice, and the stories of our spouses and of the mental health needs of our military community. As I reflect on my time in the MSOY program, I'm proud of my accomplishment, the doors it has opened, and the difference it has made. My network and sphere of influence has grown tremendously, allowing me to do more and more for military spouse clinicians and for the mental health of our community. I couldn't be more grateful and I look forward to the road ahead, one where we will no longer suffer the losses to suicide within our community and where our military spouses will become a vital part of the landscape of mental health professionals helping our military service members, veterans and their families.

Ingrid Herrera-Yee, PhD is an Army Reserve spouse, mother of three boys and a clinical and research psychologist. She has been published extensively, serves on several nonprofit boards, is a subject matter expert in military mental health and is the founder of Military Spouse Behavioral Health Clinicians network.

What a Long, Strange Trip It's Been

Jeremy Hilton

"The purpose of life is not to be happy. It is to be useful, to be honorable, to be compassionate, to have it make some difference that you have lived and lived well." -Ralph Waldo Emerson

With apologies to the Grateful Dead, I suspect I'm not alone as I think about our military family's "adventures" these last many years. As I reflect on the past fifteen years, I can't help but wonder what might have been had our lives taken a different path. Just because I wonder doesn't mean I would have wanted a different path. I am convinced our story and the lessons we've learned serve a purpose. I hope my insight provides some measure of understanding of my advocacy, rules of the road, and how important the voice of our military community is day-in and day-out.

September 11th, 2001

I remember the morning of September 11, 2001, quite well. I was on shore duty as a Navy lieutenant, stationed at the Washington Navy Yard, in downtown DC. It had been surprisingly crisp that beautiful, clear morning. My wife Renae, an Air Force OSI agent, was working a forensics case in California. I had worked out that morning and had been at my desk for an hour or so, when a colleague said something about a plane hitting one of the World Trade Center buildings. As a friend and I were listening to the radio, as soon as the second tower was hit, we knew we were at war. But while my wife and many of my friends would be actively participating in the longest armed conflict in our nation's history, I would not. That was not the direction my life would take.

It ends up I had a different battle to face.

The day after the attack, my wife caught a military transport plane carrying a general officer back to DC, a good thing as all commercial flights were grounded. She and her OSI partner did back-to-back day and night shifts for the next two weeks outside the Pentagon. They processed evidence and ensured the bodies of those killed were taken care of appropriately. As we touched base each day, I going to work and she going to bed, it was perhaps one of the most surreal times in our marriage. I also think back to that period in her life and wonder what she might have been exposed to as she was doing her job ... a question that would become very important shortly.

In the fall of 2002, I'll never forget how proud I was, when Renae, now pregnant with our first born, was honored as that year's top female federal law enforcement agent for her work at the Pentagon after Sept 11th. I had no idea how dramatically our life was about to change.

Kate

A little over a month later, we were at a friend's house when my wife said, "We have to leave, my water broke!"
We rushed to Bethesda Naval Hospital where the doctors induced my wife and after 40 hours of unsuccessful labor later, our daughter Kate was born via C-section. Unfortunately, there was a reason she would have never made it out via normal pathways, as she was born with massive hydrocephalus, with her ventricles swelling her head to the size of a three year old's.

The next month in the NICU was, to put it mildly, nuts. Ventricular punctures, bradycardia, seizures, and feedings in milliliters became our life. Kate's prognosis was unknown but I remember distinctly a well-meaning doctor and friend suggesting that Kate would never be more than a vegetable and we should consider placing her in an institution.

Well, that clearly wasn't about to happen, but it was obvious to Renae and I that this little girl was going to need a lot of help; help that was less likely to be there with two active duty parents. Given the deployment cycle for Navy submariners versus Air Force OSI agents (particularly at that time), we knew it made more sense for me to get out of the Navy.

Stay-at-Home Dad

People often ask me, "Why did you get out instead of Renae?" or tell me, "What you did was amazing!"

I typically give a brief answer or comment, but I really don't like to discuss why I left the service. I am not a martyr. I am a father. My wife and I are a team and we make decisions based on the best interests of our family. There have been plenty of times Renae wishes she could be home with our kids and there have been plenty of times over Kate's last fourteen years where I would have loved to have been able to work in a traditional environment (because trust me, being at home has been work).

Honestly, I think I was well suited, at least for a time, to the role I was given taking care of Kate, particularly in those first six years of her life. I focused exclusively on the day-to-day necessities of ensuring Kate was receiving all she needed to maximize her quality of life. I juggled therapists, doctor visits, and the normal craziness of a household, many times while my wife was either training to deploy, deploying, or working what seemed to be an insane number of hours each day at work. In that first six years, Kate had nine surgeries, a couple being what can only be described as very intense. More than once, we wondered if she would survive.

But through it all, I felt like I had a mission, not unlike my military career. Moving our little family five times in those five years, with two deployments, a command job for Renae, and ten months of school in Alabama put my every skill to the test.

Each time a family like ours moves, it takes about six to nine months to re-establish the medical and educational team necessary to ensure our family thrives. It didn't help that I was having my own significant medical concerns. Finally, with Kate's medical condition seemingly stabilized and Renae landing a Pentagon job in the summer of 2008, we took our collective breath, just in time to add a little guy, Jackson, to our household in 2009.

Advocacy

After we unpacked our boxes and settled into a routine in DC, one of the first things I did was sign up for a program called Partners in Policymaking. PiP, as it's known, is a one year, very intensive, competency-based training which teaches family members and individuals with disabilities how to effectively work with policymakers at the local, state, and national levels to promote systems change.

Over the course of the program, I started to think about what advocacy meant, both to me and my family, but just as importantly, to those in similar situations. I thought about what we had experienced as a family during the first six years of Kate's life, and I began to see how I might apply the lessons we learned to help others.

The first issue that came to my mind was the difficulty we had experienced as our family moved across the country the past five years. The Air Force has a program, called the Exceptional Family Member Program (EFMP), which is supposed to help military families like ours. It didn't help. In fact, it did the opposite, making our moves more difficult, while providing little to no support.

In online forums, other families expressed similar experiences. I attempted to work within the Air Force community, participating in focus groups. However, at the end of the day, it became apparent that nothing would change. Then, one day I thought, "I wonder what the Air Force instruction on EFMP says?"

Air Force Instructions are orders with specific requirements. They aren't suggestions or pieces of papers to be followed when convenient. Coming from the nuclear side of the Navy, the importance of following procedure had been ingrained in me; one does not skip steps when starting up a reactor or working with radioactive material.

Somewhat surprisingly to me, the instruction detailed a whole host of action items the Air Force was responsible for but that they had obviously skipped with my own and others' families. So, I took a controversial step when I wrote and then filed a DoD Inspector General complaint against the Air Force's Exceptional Family Member program on behalf of 16 Air Force families. A couple of months later, findings in our favor were issued: systemic non-compliance across the Air Force in its administration of the EFMP system. To be honest, that success gave me the advocacy bug. With hard work and dedicated military parents, we found that we could make a difference.

I have spent the last seven years in this advocacy space, doing my best to make that difference in military families' lives. Frankly, it's been a full-time job. And that's on top of my other full-time job, taking care of our family.

I'd like to highlight two initiatives I've worked on:

- **Keep Your Promise:** Four military spouses and I co-founded what eventually became the #Keep Your Promise movement, an enormous undertaking after Congress passed the 2013 Bipartisan Budget Act, which reduced the value of military retirements by tens of thousands of dollars for every military retiree. At its peak, we were working full time with 16 military service organizations, leveraging a grassroots advocacy campaign aimed at uniting hundreds of thousands of military and veteran families. We developed a no-cost social media campaign and town halls on Facebook and Twitter. Amazingly, our efforts went viral, reaching more than 157 million timeline hits on Twitter and over a hundred thousand Facebook followers. Our efforts played a key role in ultimately overturning the military retirement cuts 61 days after they were made law. One editorial compared our efforts to that of the National Rifle Association, an organization with a fully paid staff. Please never tell me military spouses don't make a difference.

- **TRICARE for Kids:** Based on a 2013 bill for which I advocated, TRICARE for Kids consists of military and veteran service organizations and military families who advocate for health care and support for children of military families, including those impacted by special needs (www.tricareforkids.org). We have had success in the last four years working with Congress to enact appropriate legislation as well as ensure that the Defense Health Agency and DoD are held accountable.

Both initiatives were created in response to a need to collectively raise our voices on significant issues impacting military families. I think it's fair to say that advocacy, in large part due to the digital age and social media, has changed significantly in a short number of years. While military spouses a generation ago would gather around a kitchen table (literally how the National Military Family Association was created in 1969), today they gather around a virtual table. The internet age and the speed at which information travels has changed the advocacy environment. At the same time, some things haven't changed at all and they relate to the way advocacy should be accomplished.

Effective advocacy takes practical, purposeful steps. While the following is not all-inclusive (and I've violated them all at some point), I hope the list I've come to call "Jeremy's Eight Rules for Military Spouse Advocacy" is helpful.

Eight Rules for Great Military Spouse Advocacy

1. If the people who are affected by a decision or policy change aren't at the table, you are doing something wrong. In the disability movement, there is a famous phrase, "*Nothing about us without us.*" When it comes to bureaucracies, many times this concept is purposefully overlooked. Whether it's in a spouse club, wing commander meeting, or in the Pentagon, those most impacted by a policy should have a seat at the table. I'm not suggesting that the decision must be in the advocates' favor, but that their input is considered. In the end, doing so is in everyone's best interest as the decision or policy change will be better for having taken this step. Sometimes our leadership just needs that reminder.

2. We need to appreciate everyone for what they are doing, not for what we want them to do. Kids or no kids, job or no job, both sides should respect the other's situation in life. We will all move in and out of our capability levels over time.

    As an advocate, we need to meet people where they are at, not where we want them to be. There are all different kinds of capabilities and different levels of support. Be prepared when you are told "no" (and consider rule three). We should be thankful for any help a fellow military spouse can provide and not chastise them for not meeting our preconceived notion of what they should be doing.

3. Learn to say no. Not every idea is a good one. I've learned that many times one's first intuition about a person or idea is usually a

good one. Learn to say "no" to that person or idea. In the advocacy world, you are guaranteed to make mistakes, but always remember that your reputation, particularly as it relates to trust, is the most important currency you have.

The other piece of saying "no" is that you need to maintain focus. Being an expert in one policy area is better than being an amateur in two or three.

4. When you see a fellow military spouse who wants to learn or expand their repertoire, take them under your wing and help them learn the ropes. We should be training the next generation of military spouse advocates. We certainly didn't get to where we are without lots of support from the generations that came before us. Pay it forward.

5. You don't need to, nor should you, be doing it all. Almost none of us are being paid for this advocacy work. When you stop liking what you are working on, take a break or try something else. Your family and your military family needs you around for the long haul and it is exceptionally easy to get burned out.

6. Professional and concise is the order of the day. Hone your message and then deliver it. Craft your thirty-second elevator speech. Creating relationships is important but remember, the message is why you are there. Sometimes our leadership, Congress, or whomever you are speaking with would love to talk about anything but the issue at hand.

7. Senior spouses have lots to offer … so do junior spouses. Both need to listen and learn from each other.

Really listening is a gift and we have so much to teach each other. Don't get hung up on the officer-enlisted divide, the "old" versus "young" spouse issue, or whether one spouse has a college degree or not. Experience really does count for something, so listen when that senior spouse provides input. You aren't obligated to follow their counsel, but I would recommend you consider it. Likewise, many junior spouses are much more connected to what's happening on the ground and can provide amazing input on what really matters to today's military families.

8. We are stronger together than we are apart. "No kidding," I'm sure you are saying. However, for whatever reason, it's a lesson we military spouses seem to forget far too often. We don't always have to agree at the tactical level, but when it comes to strategically advocating for our families, we need to keep this rule in the back of our collective minds. In the end, we need to find a way to support each other, even when we disagree.

Some of you won't like this list. That's fine – make your own. Do what works for you. But get involved. We are heading into some tough times, both as a military and as a country.

In the many years I've been doing this type of work, I know I've ruffled some feathers. Sometimes, it's been because I'm pushing people to change in ways they don't find comfortable. Sometimes, it's because I've violated one of the above rules. I've heard the argument that military families should be happy for what we have, and that if the Defense Department (or others) gets it wrong, our "job" as spouses is to hold our noses and support the chain of command. I also suspect there are some "old school" military spouses who don't believe that military spouses should be stepping out of our lane by becoming advocates on issues we care about. They don't see it as our place.

I don't hold to either philosophy.

We military spouses have a responsibility to act to right a wrong or to fix a law, regulation, or policy that is negatively impacting military families.

Looking back, I hope my advocacy made a difference. But just as importantly, I hope our story emboldens those who read this to understand that what they do on behalf of others is so critical to our future. Has every day been easy? No. But that's okay … none of this was meant to be easy.

Jeremy Hilton is a Navy veteran, Air Force spouse, author, and advocate. He helped repeal the military retirement cuts in the 2013 Budget Control Act as a #KeepYourPromise Cofounder and is currently working to reform military pediatric healthcare as a "TRICARE for Kids" Champion. For his work, he was selected as the 2012 Armed Forces Insurance Military Spouse of the Year. Besides the Huffington Post, Jeremy has written for Time, Military Spouse magazine, USAA, and Exceptional Parent magazine.

Keeping Pace

Nicole Maddock

When I first saw Erik it was on a Christian online dating site. I'll be honest – the uniform made my heart flitter-flutter. Erik and I met in person about four weeks after we first started talking. I was a second year law student – he was a recent returnee from Iraq, a submarine officer in the Navy, and stationed at a shore duty in Evanston. Being just north of my favorite city at the time and about three hours from where I lived, I figured I could give it a chance. The advantage to online dating is that you can ask anything and the other person has all the time in the world to respond – if they do at all. Erik told me of his love for the Navy, but his decision to take his career a different direction and transfer to the Navy Reserve. He wanted to settle down in his home state of Michigan and raise a family – this was convenient as I currently lived in Michigan and our families, we discovered, lived only two hours apart. When I first saw him I was head over heels; he was tall, handsome, and climbing out of a beautiful sports car. We dated for five months before we were engaged. Seven months later we got married in a dream-come-true military/Protestant service.

I knew I was in over my head, however, when I walked under the sword arch and was whapped on the backside by his commanding officer with a sword and a hearty, "Welcome to the Navy, Mrs. Maddock!" I then experienced my first move with Erik. I got to move in with Erik after we returned from our honeymoon. I had one semester left of law school and so my start as a Navy wife was as a transient – half the week I lived in our little apartment, then I'd climb on Amtrak, ride the three hours back to the city I was interning in, intern three days a week, go to class in the evenings, and at the end ride back to my new husband.

When I graduated four months after we got married, we started very seriously acknowledging the truth – our plan for the future was looking a bit shaky. Erik was going back to graduate school in Detroit full time and I was looking for work, hopefully in a commutable range. I found work that summer in my dream job working as a prosecuting attorney for a wonderful county 90 minutes north of where Erik went to school. I moved back to Michigan and lived temporarily with a new coworker while Erik finished up his active duty assignment, and we worked on purchasing a house in Michigan. We thought we had started the path to eternity. We got a new puppy and new kitten the same week that we purchased a new car (and traded in my husband's beautiful GTO for a grocery-getting Equinox.) Erik was working a two-year program and I was learning the ropes at a job I felt passionate about. Erik's Reserve career started and he found himself learning the ropes at the base that was thankfully just six miles from our front door. We thought we had figured it all out. Then a little more than a year into our new gig, I excitedly found that we were expecting our first child and Erik nervously started looking for work. Two weeks before my due date with our son, we moved 140 miles away for what would be our only in-state move. Erik found what seemed to be an awesome civilian employer who was excited about his Navy experience and I got to settle in an area a little closer to my family. I quit my job expecting to find work after the baby came and then Sammy made his entrance into the world.

I was totally overwhelmed as most new parents are. About three weeks after he was born, Erik headed off for his first drill weekend. Faced with what felt like the unbearable prospects of a new baby, a new house (under renovations on most of the main floor), a new community, and being alone for a full weekend, I fled to my mom's house where I was sure I'd at least eat. Slowly over the next two years as Sammy and I became more stable, I began to find a group of friends – other moms at our church that I depended on more and more for support and humor. This tribe became critical in my abilities to keep us all alive and happy in our home.

We made it through the first year by what felt like the skin of our teeth, emotionally and financially. I decided that I really needed to start working again (plus I missed "grown up time.") I could pick up cases on a part-time basis at the county courthouse doing contract criminal defense work. I finally felt like we were maybe going in the direction we thought we would be when we first met. We made it through the 18 months of this job. The turning point for us came when his employer threatened contract reneging when it came to the two weeks of Navy Reserve drill that was required of him. It became more and more obvious that this position was not for him and although he had been looking for work for more than a year, there was nothing that sparked the fire of his intelligence or fit the bill for our budget needs. After long talks, we realized we'd have to expand our horizons if we wanted to find work that fit the bill. We might have to move – again. Erik's calling was to return to the work he had studied in graduate school, medical physics, and to work in a hospital setting. We hoped that we had found a great position for him in Ohio, about an hour from his parents and three from mine, but when he started negotiating his contract, they rescinded it and left us in shock. We had a backup plan but one that I didn't think we were honestly ever going to take: the

Navy wanted Erik back for a one-year recall. Our family was moving to Montgomery, Alabama.

We sold our house, loaded another truck and went on our adventure. Erik was happy to be able to walk away from his employer to essentially go back to school for another graduate degree. I was happy that our stresses from his employer and our tight financial situation got a shakeup. In July, we rolled down to our new home only to find it completely unready for us. The house on the base at the address we had forwarded all of our mail was a wreck. Wires were hanging from the walls, it was dirty, and the carpet was either being torn out or torn up. We thought it'd be nothing, that they'd just find us a different place! But, they were still working on the alternative so we stayed in our one bedroom hotel room for 10 days with our 95-pound Goldendoodle, cat, and toddler while my husband started his schooling. Not quite the way I had imagined our "big adventure" starting. I have since started telling my young son when something goes awry on an adventure that the chances of things going wrong are what make it an adventure and those "mistakes" will make the funny stories down the road. We did eventually settle into our new home in Alabama.

When I went to the school's spouse orientation a week after moving into our new home, I sat next to two of what would be the best friends a girl could ask for. Halfway through a spouse's presentation about the Halloween party started getting into how much they needed help I leaned over and said, "Yeah, I did high school. The point was I made it out alive. I'm not doing it again." My new friend Kelly laughed and said, "Girl, I knew we'd be best friends." I felt like although I had left my tribe back in Michigan, I would be able to establish a new one and learn to love our life in Alabama just as I had back home.

We settled into the pace at school and soon were delighted to find ourselves expecting a second time. Having had a stress-free pregnancy with our oldest, Sammy, I was surprised to find periodic bleeding. I did my best to live in the moment taking care of him and taking advantage of the sunny weather and close knit community being at a military school afforded us. It also felt a little bit more like home when my stepbrother who was an enlisted Air National Guard member came down to the same base for school. I tried to imagine what the chances of an activated Navy Reservist and a senior enlisted Air National Guard member from Michigan lining up at the same base in Alabama. My mom and step-dad came down for his graduation (he was at a much shorter school.) I had so been looking forward to their visit, which was my mom's first since we moved, but the truth was I was as sick as a dog the whole time she was in town.

Two weeks later I drove to my 20-week ultrasound. My husband stayed at home to finish packing the car for our trip for Christmas. My doctor took a good guess as to why I was so sick – my water had already broken with this pregnancy and my body was trying hard to stay pregnant. All plans for travel were immediately scrapped and instead of going home for Christmas, I was off to Birmingham for testing from a maternal fetal specialist. We were in complete shock. I talked to our family and explained we would not be coming home for Christmas. The next morning I was off to the specialist with my husband while Sammy stayed with Kelly. The doctors told me the chances of making it to viability were exceptionally low, but if I did I'd have to go in-patient in the hospital in Birmingham when I reached 23 weeks until I gave birth, whenever that was. Our heads were spinning; I had never been away from Sammy for three nights (and had only JUST been away for two a little more than a month before on our first marriage retreat.) Erik had to go to school and Birmingham was 90 minutes away from our home. Our family was still in Michigan nearly fifteen hours away. We cried, and prayed, and cried and reached out to command. We explained with the best of our understanding (which now having talked to others is a case by case basis) our needs, our worries, and our question marks. A position for Sammy was opened at the Child Development Center (the military's childcare) and my mom drove down to care for us as we worked our emergency contacts. I sat at Kelly's kitchen table, alternately crying and trying to figure out what would happen, as she hugged me and prayed with me. Our Bible study group flew into rescue mode also – almost all of them were also only in Alabama for the one-year school. With a flurry of activity, I was packed up at 23 weeks pregnant and sent up to the University of Alabama at Birmingham to wait – for however long – until our second son made his entrance.

At this point, I had all the time in the world to think. It was a wonderful blessing and a terrible curse all at the same time. I was able to see, however, that one of the things that was keeping me comfortable and sane as compared to many other moms in the unit was that I shared what I was going through with those around me. My "military family" was not kept in the dark; I was forced to ask for help and to receive it. I also was thankful that I had made friends from the Alabama Officer Christian Fellowship, who were central to our family's lives. I could recognize how much of a difference this network of friends made to our lives as we had moved so often.

It seemed impossibly hard at the time to sit and wait while my family needed me at home, but that is what I had to do. It was such a huge comfort to know that my husband and son were being cared for by neighbors, classmates, command, and our Bible study "family."

When our little boy made his entrance a month later it's hard to know if I was more relieved that the waiting phase was over or more concerned about what lay ahead. Again, our neighbors rallied around us and when I came home from Birmingham (for the first time in more than a month!) our kitchen had been decorated with a new wreath on the door and there was food in the fridge. Those were the kindest and most heartfelt moments we experienced as it was impossibly difficult to feel "happy" leaving our two-and-a-half-pound son in a NICU 90 minutes away. We next started the longest month of my life. Every other day, my husband and I made the trip from Montgomery up to Birmingham to visit our little son. We called morning and evening for updates and talked to doctor after doctor. Twice a week, a military member would show up at our door with dinner. And so time went.

Throughout the ordeal with Bennett, the doctors were cautious with us. Each doctor explained the probable path but explained to every rule there is an exception. The specialists praised the most minute improvements and took enormous time in explaining the plethora of machines keeping our son alive. Ten days in, the doctors told us that they confirmed what had been suspected – Bennett tested for sepsis, a blood infection. The little progress he'd made quickly evaporated and he went the other direction. We talked to specialist and doctors for hours, each compassionate but honest. He was not well. A month after he came into the world, Bennett passed from this one.

I don't think I could have made it through the first few days had it not been for my friends and family lifting us in prayer. My favorite Kelly story (and that which may exemplify the magnificence of the military wife) was my conversation with her the next morning. I had been crying, she listening. I finally confessed a fear I didn't even want to say out loud in case it proved true; I was sure I was hallucinating.

"Kelly, I don't even know how to tell you this, but I think I'm seeing things. I honestly think I've gone crazy."

"What makes you think that?"

"Well, I've been doing the grocery shopping and the cooking, but there's food in our fridge that I didn't put there. I have no idea – NO IDEA – where it came from." And then I broke down crying.

"Oh girl! I forgot to tell you! Ryan dropped it off when he let the dog out. I made leftovers for you guys. But you are my kind of crazy – you lose your mind and food shows up!"

And I laughed. Honestly laughed. Laughed for a moment's break from grief from the truest of friends.

Our next move was a little more than two months after that day – and never have I been so thankful to pack up and move out. When we moved to our next state, Erik quickly found a Reserve unit ready to take him in and a civilian career that he excelled at. Part of the new job, however, was that he had to move eight months after he started to finish his training. By this point, it has almost become a joke with our family; maybe one year our Christmas cards will have our address and not just forward stickers. As we prepare to close on our sixth house (in five states) in less than six and a half years of marriage, I lean back on what I tell Sammy – adventure isn't about it going the way I thought it'd go but about making the most of whatever comes our way. I look back at our wedding pictures and recognize that even in the few short years that Erik and I have been married, we do have a dream-come-true marriage (most days) and that I have grown more resilient, more resourceful, more adventurous, and more flexible than I could have ever dreamed. I am constantly thankful for the Navy in our family, from our pretty wedding to Tricare covering our mind-boggling medical bills for our son, Bennett; and to finding friends that are better than I could've dreamed. I had no idea what I'd find when I started down this path, but I am so, so thankful to be on it.

Nicole Maddock is the wife of Erik Maddock of nearly seven years. She has journeyed with her family from active duty Navy to Reserve spouse to activated and back. She is an attorney turned stay at home to Sammy, 4, with a second son on the way.

It Takes a Village

Nicole Spaid

I met a boy in college. Well, more specifically, I met a Texan in Alaska. We met on an Environmental Biology course which consisted of 10 days of camping in and around Juneau. He stole my heart and I have been by his side for over 25 years. If someone would have told me 26 years ago that this little, German immigrant would marry a military man, that we would maintain some semblance of calm in the eye of a storm, I would have laughed. I would have told them that I would not leave my family and essentially, grow up with this boy in the Marine Corps. I would have told them that they were crazy. But isn't that how the best stories begin?

We were married one month after graduating college and moved together to Albuquerque, New Mexico. It was the first move out of what would be 15 and counting. There, Wes worked for my father's company until the Marine Corps was ready to send us to Quantico, Virginia, for The Basic School (TBS). In retrospect, I am grateful that I began this military journey with my husband from Day 1. I learned as he learned. From the first move, I was surrounded by young spouses, like me, who were immediately welcomed, embraced, and mentored by the spouses of the Marines who were in charge of shaping our Marines.

Those first few months taught me lessons about who I wanted to be as a military spouse. Not knowing anything about the Corps, this way of life heightened my senses to my surroundings. My naiveté and a good dose of ego gave me the bravado to ask questions. I was young and dumb (I only knew I was young) and am forever grateful to these "seasoned" spouses for not pointing this fact out too often, for their sense of humor, and their unwavering determination of giving us such an excellent example to follow. They were our safe space to learn and grow.

I am even grateful for the wife of a major-select who informed me that, due to the difference in our husbands' ranks, I needed to call her, "Ma'am." It instilled in me a burning desire to never allow another spouse to feel that way in my presence. To this day, I want us to celebrate our Marine's accomplishments. Our Marines work hard for what they earn, be it in pay, rank, or awards. It is theirs. I do not recall crawling through mud, standing in yellow footprints, or taking an oath. I do not have rank. Not even on my best Jayne Wayne Day do I qualify

140

for it. I hope that the respect we earn as spouses comes from our experience, our stories, and our willingness to help one another.

It was in the early days that I learned about, and fully embraced, the Key Volunteer Network (KVN), L.I.N.K.S. (Lifestyle Insights, Networking, Knowledge and Skills), and the Navy Marine Corps Relief Society (NMCSR). I made lifelong friends who became my surrogate family and continue to help me navigate this beautiful craziness. My husband learned to be a Marine and I learned the importance of volunteerism and mentorship. They were early lessons that still shape our life today. At the time, I saw these connections as my way of survival. Looking back now, it is so much more than just survival, it is the key to thriving. It is a Marine Corps life lived well.

After TBS, we began our tour de force of moving. One would think that after a few moves we would be quite good at it, however each move presents its very own challenges. This particular move included a lengthy discussion about a bookcase that would not fit down a staircase (even though it made it up a few months before). The movers announced that it would just need to stay with the house. It did not. My most memorable move to date is the one where our truck driver was arrested for a DUI at the front gate of our base, which led to the truck and our furniture being impounded for a few days. Not funny then, hysterical now.

Sidebar: moving stories are a mild form of "battle scars" for us spouses. We could literally spend hours talking about various moves and the stories stemming from them.

My husband began flight school, which from start to finish bounced us around four times alone. Each place would present a new opportunity to volunteer. In Corpus Christi, I had the opportunity to help write and implement a program that would eventually shape into the Command Representative Program, a link between the various commands and the programs available to families and Marines. In Pensacola, Florida, I became a SAVI instructor (Sexual Assault Victim Intervention Program) at the Naval Technical Training Center. I became a LINKS mentor in Jacksonville, North Carolina. Without fail, I would work with the KVN at each duty station as well. At each opportunity, I gave my efforts and much, much more was returned to me through the people I met and the friendships, support, and guidance they gave me. While I often did not have the time to plant my roots in the town we lived, I became deeply rooted into the Marine Corps culture and the amazing families a part of it.

Our first fleet duty station brought us to San Diego, California. Fresh out of the training commands, we were excited to start "real" Marine Corps life. It was here that I began what would be a true labor of love for the next 10 years. I became our squadron's Key Volunteer coordinator. I loved the KVN. I miss it. I know there are differing opinions about it, but when a KV program was done well, it was an incredible asset to the Marine Corps.

I always thought a KVN should reflect the make-up of the unit it serves. Volunteers should come from all ranks, life experiences, cultures and lifestyles that would reflect the families of the Marines. Ultimately, one would hope to achieve a balanced pool of volunteers who were approachable by the spouses. I began to recruit at family events. I did not know, nor care much about the ranks of the spouses of our volunteers. I wanted to know the caliber of women willing to help. (Wait for it, gentlemen.) Oh, the volunteers! Oh the amazing caliber of volunteers that stepped up to help. It was, and has been since that first group, an incredible group of volunteers! Whatever stereotypes that may have existed about both officer or enlisted spouses, it was blown right out of the water from day one. We had stay-at-home moms, professionals, doctors, educators, lawyers, nurses. We had all age groups, ethnicities, and experience levels included. I was thrilled and am continuously humbled and honored to be involved with these volunteers. They went through training and we were ready! And then I got a phone call.

A spouse was concerned that bringing this diverse group of women together would encourage fraternization. What??? My heart dropped. I was told this spouse had spoken to several wives of ranking retired military and they did not think it was a good idea.

In my head all I heard was, "You should call me Ma'am."

I thanked her for her call and for her concern, I assured her that I had the support of the command and I would try it this way. I remember shaking from the frustration I was feeling. I offered her the opportunity to call me back and tell me "I told you so" if it all went to hell in a handbasket.

She never did get the opportunity to make that call.

With the CO's intent and full support, these KVs came through full force, taking a piece of ownership of the squadron and its families. They planned, executed and supported so well, I was in constant awe of them. When our squadron became reinforced to join the 13th MEU (Marine Expeditionary Unit) we grew and added more families and added their amazing volunteers into the fold. It was with this reinforcement that I learned about another untapped source of support. His name was Frank.

Frank came to us by way of his wife Kim, an incredible and dedicated Marine who would deploy with the MEU. Frank was a retired Marine and now father to a son. He was so smart with technology, computers and communications. At this time, we did not have smartphones, Skype or any of that stuff ... I know, I am ancient.

He quickly became an integral part of our families' volunteer support system. He made contact with other male spouses, explained in-depth what our Marines encountered, and even did some occasional "mansplaining" much to our delight. He taught me that support comes from everywhere. Unbeknownst to me, my perspective was too small and he helped me broaden it.

Frank passed away a few short years ago. We were so very lucky to have had him in our lives. He will always be my favorite KV and I assure you, that is no small feat because the KVs I have been surrounded by were nothing short of phenomenal.

Since that first moment with the KVN, my experience with the volunteers that made up the program was incredible. Spouses with busy lives gave their time and energy to care for one another. We were there for all of the families we could reach and formed such a cohesive group. All these families, KVs or not, came together and supported one another through the ups and downs of life. We laugh together, we cry together, we kick tires together, but mostly we laugh. We babysit, we help deliver babies, we change tires, cook meals, nurture one another. We hold onto each other in the darkest of times through the loss of too many of our Marines.

As the deployment tempo increased sharply, the Marine Corps rightly began to hire full-time civilian Family Readiness Officers who would assist the Marines in their units. The position of an FRO became too important and needed to be done efficiently and well. Not to mention, the Marines who were filling these positions were needed to deploy and be, well, Marines. I love FROs. A good FRO is worth their weight in gold. When Wes took command of Marine Medium Tiltrotor Squadron 365 we were blessed by our super-FRO, Jen. She was smart, organized, and committed to our Marines and their families. She matched my crazy. She did not even blink when I announced that I would be at the Donut Hugs and Chocolate Kisses event she set up to lend immediate support to the families that were dropping off their Blue Knight to deploy. We started at 3 a.m. that morning and finished at 4 p.m., hugging spouses, holding their kids, and wiping the tears. She worked her tail off to make sure our families were well informed, taken care of, and entertained. She was flawless to me and I know that without her and our amazing volunteers this deployment would not have been as successful as it was. I believe this is exactly how most commands feel about their FRO.

With creation of the FRO Program, the KVN disbanded and we lost a program that gave an opportunity for families to pour into one another. I miss it greatly and I think we still have to figure out a way to help connect our families more closely within the units that their Marine serves.

Throughout this time, our family grew. Kate was born in 1997. She was three when Wes first deployed. It was the first of 7? 8? Is it crazy that I can't remember? They all seem to turn into one big deployment after a while. We took her to the ship several times so she could see where Daddy would be living. Who knew how much of it actually sank in at the time. Well, we would find out shortly. The day of departure, we kissed and hugged her Daddy. Surrounded by our squadron families, all of us trying to be brave, we waved and smiled. When the ship began to push off a shocked Kate began to cry and yell out, "DADDY!! Daddy, don't go!!" Yup … still brings me to tears. Any semblance of bravery melted and everyone, I do mean everyone, in our vicinity began to cry. What a sendoff.

Our military children are incredible creatures. If you ask most military parents, they will agree that we desire to create as much stability for our children as we can. Our lives are chaotic enough with each deployment, temporary additional duties (TADs) and the many moves. We have to learn quickly how to integrate our kids into the community we reside in for whatever length of time that may be. I think for us it was sports. Sports or other extracurricular activities like cheer, dance, and art have always provided my kids an instant connection to other kids their age. Through these activities, they often make friends who then go to their schools, and having a few familiar faces in the crowd is always a good thing. A good thing about a small Marine Corps is that you eventually come to a time when your kids will have friends at whichever duty station you are sent. We know that should we go to San Diego, we have friends there. Jacksonville? Covered. It makes the moves that happen later, at a more difficult age for the kids, a little easier.

Throughout our moves, my kids (1 girl and 2 boys) have become incredibly close. There are times when all they have is each other and it has formed an incredible bond between them. Just recently, as we found ourselves back in Texas for a year, we have been given orders to move to Portugal. My daughter is in college in South Carolina and is excited about her new vacation spot over the summer. Ross, my youngest, is still young enough to be content to just be with us. I was most concerned about what Jack, my 14-year-old would think. Thankfully, Portugal is a soccer haven and my boys love soccer. He knows this will be an amazing opportunity to play at a high level and receive an excellent education through an international school there. He just smiled and said, "What? Seems right. I just got here, found a good team to play with, made the varsity soccer team and made a few friends. It sounds right that we should move now so I can be lonely and socially awkward again." Did I mention you have to have a great sense of humor in life? He will be fine. He is Jack Effing

Spaid, and he always lands on his big, athletic feet. This life has also taught them about diversity and not to fear change. It is a great lesson to teach children and I am in constant awe of how well my kids have rolled with the punches throughout their lives.

Jack was born in Albuquerque while Wes was deployed as an air officer with the 3rd Battalion 5th Marines. As sad as it may have been that Wes was not there, babies have a funny way of being born no matter who is in that delivery room! As much as I missed Wes, we thankfully had nurses and a doctor, to catch my little man. Kate and I lived with my parents for six weeks prior to my son's birth, which leads me to another point. It is not only the service member that serves. It is not only the spouse and children that sacrifice. When the pebble is cast into the pond, the ripples span much further than the original point of impact. Parents, siblings, aunts, uncles, cousins, and friends all have a vested interest and their support has been invaluable. My parents, specifically for me, have been such an incredible and unconditional source of support and love for my family. I will never be able to thank them enough.

2003 found us in the midst of Wes attending Expeditionary War School, a 9-month career-level professional military school in Quantico, Virginia. We lived on base, Kate started kindergarten there, and Jack was trying to crawl. It was an easy time, post-deployment, for our little family. We became friends with the students and instructors of the school and they became our community. It was also at this time that the Beltway Sniper attacks were occurring around us, so we stayed put in our well-guarded "gated" neighborhood. We had heard the rumblings of what would become the invasion of Iraq. I did not think too much of it because Marines attending schools are rarely pulled, not to mention my husband was a pilot and needed to go through a refresher course before going back into the cockpit. Much to my husband's chagrin, we were "safe."

Wes would come home with stories about the frustration the Marines felt about having to sit this one out. They all wanted the chance to do what it is they relentlessly train to do. And then one day, Wes came home to tell me that he would be dropping out of school and joining the 3rd Battalion 5th Marines as their air officer within the week. You see, Wes's last deployment was with 3/5. He knew the battalion, he knew the position, and he had much respect for the CO. They needed an air officer and they wanted Wes. My husband was going.

To this day, I am not sure if it was a blessing or a curse that I was removed from the fleet families through this. I stayed with the kids in Quantico even though EWS students would graduate and the families who had become my friends would move on. Thankfully the instructors remained and supported me with fervor. To be quite honest, that time is a bit of a blur. I remember focusing on Kate and Jack. I remember watching the news incessantly until my desire to crawl through the screen and strangle some of the journalists became overwhelming and unhealthy. I then prescribed myself to a rule I still hold to in times like these. Thirty minutes in the morning and 30 minutes at night would give me a sufficient picture of the events. We told Kate that Daddy was going back to work with 3/5 for a few months and he was headed to Kuwait. We felt that was more than enough for her to handle.

A few weeks after Wes left, I took the kids to our favorite pizza place to pick up dinner. It was crowded and I busied myself with ordering our food. Kate sat in a booth while I ordered. I did not see the TV, not that it was on a news channel. All I knew was that all of a sudden Kate was standing on the booth pointing at the TV asking if that was Daddy's work and if he was okay. A hush fell over the restaurant and people stared at us. I looked up to see the television with reports coming in that 3/5 was in a firefight and taking casualties. It seemed like we all froze and Kate just kept asking if that was the same 3/5 that her father was with. Thankfully, the man behind the counter shoved a boxed pizza at me and told me to not worry about paying. I grabbed Kate, Jack, and the pizza, and ran out the door. She does not remember that day. I will never forget it.

My husband returned a few months later. It was late at night and because he augmented with 3rd Battalion 5th Marines out of California, he would fly back to us alone on a commercial flight into Washington, DC. My parents had travelled to welcome him home alongside us. We were at Reagan National Airport. It was around 10 p.m. The airport was empty, the stores were closed and we were still able to walk to the gate those days. The TVs around us were showing the return of the soldiers that were captured by Iraqi forces. There were scores of people waving flags and cheering. It was a stark difference to this dark, empty airport. I saw him walking down the gateway. He was painfully thin. He looked tired. He looked different.

It took several years for him to fully let go of the weight he carried back with him from the war. It was a weight I could not help him carry, even if he would have wanted me to, which he did not. I am grateful to those who have and continue to fight for those veterans who suffer from the aftermath of the deployments into combat zones, both physical and emotionally. I am grateful to the other Marines that understood and listened.

And so this is how life in the Marine Corps ebbs and flows. Deployments come and go. We move, we get settled, we move again. I am certain that those Marines who did not get that first chance to go to a combat zone have each done so many times over. We continue to support, to celebrate their accomplishments, and to mourn their losses. Throughout the years, we sometimes have to rely on the energy of others because there are days, weeks or even months that we, as a military family, are just tired. We push on.

The support that is available to our families is unmatched. After the birth of my son, Ross, I was diagnosed with stage III breast cancer. Ross was a surprise baby and I think God sent him to save my life. We were in Jacksonville, North Carolina, and my husband flew for the VMM-263 Thunder Chickens. Through Tricare, I was able to be seen by the UNC Lineberger Comprehensive Cancer Center, arguably one of the top cancer centers in the world. My parents came to live with us to help with my babies. The support from the squadron and the Marine Corps was instant and powerful. Our CO at the time was Lt. Col. Paul 'Rocket' Rock. He and his wife Maria made sure that we were taken care of. Wes was able to come to every appointment, every chemo session, every surgery. When the chemo had taken its toll and my hair began to fall out, Rocket announced that he would also shave his head. Then another Thunder Chicken announced he would shave his head. Then another. Rocket, in all of his wisdom, decided that we would have a fundraiser. He allotted an hour for all of the Thunder Chickens wanting to participate to gather in the hangar and "bid" on each other's hair. If someone bid for the opportunity to shave a Marine's head, that Marine could out bid him not to have to do so. It was hysterical! Chairs were lined up and our beloved New River Barber, Mr. Heuston Hall, brought several clippers to do the job. It was a bidding frenzy. I know Marines can only have 3 inches of hair anyway, but they are very proud of that 3 inches. Within an hour we raised around $3,000 for the Livestrong Foundation. The newly shorn heads included our CO, XO, sergeant major and even the Marine Aircraft Group commanding officer gave up his hair. I have never, nor will I ever, experience such an outpouring of support. My husband told me that even after I left, Marines were still lining up to get their heads shaved. Can you believe it? Rocket is now a general in the Marine Corps. I will always strive to be the kind of people he and Maria are. The Thunder Chickens will always hold a special place in my heart. Right next to my beloved Blue Knights.

If I have learned anything these past 20 years, it is that I would not trade this life for anything. We are closer to the end of our military life than we are in the beginning or middle of it. It is the only life we know. We married young and the Marine Corps has become our home, our family, and our lifestyle. I value and cherish it. I want to continue to serve, mentor, and protect our Marine Corps families. I often tell other spouses to remember that we have a responsibility to take care of each other. To those who have been here a while, we have to help raise the next generation of spouses to become strong, independent, and great mentors to those that come after them. Sometimes this means we humble ourselves to answer even the questions we find silly. As a new spouse, it means to humble ourselves and listen to those that have more experience. I have found one of the greatest assets that the military has lies within the military spouse. They are movers and shakers. They are strong, resilient, diverse, and a force to be reckoned with. I am small compared to the greatness I have seen among them. They do everything from creating a home in whatever environment they are in, to creating and owning their own businesses, to working full time, to going to school, to creating nonprofits to help others, to fighting for our veterans suffering from PTSD. They take care of those close by and when they can, they reach further to take care of many more. They are even known to testify in front of Congress and camp out in legislators' offices until the rights of our veterans, our spouses, our families, and our special needs communities are met as well. And they do this while still achieving their greatest accomplishment yet – taking care of their service members and their children.

Go out. Volunteer. Become a part of something greater than just you. Help each other. You are amazing creatures, you military spouses. I thank God for you. Every. Single. Day.

Nicole Spaid is first and foremost a wife and mother who is incredibly thankful for her family. She loves God. She is the 2015 Armed Forces Insurance Marine Corps Spouse of the Year, which she feels really belongs to all the Marines and their military spouses who have shaped, taught and inspired her along the way.

Standing Tall

Lakesha Cole

"Stand tall, pretty girl with your shoulders back."
Those were the words my Grandpa John repeatedly said to me while inspiring me to pursue big dreams. Grandpa was everyone's best friend. He was my Heathcliff Huxtable. He often sported colorful sweaters and his favorite blue and gold baseball cap with a perfectly bent brim. Grandpa loved jazz and a good sandwich. "Smile, it's free," he said. He greeted everyone with the same smile and casual handshake. He loved his family and friends immensely and was a strong advocate of education.

My parents were teenagers when they had me so I spent a lot of time with my grandparents. One of my fondest memories of childhood was going to the "candy lady." Every neighborhood had one, but we had the best one. Her name was Ms. Rocket. She was elderly, well at least to us kids. She was our friendly neighborhood store owner and sold mostly snacks from her brick house located across the street from the elementary school. On the menu was some of my favorite candy – Boston Baked Beans, Lemonheads, Chick-O-Sticks and sour apple Now & Laters, to name a few. She also had butter ring cookies, chips, pickles, peppermint sticks, soda and iceberg cups. For those of you not familiar with an iceberg cup, it's extremely sweet Kool-Aid, frozen in a Styrofoam cup. Grape was my favorite. During those hot Virginia summer months, Ms. Rocket would also sell homemade vanilla ice cream, and push-up pops for just a few cents.

Going to the candy lady was a daily thing. After homework, we would ride our bikes until our legs were sore. We picked refreshingly succulent, tart and sweet mulberries that grew on our property. We played outside until the street lights flickered on. At night, we watched our grandparents cook our family dinner together, shared our candy and snacks from the candy lady, choreographed dance moves to the latest New Edition song, and dreamed many dreams of what life would be like when we grew up. When I got older, I wondered why we flocked to the candy lady every day. We could have easily gone to 7-Eleven and bought the same items, but Ms. Rocket was something special. She knew our names, or more like, "You're Sylvia's daughter." She knew our entire family and gave us a free piece of candy on our birthday. During the busy summer months, she would bring in all of our favorite flavors and new ones to try.

Ms. Rocket was my first introduction to entrepreneurship and the human-to-human connection in business. My dad later opened Wright's Wright Hand Service, a local carpet cleaning business, and my uncle owned several peddler businesses. An early exposure to the entrepreneurial mindset made a world of difference for me in knowing that entrepreneurial success is possible.

I heeded my grandpa's advice and pursued higher education at North Carolina A&T State University, where I majored in journalism. My maternal grandparents were both school teachers. My paternal grandparents both worked for the city. Growing up we were taught we could be anything we wanted to be. We only knew of two career paths – attend college or join the military.

Not doing anything simply wasn't allowed.

Every Sunday grandpa made us watch "Crossfire" and Tim Russert on "Meet the Press." I remember thinking, "Who is this old white man on TV and why do we have to watch him every single week?" Little did I know that these moments would later inspire me to become a journalist and spark my love-hate relationship with politics. Grandpa made sure we stayed informed. He often explained how most people don't pay enough attention to the news. Some may follow local happenings, but they have little or no interest in national and international affairs and are not concerned about the details of how these decisions impact our day-to-day living.

Registering to vote was a significant life milestone. We were taught at a very young age to support our beliefs in elections; to take note of the challenges and problems within our community and see them as opportunities and not as setbacks. We were encouraged to be activists – to have a voice and know how to use it for good; to always stand up for yourself and others, and to be good citizens.

Today, I indeed stand tall and confident just like my grandpa taught me, flanked next to my Marine Corps gunnery sergeant and husband of 15 years. I'm a 37-year-old mom of three, entrepreneur, and mentor who is committed to supporting and impacting the military community.

I began dating my husband Deonte while in college. I was determined to graduate before getting married. It wasn't a matter of if I was going to marry him – it was a matter of when. Two months after graduation we tied the knot at the justice of the peace. One month later he deployed overseas. Six months away turned into 11 long months. I was busy planning his homecoming when I got the news about him sailing into the Iraq War. My first reaction was to ball up and cry.

Our only sense of the country going to war was Desert Storm, and we were just 11 years old at the time. I had no real concept of what going to war meant for us. You think of people dying and you see horrific images on TV. Looking back, I now know staying glued to round-the-clock news coverage of the war was the worst thing I could have done.

So, I spent the first 11 months of our marriage learning to cope with loneliness and the adjustment of being a military spouse. I admit to freaking out at times wondering if he would ever make it back home. But thank goodness for my fellow military wives for helping me get through those moments of uncertainty. There were lonely, sleepless nights of crying myself to sleep. The emotional cycle of deployment before, during, and after war is draining. There's a range of intense emotions and feelings – anger, fear, loneliness, sadness, overwhelmed, helplessness – all while taking care of the home front. I had to let him know I was okay at home so that he could focus on the mission. I had to get to a place where I would be okay.

It was during this difficult time that I also learned the benefit of filling my days, weeks and months with work and volunteering, and how crucial it was to start creating a career path of my own. I used to work for the federal government, in local government, and in the nonprofit sector.

Choosing entrepreneurship as an alternative to traditional employment was a natural fit for me. Four years ago while stationed in Okinawa, Japan, I made the transition from employee to employer. I could not have done this without setting and pursuing strict goals around the demands of military life.

I've been fortunate enough to have worked for many great companies and organizations. I made a lot of cash at a very young age. Stock options, security, travel, paid leave, education, health benefits, the big house, and my dream car, a black CLS-500 with black leather interior; you name it, I had it. I quickly mastered my jobs and was often praised as a high performer. I was content and comfortable and enjoyed living my young and fabulous life. Why did I leave?

I was bored. Working in that capacity felt like a never-ending chore. I couldn't take another pointless meeting to discuss the next meeting. The thought of having to format another monthly Excel report made me ill. And to use the words "vision," "purpose," and "mission" in yet another PowerPoint presentation made my skin crawl. Bottom line, my heart wasn't in it. My heart was never in it.

Seven years ago I started experimenting with different business ideas. Some were successful, others were not. I didn't discover my true passion until 2010 when I launched She Swank Too, a curated shop for girls featuring imaginative clothing and accessories that embrace the innocence and fun of childhood. My dream-to-reality of owning a boutique started as an idea while sitting in our on-base apartment at Camp Pendleton. I was unemployed with a 3 year old, a deployed spouse and all my family 2,000 plus miles away. I started She Swank Too with $500 during the 2009 recession while working and attending school full-time, followed by three more deployments and three PCS moves, including overseas. I had no real clue about what I was doing. I had no real clue about what I was doing. Before owning a business, I had never hired or fired someone. I had never collaborated with a national retailer, composed a profit-and-loss statement, or analyzed a balance sheet. I had never built a website or negotiated in a foreign currency. I had never manufactured products. And the most terrifying of it all, I had never been responsible for anyone's paycheck. Yet my biggest struggle was and is always time and balance.

Finding that balance as an employee was always easy for me. I lived by "if I don't do it today, it'll be here tomorrow" motto. That logic no longer applies. There's no administrative assistant to handle the day-to-day tasks. There's no IT specialist to call when the computer stalls. There's no payroll department to ensure you get paid on time. And there's no one to hold you accountable to your deadlines and commitments. You don't just wear many hats; you must wear them all. Several of which you may have zero qualifications for or experience in handling.

The truth is I've never been so busy and so overwhelmed, yet so driven by my progress and even my failures. Most of my days are long, and my off days seem even longer. I'm constantly thinking about what's next, how to make payroll, and when my next big break will come. I'm always working.

Most entrepreneurs say starting a business is like having a baby. I used to laugh when I heard this comparison because it often came from older white-collar men who have obviously never experienced the joy and pain of childbirth. But theoretically, there are a few similarities. Once you give birth to an idea, you have to name it, care for it, nurture it, and in most cases, finance it. It's one of the most stressful things you can do in life but one of the most rewarding.

But when I truthfully ask myself what I miss about my corporate life, nothing comes to mind. I am doing what I love, and I have no regrets.

Here are five quotes that I've lived by and the lessons I've learned during my first year as a full-time entrepreneur:

1. *Find out who you are and do it on purpose.* Let's be honest. Being a mom and entrepreneur is two of the hardest jobs ever.

And at some point, both roles will do a number on your self-confidence and bring you face-to-face with every insecurity you have and reveal some you didn't even know you had. Business coach Dan Sullivan says that protecting our confidence is our greatest duty as business owners. I used to have feelings of incompetence and self-doubt when I introduced a new product or started a new project. And, to be honest, those feelings still try to creep in every so often. I question if I'm cut out to be an entrepreneur. I question if I'm as good as my competitors. To be successful, you have to believe in yourself and your ideas. It takes confidence to sell a product you've created to people you've never met. It takes confidence to know you can exist outside of your comfort zone. You need the confidence to take risks, fail, and then get back on your feet to take even more risks to grow your business.

2. *If opportunity doesn't knock, build a door.* Get up and do something. Anything. Stop waiting for a hook-up or a handout or the perfect day, the perfect year, the perfect time. There's no such thing. If an opportunity doesn't present itself, don't just sit around waiting for it to come knocking on your door. That only happens in movies. Find ways to put yourself in the right place at that right time. Align yourself with like-minded people that can help you get to where you're trying to go. How you work determines the quality and quantity of your rewards. Work as hard as you can, and then work harder.

3. *Failing is not always failure.* Perseverance and emotional strength are needed to be a successful entrepreneur. It is the one defining thing that keeps you moving forward and closer to your goals regardless of circumstances. Everything will not always work in your favor. Accept it and get over it. Meeting challenges is a daily requirement. Welcome it. Embrace it. Many people don't take the first step because they fear failure. But failure is only guaranteed when you don't take the first step.

4. *If your goals don't scare you, they aren't big enough.* We all have that place where we feel safe and comfortable. It's small and limited and usually comes in the form of a box, also known as our comfort zone. The problem is if you stay within your comfort zone you will not grow. Dreams that require you to take risks and step into the unknown and overcome fears are the ones that make you grow. You have to learn how to be

comfortable with being a little uncomfortable. Put yourself in unfamiliar situations and stay there until you get used to it.

Over the years, I've shared my experiences to assist spouses in starting, surviving and succeeding in small business, while handling the daily challenges of the chaotic but blessed life we all choose to live. When we moved to Okinawa, I took notice of the lack of business opportunities for military spouses and founded Milspousepreneur, an organization on a mission to cultivate a learn-by-doing business experience for military spouse entrepreneurs living abroad by providing workable business solutions through leadership, live events, education, advocacy, and networking support.

I came to Okinawa with one goal in mind: to expand and test my business in a way I had never done before. I succeeded in doing so when I landed a short-term contract with the Exchange to operate She Swank Too on base. The path I created allowed me to do such while opening the door for other military spouses to start or grow their own businesses.

Today the She Swank Too brand has traveled to customers in 50 states and five countries, paving the way for our first U.S. flagship store in Jacksonville, NC.

My advice to other military spouse entrepreneurs is simple: Don't just be in, be all in. Get involved in your community. How you contribute to your community (or not) is a direct reflection of your business. Giving back is always good for business. Monetary donations are great. Giving your time and sharing your knowledge is priceless.

Lakesha Cole is an author, mom, military spouse, business owner and mentor with a mission to help mom's discover how to use their passions, interests and experience to start a business. She's the owner of She Swank Too, a curated boutique for girls; and founder of Milspousepreneur, which works to inspire other military spouses to build their own businesses.

Journey of an Air Force Spouse

Jana Raye Kingery

Humble Beginnings

Growing up in the Midwest, mostly in the small town of Odin, Illinois, limited the amount of exposure that I had of the sacrifices and contributions of our military. I was proud to be an American and loved learning about the history of the United States in school, but that was the extent of my understanding. In this township, the community allowed me to thrive with my disability. I moved to this school the summer before my eighth grade year. Anxious to meet my fellow classmates, I hoped I would be accepted. The previous year I received hearing aids in both ears due to bilateral nerve deafness. Wow! I felt like I was awake for the first time in my life. I could hear ... the birds (beautiful), the school bell (no more looking at the clock), the lockers (ouch), peeing (gross), and my own voice! This year was a brand new start for me. After much anticipation, the school year began. I gained friendship, understanding, and no judgment from students and teachers which I give complete credit for the reason for I excelled in academics and in confidence. I continued into high school staying active and involved in many after-school activities and functions.

During my sophomore year, I met my future husband, Matt, through mutual friends of my church's youth group in a neighboring town. It was not until my senior year that our friendship commenced when he and a group friends came to watch my volleyball game. We talked, laughed, and jumped on my trampoline. Eventually, he asked me to go rollerblading around town (which was the cool thing to do). He makes me laugh. He has wrinkles around his eyes when he smiles. He saw me. Our relationship deepened as I started my first year of college. During that year, he enlisted into the United States Air Force and left for basic training in March, which starts the tiny steps into my journey. The first phone call from BMT (this started the famous acronyms of the military ... Basic Military Training) was quite upsetting to say the least ... he was yelling at me to get a paper and pencil for his address. What?! Where was the love? I have difficulty understanding speech on the phone when someone is talking like a sane person so THIS was confusing. Needless to say, I did not get the address. After a brief delay, I received his address and begin the writing back and forth. In his first letter, he informed that he had to hide the note in his boot to keep it safe … safe from?? I also realized what horrible handwriting he has, but I treasured getting letters! Once he finished boot camp and started tech school, we started the long distance telephone relationship. We talked every moment we could; I do NOT want to know what we spent in phone cards and telephone bills. It was worth every penny!

Fourth of July weekend was his first visit home for a couple of days since he left. We had some serious conversation about the direction that we wanted to take our lives together. After an unexpected circumstance, he was able to fly home again the first week of August in which he proposed to me in the location where we first started rollerblading and where he first took my hand to help pull me along. We had to plan our wedding entirely around his tech school and my second year of college. We were married on December 27, 1997, in the church where we met through mutual friends. After we both graduated from our respective schools in May 1998, we PCSed to Dyess AFB in Abilene, Texas, our new home.

New Marriage, New Apartment, New College:
A New Life Including a New Cat

After trekking across Abilene without a car, Matt found an apartment for us to rent before I arrived there after putting our names on the housing list that had an extensive wait. He came back to Illinois to pick up me, his car, and all of our household goods and off to Texas we went. Once I viewed our new apartment, I was quite impressed by the area he chose for our beginnings. Since I graduated college with an associate degree in Science, I began to search for a new college to complete my teacher education program. I choose to attend McMurry University due to its excellent reputation in education. While registering for my classes, I learned some of the benefits available for military spouses for tuition assistance that applied on top of the scholarship I was awarded. This was a tremendous help to us as a young couple.

Trying to juggle classes, work, our apartment, our life, we decided to take on our first pet, a cat named Willy. Willy was meant to be a military cat. He managed to find Matt's helmet and uniforms and "mark his territory" by peeing on them. It was quite a spectacle … no accidents anywhere else but his gear. Through all the many loads of laundry, I caught a glimpse of the structure and pride that goes into wearing that uniform. We attended events together in that uniform where I started to learn about protocol, rank, and customs including our spirited Air Force song.

It was during this new phase that I graduated with honors with a degree in Biology and English and began my first teaching job as a high school Biology teacher and assistant softball coach in Sweetwater, Texas. This first job was a challenge and made me want to pull my hair out more than I cared to admit, but it was so rewarding. I loved teaching. It was during my first year of teaching that the tragedy of 9/11 occurred. One of my students came into my classroom and instructed us to turn on the TV immediately. It was the manner in which he announced it that was eerie. After turning on the television, we gazed at what we saw in shock ... the second plane flying into the second building. I had never seen my students so quiet, so heartbroken by an occurrence out of their control. These students matured that day in a way they should not have had to; they walked the halls in tears and shaking hands as if passing strength to one another.

That afternoon, I drove home to our house on base that we accepted and recently moved into feeling tired and worried about the unknown, but I knew the Air Force and the rest of the military would be forever changed. Coming on base had new security measures which I was not accustomed to. I waited for my husband for information on what came next for him and all of the United States military. We watched friends pack up and leave in a moments' notice, families said unexpected goodbyes, and some of my students came to school the next day with one less parent at home. Quite an impact this new life has made.

A Birth of a Family

After being married for seven years and moving to our next base, Schriever Air Force Base in Colorado Springs, Colorado, where we bought our first beautiful home with a VA loan, another benefit of being in the Air Force, we decided to begin our family. During this time, I continued to teach Biology to students now at Widefield High School. This teaching assignment was one of the hardest to leave because I absolutely loved our science department, especially our department chair, our entire staff, and of course, the students. I can't believe how many of these students and the ones from Sweetwater that I am able to watch their successes and their families through social media.

Our sweet girl, Gillian Brooke, was born in September of 2004. Having her was one of the most terrifying and one of the most joyous times of my life. After being diagnosed with diabetes in 2001, I had to adapt my lifestyle and start a medicine regimen that has had to have been adjusted throughout the years. Being diabetic and pregnant poses additional risks that I had to overcome. I had to see my OB doctor EVERY single week until the last two months in which I went three times a week, and I had to give myself four shots of insulin

157

EVERY single day. I was exhausted! I was scheduled to be induced on a Friday before Gillian was due to help the doctors remain in control of the risks. Early on after starting the Pitocin, I was having contractions as shown by the monitor, but I could not feel them so I thought maybe it wouldn't be as painful as I thought. Boy, was I wrong! It was excruciating ... but the Army doctor came in to administer my epidural after what seemed like an eternity. All was right in the world again for a brief moment. The OB doctor decided to give me magnesium to regulate my blood pressure since it was elevated. This evil drug caused every inch of my body to start burning – NO – searing in flames, and this nurse, who is probably a really nice lady, kept rubbing my leg telling me it was going to be okay. All I could think of was STOP touching me; I do NOT like to be touched when I am in pain. Good thing my mom, who is the best nurse in the world, was there, or I may have been a bit violent by chopping off her hand. Needless to say, a couple of hours later, our beautiful girl was born at 1 o'clock in the morning. I think Matt was a bit traumatized by the entire situation, but he was by my side, holding my hand, through it all. His duty was about to come early the next morning. It was at this moment our little innocent precious child decided to have her first bowel movement, or should I say movements. Matt had barely even held her or any baby for that matter let alone change a diaper. The chocolate factory began ... he cleaned it up, he walked away to throw it in the trash, he came back to more, he walked away to throw it in the trash, he came back to more. The Tootsie Rolls were never ending. He looked at me in horror realizing what the next few years were going to be like. She captured our hearts and we knew this child would light up our life in such wonderful ways. We laughed at this moment; our family was born.

We made the long trek to Elmendorf Air Force Base in Anchorage, Alaska, in 2006 as our home for the next three years. Enter Declan Joseph in 2007, our clever, mischievous little boy. My pregnancy with Declan was considered high risk like with Gillian, but the precautions that I had to take were not as extreme. The doctor visits were not as frequent, but the shots were just as many. Declan's entrance proved to be more dramatic than his sister's. I had an induction planned, however it never occurred to me that he could actually be ready to come out before that date. He did. Around 2 o'clock in the morning on a Monday in August, my water broke while Matt and I were sleeping. I remember waking up, grabbing his arm, and scaring him to death. I told him something happened ... either I was peeing my pants and I could not stop it OR this fluid meant the baby was coming. We rushed to the hospital on base in the middle of the night and were held up by slow, giant porcupine making his way across the road. In my heart, I believe that porcupine foreshadowed the type of son that we were going to have. I mean that in the best of ways. You must understand, I adore porcupines. I think they are cuddly, clever, and oftentimes, up to no good, but always full of heart. Once we arrived to labor and delivery, my contractions were strong and fast. It was time to push. This time around, it was only Matt and me so he had to be my strong coach through this process. So, as he was holding my hands as I was slouched over the side of the hospital bed preparing for my epidural, I was squeezing his hands so strongly that I caused him to become light-headed. He ended up providing the perfect distraction because I had to worry if he was okay. Alas, he recovered quickly and was at my side once again. In the midst of pushing, Declan's fairly large head became stuck which caused his heart rate to decline. Once my OB doctor arrived, he was able to safely deliver our boy. Because I was diabetic, Declan had a little trouble adjusting his sugar level during his first few hours of life. The doctors and nurses had to take him away to insert an IV to administer sugar water. Watching them tourniquet his arms, legs, and head trying desperately to find a vein while he was screaming was a struggle to watch. The next day Declan stabilized and was strong. We brought Gillian to see her new baby brother that day; she swooned over him just like we did. Our family was complete.

A Time of Service

After a short residency at Goodfellow Air Force Base in San Angelo, Texas, where I had the honor of teaching the students at Lakeview High School. I had not quite one year to make a difference at this school, but I worked as hard as I could to make an impact on each student's education. We received orders to Beale Air Force Base in California where we currently reside. We have been stationed at Beale for over seven years. This community reminds me of my small town growing up. It is family oriented in addition to being surrounded by farming.

The challenges I have faced during this assignment have been the most frustrating of all the bases we lived. This was the first location that I was not able to find a job teaching soon after we arrived. I was devastated and probably was a bit depressed as well. I have known since I was in middle school that I wanted to be a teacher, and I have worked so hard to maintain current training to build my résumé and expertise. I have to admit I was a bit mad at the Air Force and Matt because I already had to accept retirement loss with each new PCS due to state retirement systems not transferring 100 percent for military spouses. I also had to recertify again, security check again, test again, not to mention how much money each of these costs for me to do without even having a guaranteed job. I searched in the surrounding communities daily for teaching openings with no luck. The neighboring districts were letting teachers go at an alarming rate so they certainly were not hiring.

My daughter started kindergarten the first year we were at Beale. It was a precious milestone for our first child. We were full of pride dropping her off to her new classroom and new teachers. She was all smiles. After not being able to find employment the first two months of school, I decided to focus my energy in helping Gillian's kindergarten teacher. This was the pivotal point in my beginnings as a volunteer. I was there every day teaching small groups, teaching science, teaching kids. As I look back now, I am so lucky to have been able to be there for both Gillian and Declan during their younger elementary years and form friendships with the teachers of Lone Tree Elementary.

From this moment on, still jobless, I focused on serving my children's school. I was excited to be involved at Lone Tree. After being elected to the site council, I introduced the idea of a volunteer program for the school since there was no PTA. In my experience, military families are some of the most giving and supportive even during difficult times. The program was approved, and I developed the first Team Lone Tree Volunteer program, a parent/guardian volunteer database to assist the school in functions, help with fundraisers, and provide morale to the staff through potlucks and teacher appreciation. As the kids entered each new grade, I completed science demonstrations and experiments to increase learning and provide hands-on activities. The most eventful activity was the earthworm lab. Imagine young kids performing tests on live worms to determine soil preferences. The extension of this project was the fact that worms are actually edible and full of protein. So, in my marvelous expertise, I baked homemade earthworm cookies like I did in my high school classes after we did the earthworm dissection. The kids loved the cookies that had dehydrated earthworms that I dried and crumbled into a fine powder. But … I learned that year that I need parent permission for their children to eat earthworms because some parents thought I was teaching the kids that it was normal to eat worms right out of the ground. No, I did not do that, but the memories from the awesome experiment remain strong.

I focused on serving my husband's squadron. A couple of close friends introduced me to the Key Spouse program. This program is a sort of support and information role between the commander and the spouses in the 13th Intelligence Squadron. Our group of spouses thrived and developed a close relationship of helping each other. Participation grew exponentially. We were able to start quarterly crew feeds to serve meals to our airmen that worked around the clock operations. Morale improved, the effort was ongoing. I offered assistance to the booster club as well through joining other spouses to help with bake sales and fundraisers and gathering donations for our 13IS airmen and their families. We embraced the local community, and businesses were more than willing to support our mission. As a Key Spouse and a booster club member, I participated or supported squadron functions in any way that I could. Reaching out to the spouses of the deployed, newcomer spouses, or spouses who just might need someone to listen became my call. I was able to be a part of so many of these families' lives through tough deployments, sickness, marriage issues, feelings of suicide, and births of children that I truly feel like this is my family outside of my family.

Because of my service, I was nominated for awards and medals that I hold dear to my heart, but not for the title, but rather for the insight it has given me. In 2015, I was selected as the Armed Forces Insurance Air Force Spouse of the Year due to my volunteerism and service of others. Meeting the recipients of the other branches, Army, Marine, National Guard, Coast Guard, and Navy, turned into a sisterhood I never expected. The support and cheering on that we do for each other has no bounds. We were treated to trips where we met with important people, shared common goals, and created unbreakable bonds with other military spouses. Having Mother's Day Tea at the White House while meeting Michelle Obama and Dr. Jill Biden, being invited to dinner at the historical Air House with General and Betty Welsh while the Air Force Band performed the outstanding "The Devil Went Down to Georgia," attending the Armed Forces Bowl in which the Air Force played in, touring DC with my MSOY sisters ... no words can express how dear I hold this achievement. The most powerful part of this journey was when I was invited to speak at the Air Force Corona at the Air Force Academy. Our Air Force leaders requested ME to speak on behalf of our Air Force families. I was truly honored.

What happened next will impact my life forever; we had lunch with five Wounded Warrior families. After we ate, one airman shared his story of losing three of his fellow troops while he was in Afghanistan. He shared his loss, his injury, his trauma, and I could feel completely the pain that he was reflecting. This strong man spoke of the moment he sat in a chair at his house with a beer bottle in one hand and a gun in the other contemplating ending his life. His wife was able to reach him, and through the program he enrolled in, he was able to survive. I thanked them for their sacrifice and their service and sobbed as I told them how much of an impact and inspiration they were to me. These brave warriors took us out to the horse stables to ride the trails. I had never been on a horse in my life. These brave warriors taught me, guided me, and comforted me. The horses were a source of comfort and reconnection for them, service members of PTSD. This was a sight to see. Even though I was the one that received this award, I was the one rewarded beyond measure!

Building a Village

In the summer of 2015, teaching opportunities became available. I received three different offers and accepted the one that I thought was best for me and my family. On the first day of teaching at this new job, I felt off. I chalked it up to being extremely nervous and not sleeping well the night before. My classes were going really well, but I just could NOT catch my breath, similar to being out of breath after sprinting. At lunch, I started to get heartburn and become nauseated so I rested my head on my desk briefly. The day ended on a positive note with the students so I packed up and walked through the office to head home. I walked by the principal and another science teacher who had asked me how my day was. I was honest ... the students were great, but I just could NOT catch my breath. I told them that I was going home to sleep. The science teacher suggested that I go to the ER because breathing issues should not be taken lightly. I brushed it off, telling myself that I just needed to lay down. As I walked to my car, a little doubt grew in my head so I decided to call the nurse advice line to ask for direction. The minute that the nurse started talking to me she contacted the nurse manager, and both spoke with me at the same time. She directed me to go back into the office immediately and have them call 911. Rolling my eyes, I was determined to drive myself because the hospital was not very far and because I did not think it was that serious. The nurse manager refused to accept that and demanded again for me to go inside and that she would not hang up until I gave the phone to one of the office workers to verify. So, I grabbed my purse and headed back in, phone in hand and on speaker. I guess I must have looked sickly because my principal ran to grab me and carried me to his office while I was slurring that the nurse said to call 911. The paramedics arrived and took my vitals. My vitals were stable. My oxygen was normal even though I could not breathe correctly so off to the ER we went. My principal that I had only known for a few days followed the ambulance there and contacted Matt. It was not the first day that he was expecting.

The first ER doctor I saw did not know what was wrong with me. Of course, I explained my medical issues including the new diabetic medication that I was taking. This doctor diagnosed me with having a panic attack ... I have never had a panic attack before and

162

was curious if the attacks can last for over eight hours. He injected me with a dose of Ativan to "calm" me down, but it had no effect on my breathing so he consulted an intensivist, a critical care doctor. This new doctor drew blood from my wrist immediately which was quite painful and connected that I had diabetic ketoacidosis. The last thing I remember is telling Matt that it looked like his face was melting. The next event that happened terrified the ones that love and depend on me. The intensivist escorted Matt from the room and informed him that they needed to intubate me NOW! That night, I was in the ICU on dialysis, on a ventilator, and Matt not knowing if I would recover. It was this moment that my family needed the village that I created through my service to others: the village that would step up and serve us.

My husband called on my dear friend, Mandy. She stayed until the early hours of the morning on my couch with my kids. Matt tried to get a few hours of rest. I am sure he did not. I am not sure what his thoughts were, but I know he was trying to be strong for himself and for our children. He drove the kids to their second day of school and informed their teachers of the situation. Later, I found out he cried when he told my son's teacher so I know how scared he really was. He returned to the hospital and spent the day at my side while I was still unconscious, still on the ventilator, still on dialysis with no real updates. It was Declan's birthday so I am forever grateful for Mandy taking him and Gillian out to celebrate and keeping them distracted from what was going on. Matt returned home that evening with the prognosis that I would pull through and be off the ventilator in the morning even though I had not awakened yet. The second part of my village was my amazing friend, Goldie, who watched my kids the rest of the time that I was in the hospital. She made Gillian and Declan laugh and smile the entire time they spent with her. I am forever grateful to her for that.

After two days on the ventilator, I woke up. I could not fathom what had happened. My hands were tied down, a tube was down my throat so I could not talk, and I could not hear any sounds. The nurse kept asking me questions, but I could not understand what he was saying. I kept motioning with my hand for a pencil to write with, but the nurse could not understand me. I tried to talk, but I could not. Tears began to roll down my cheeks because I could not communicate. After several writing hand motions, the nurse figured it out. I wrote the words I CAN'T HEAR YOU. The nurse wrote AT ALL? I wrote BATTERIES DEAD. He let me know Matt was on his way. I, then, wrote VENT OUT NOW! The removal of the vent tube hurt, but I needed it. I remained in ICU recovering for the next week. Matt snuck Gillian and Declan in for a visit. I missed them with my whole being. I worried if seeing me with all these tubes and machines would be too

163

much for them, but they needed to see me and I them. I predicted both of their reactions … Declan would cry because he wears his heart on his sleeve; Gillian would internalize it by trying to be strong for me, so I comforted Declan through the tears, and consoled Gillian after she threw up for holding it all in.

My life altered after this near-death experience. I had to resign from my new job to spend the next few months to recover, and I became insulin dependent which means four shots every day for the rest of my life with constant checking of my sugar levels. I was thankful for the health insurance I have through the military because I can only imagine the costs of the medical care that I received. I did recover, my family recovered, but it taught me how lucky I am to have such a strong village.

Words of Wisdom

My journey continues. In the summer of 2016, I accepted a job at Riverside Meadows Intermediate to develop curriculum and teach STEM classes. I LOVE it! I still serve others as a volunteer, but I have taken a step back with some roles to focus on my new role. Looking back, there were definite struggles that I had to overcome that are unique to military spouses such as Matt's deployments, his remote tours, and his extended TDYs, but I choose to concentrate on the events that built me up. I still maintain that I was not made to be a military spouse. I want to plan, I need details, I resist change. However, I would not exchange my experiences. Those moments live inside of me influencing my daily choices.

My Words of Wisdom: I challenge my fellow military spouses to always be present in their own life as well as their families. I challenge myself to always impart knowledge, kindness, and service to my children so that they may be inclusive, empathetic, and caring. I wholeheartedly thank Matt, my airman, my hero, my continuity in my journey as an Air Force spouse.

Jana Raye Kingery is the 2015 Armed Forces Insurance Air Force Spouse of the Year, key spouse of 8 years, science teacher, and dedicated volunteer. She was born to her strong mother, Janice. She has been married to her supportive husband Matthew for 20 years and has been an Air Force spouse for those 20 years. She is proud mom of her two children, Gillian and Declan.

Paying It Forward

Verenice Castillo

Always Grateful

Some of us never get out of our comfort zone; for some of us, getting out of our comfort zone becomes part of our lives - a process that helps to live life fully. The experiences I faced moving outside of my comfort zone changed and influenced my outlook on life. I have been blessed with challenges in my life that have made me who I am today. I am a woman full of qualities - integrity, selfless, serving; but I am the total package with flaws, dreams, and fears, successes, and failures.

I went from being an immigrant in a foreign country where I didn't know the language, to marrying a member of the Armed Forces and having two kids, to being the founder and president of a non-profit organization. This is the story of my success and blessings. A story that summarizes everything I have achieved – my personal and professional accomplishments, the opportunities to chase and reach my dreams, and the times when I had to turn difficult challenges into positive learning experiences. I have learned a lot in my pursuit of purpose and happiness. I have learned all about passion, purpose, honor, dedication, patriotism and honor. When I got married, I had to leave my extended family behind, but I gained a much larger extended family – my military family, in which I discovered the real meaning of resilience, support, and the opportunity to dedicate my time to help others and make a difference in their lives. Sometimes I look back reflecting on how far I have come, and all I feel is gratitude and a desire to continue to do the things I do.

My Life as an Immigrant

I came to the Unites States from Mexico when I was 16 years old in pursuit of a dream: the American dream. My parents wanted my brother and I to have a better life. They wanted us to be in a place where they knew we would have plenty of opportunities to succeed and follow our dreams.

I still remember the day my parents told me that it was time to move; I cried like a baby! It was not an easy thing to do. It was difficult because it meant I would have to leave my extended family and friends. I also thought about the difficulties in moving to a new place where I did not know the language and although I lived in a border city and we were just going across the border, it was a different culture. The idea of starting high school where I did not know anyone was very frightening. I was going to be the "new kid in town." It was hard to understand why my parents were making me do this, but I had to be okay with it and move forward.

Although I was nervous and scared, I was also very optimistic and excited about this new place where I was going to fulfill my potential.

My first year in high school was very challenging, but I was brave enough to fight through and overcome the trials which eventually made me stronger. The rest of my high school years were much better. I got great grades, became a part of the modern dance team, and I won various awards from competitions. I never imagined that in such a short time I would have accomplished so much and settled easily. I started to feel at home and felt that I was finally in the place where my parents said I belonged.

An Experience That Changed My Life

Life doesn't always go as expected, and sometimes we experience both good and bad times. I am a positive person and always try to look for the bright side even when experiences are challenging and dark. My philosophy in life is to always be grateful for all of my blessings, including the ones that come with hard challenges, and to try not to miss any opportunities to learn something new and turn things around.

During my last year in high school, I got to experience something wonderful, unforgettable, and life changing. I was given the honor to represent the state of Texas during a one-week trip to Washington, DC I was sponsored by a great foundation that provided a chance to learn about the American government and democracy to new Americans. I had the opportunity to visit the White House and Capitol Hill, and meet with state representatives. I learned about the Constitution, democracy, and American values. I had never experienced such an honor; not only was I proud to live in America, I was also thankful my high school teachers had the confidence to give me the chance to reinforce my commitment to being an American.

This is when I understood the reasons my parents brought me to America; it is the best place to be free and dream without limitations. Then and there I decided that in the future I would pay-it-forward, and not only become a good, productive American citizen but to do my best to make a difference in the lives of others. Without consciously knowing it, moving to the United States shaped my future and became the foundation of my dreams and purpose in life. This trip opened my eyes and helped me understand what it was that I wanted to do when I grew up. The experience reinforced my desire to help others and make a real difference in their in lives. I never imagined that I would someday find myself in a role where I would make a difference and be a part of meaningful change in the lives of so many people.

After I graduated from high school, I went to college. I was a full-time student and was a work-study student in the Financial Aid office. A couple of years afterward, I found myself working as a full-time employee at the same place while continuing my education in the field of social psychology. I was always fascinated to find ways to help others, so I knew that studying social psychology was going to prepare me to do that and much more.

One day while out and about, I met Tony Castillo, a handsome and smart guy who was also an active duty member in the Unites States Army. We dated for a few months and got married. I had absolutely no clue what my new military lifestyle would be all about since Tony was the first military member I had known. As with many military couples, there was no time for a honeymoon. We got married on a Saturday and he was off to the field the following Monday. Seventeen years later, I still give him a hard time about it. We lived in my hometown for just a year before it was time for my first Permanent Change of Station (PCS). I continued to work and go to school, and I missed my husband a lot because he spent long periods of time in the field. I had a hard time adjusting and comprehending my role as a military spouse. We all know that marriage can be challenging and you need to work at it every day. Now imagine throwing more challenges into it due to the military lifestyle ... not an easy thing to do, but not impossible! We were married before the tragedy that changed America and when we were not at war.

On September 11, 2000, we were blessed with the birth of our first son, Tony III. Within a year I got married, had a child, worked full time and went to school. This was my new life. At times, it was overwhelming and I found myself wondering if I was going to be strong enough to handle everything ... without knowing, once again that these trials were just the beginning of a new fundamental era of our lives.

A year later, the tragedy of 9/11 happened. I still remember that morning; not only was it our son's first birthday but we were experiencing the worst tragedy that our country had ever seen. My husband called me at work to let me know that he was considering transitioning from the Army to the Air Force. The Air Force was giving him the prospect to serve in Security Forces. It was something he had always wanted to do. It was a scary day for our country and for all military families as we were experiencing a lot of uncertainty, and we wondered what was going to happen to our spouses. A few months later, the transition to the Air Force was complete. My husband was no longer a soldier, he was now an airman and America was at war.

This new move was very difficult as we had to go through the process of starting all over again. Tony was going to be gone a long time for training and we were going to have to move again. I was going to have to leave my job and my friends and start new all over again in a different military branch and culture. I had to learn how the Air Force worked, and it was a bit difficult as I was just getting used to the Army. Believe it or not, they are both totally different from each other. Both branches use different terminology, ranks are different, the military installation is no longer a post but a base, and the programs and readiness centers for families are also different. We held on, took it all in and we made it through, and the experience made us stronger and resilient.

As with many military spouses after 9/11, I would often find myself thinking about the potential dangers that could arise. Dangers like losing my husband at war.

After our first PCS as an Air Force family, we found out that we were pregnant with our second child. A few months later, a day before Thanksgiving, Alexander was born. It was a day of mixed feelings; I was happy with our new baby, but I was sad because Tony was not with me – he was deployed.

Just like many other military spouses, I made the decision to be a stay-at-home mom. Although I was very determined to take care of my family, I also liked the feeling of being meaningfully engaged at every point in my life. My desire to graduate from college and have a good job was not possible at the time as I found myself fulfilling the roles of both mom and dad, making sure that our home and family were taken care of.

Military spouses face a lot of tests and many times these challenges can be stumbling blocks in pursuit of individual goals and aspirations in life. Goals like finding permanent, meaningful employment were mostly unattainable. I always had to leave my job and go through the stressful process of securing another during each move. Other challenges were finding a good school, day care services for the boys, and so much more. The most challenging memories however, were the extended periods of loneliness. For a few years I felt resentful toward the military because even after a few years of marriage, I was having a hard time adjusting each time we had to move. I was resentful because my husband was gone a lot. I felt like an outsider.

I remember telling my husband more than once that I would never volunteer or be engaged with the military community because my first impression of the military was nothing close to what I had expected. I did not have someone to mentor me or help me with tough situations. My husband helped me to keep my spirits up and motivate me to go through those challenges.

Supporting Military Families as a Volunteer – Team Work at Its Best

As the years passed and my kids got older, I decided to go back to school and try to finish what I had initially started. Then in 2012 my husband took command of the 42nd Security Forces Squadron. Even as I was a bit reluctant to volunteer, I started volunteer work and boy did I enjoy every single part of it! While volunteering, I thought about how amazed I was that this was the same opportunity I had originally rejected. In the past, I had said that I was not going to volunteer and suddenly the light bulb went on and I realized that I had let my indecisiveness get the best of me; I discovered that I had been convincing myself that volunteering was not the opportunity I had always wanted. As I course corrected and helping within the unit, I was overcome by a sense of motivation to help others and make a difference in their lives.

I was actively engaged in volunteering and went 100 miles an hour with many plans in mind and lots of goals to accomplish. I became a Key Spouse mentor for my husband's squadron. I became very passionate about the job and for the first time in a long while, I felt fulfilled … and I was finally doing what I loved. My husband and I were a team dedicated to supporting others. It was a great way to spend time with my husband while we looked for ways to help families in our squadron.

I had the chance to help other spouses and make sure that they never felt alone or out of place like I had many times. My duties included providing guidance on Air Force programs and also provided resources to aid Air Force families, especially those families with members deployed. My commitment to helping Air Force families was the foundation of the focus needed to create and deliver resiliency tools for spouses.

In the fall of 2012, the Strength for Spouses program was born. With the assistance of our installation's Family Readiness Center and my husband, I developed and executed this program in collaboration with our unit Key Spouses and the installation's Airman and Family Readiness Center (A&FRC). The success of Strength for Spouses caught base leadership's attention and eventually became a benchmarked effort that was replicated at other Air Force installations. Eventually, this program was used by the Air Force as a platform to create its own resiliency program for all Air Force spouses. On the heels of Strength for Spouses, my Key Spouse team and I followed up with another program– it was another home run effort known as the Key Spouse Crisis Intervention Course. The course features training that provides Key Spouses skill sets to identify signs of maltreatment and PTSD, and reinforces the importance of self-care. This training majorly transformed the role of Key Spouses across the Air Force.

In 2013, I was honored as the Armed Forces Insurance Air Force Spouse of the Year. This award was the opportunity of a lifetime that opened many doors for me to continue to reach out and provide support to more military spouses. Because of this amazing recognition, I was able to go back to Washington, DC. While back in the nation's capital, I had the opportunity to go to the White House ... again! However, this time I was actually meeting the First Lady of the United States at a beautiful tea party to be recognized for my volunteer efforts. Throughout 2013, I used my title to advocate for others. I dedicated myself to accomplish my mission of support for Air Force families. As I moved along my path, families from other military branches started reaching out for assistance. At that moment, I realized I could organize a group of volunteers that I could train on executing ideas, projects and programs supporting military families. The end goal was to expand the scope to assist more families, enhance outreach, and deliver effective and efficient services to military families at military installations across the Department of Defense. I developed a plan, training, and programs to build a network of volunteers that shared my passion and vision. Within a few months, the group was so big that I could no longer handle the fiscal demands of the network; I realized it was time to go big and grow larger. It was time to go the non-profit route.

This is when the Military Spouse Advocacy Network (MSAN) was born – a non-profit with a mission to create stronger military families through education, empowerment and support. MSAN is a non-profit organization that understands the challenges military families and spouses face on a daily basis. MSAN advocates provide peer-to-peer mentorship, resources and programs to overcome challenges spouses encounter when they are new to the military. MSAN focuses on delivering support in the areas of caregiving, finance, education, career and employment, deployments, reintegration, resilience, mental health, and military to civilian transition.

I remember being afraid to start and be the founder of a non-profit organization. In the beginning, I was intimidated by distractions of the challenges of running a non-profit and being afraid of losing my focus and vision. But in the end, the experience was the complete opposite. I had an amazing team of volunteers that helped me launch this wonderful project and it was a huge success. Since the founding of the Military Support Advocacy Network, I have had the opportunity to care, provide and advocate for military families, both locally and internationally; had the privilege and opportunity to meet with leaders and members of Congress; and supported and joined initiatives at the White House while supporting and partnering with other organizations. My dedication to selfless service and being supportive of others led me to where I am today. I had absolutely no idea that my project would become this big and I am literally blown away. In the words of Thomas Edison, "If we did all the things we are capable of, we would literally astound ourselves." Prior to the start of my volunteer project, I would never have imagined a situation where I would be leading a team every day reaching out to military families in need of encouragement, mentorship, and support.

In 2015, I was awarded the Volunteer Excellence Award presented by the Chief of Staff of the Air Force. I was also a contributing participant on various panels briefing senior military leaders and their spouses on the importance of supporting military families. I granted interviews, was featured in magazines, newspapers and more. I felt grateful not because I was beginning to garner public attention or interest, but because a project I grew from nothing was turning into a success story.

Future Plans

As MSAN continues to grow and remains one of the fastest growing networks of advocates and mentors serving military families, my resounding dedication to support others will never fade; I plan to ensure that its continuity is maintained. I plan on extending and growing the support and mentorship we provide to military families to other countries, to spread our influence and extend our capabilities to other areas. On a personal level, I want to continue to do the things I'm currently doing; I want to learn and re-learn new things, undertake new, life changing projects. I want to have the opportunity to reach out to many more new military spouses and share my experiences with them, encouraging and letting them know that they are not alone. I want to let them know that this new military lifestyle is unique and wonderful despite the challenges faced on a daily basis and all we need to do is take advantage of opportunities to grow and reach our potential.

I imagine a future where new and seasoned military spouses will come together and create new groups, grow and interact with each other to change the world and live fantastic life-changing experiences. Sometime in the near future, the MSAN will launch a new program that promises a foundation for spouses to gather and provide mutual support for one another no matter the service, anywhere in the world.

Conclusion

My life has been filled with events and milestones that have molded me into the person that I have become.

I have been blessed with the grace of having a beautiful and supportive family, and wonderful friends, mentors, peers, and volunteers. We can never limit ourselves to dream big because our limits are beyond the sky. I have never placed any limitations on my dreams and I think nothing is too far or too big to achieve, and all I have to do is just start and keep pushing until I accomplish all my goals in life.

Finding my passion in life and making it part of my existence is an incredible feeling and words cannot describe that feeling. Among the things I hope for, a major dream is to continue to advocate for military families. I also hope to make my family and loved ones proud and that my boys not only appreciate the sacrifice and service that their father makes in order to fight for our freedom but also understand that supporting those in need is a way of serving.

Lastly, I feel a deep sense of satisfaction that I have truly lived and I am living my dreams. I feel fulfilled knowing the fact that I decided to risk it all and with extreme dedication I followed my passion and with the right dose of commitment I have been able to make some small amount of success out of it. I feel happy knowing that I'm a mother of two strong and handsome boys, that I have a wonderful husband that supports all of my dreams, and that I was given so many opportunities to make a difference in this world. The most important lesson is to never let go of your dreams no matter what the circumstances might look like. One just has to find a way to stay motivated and keep pushing and taking those baby steps until those lights at the end of the tunnel start blinking.

I sincerely hope that my story empowers others to be persistent and pursue their dreams. I hope my readers get to appreciate themselves every step of the way and keep a positive outlook on everything that happens because it is essential in the accomplishment of one's goals. Nobody has ever accomplished anything by keeping negative views or having a negative mind set. I hope everyone gets to discover their mission and purpose in life. Being a military spouse is not easy and comes with many challenges, but those challenges are nothing compared to the beautiful experience of patriotism, honor, and dedication. I will always be thankful that I had the faith and strength to deal with difficult challenges and that I received opportunities of a lifetime to make a difference and pay it forward!

Verenice Castillo is the 2013 Armed Forces Insurance Air Force Spouse of the Year, recipient of the Volunteer Excellence Award presented by the Chief of Staff of the Air Force and the Founder & President of the Military Spouse Advocacy Network (MSAN). Married to Lt Col. Tony Castillo, Jr. and they have two sons, Tony III & Alexander.

Right Where I Belong

Corie B. Weathers

When my husband Matthew came home one day and told me he wanted to be in the Army, I said "no." It wasn't my best moment in marriage, but I was in shock. The military had never been an option on the table and not a thought in our minds. We had been taking turns putting each other through graduate school. I didn't see myself as a military spouse. When he said that, every worst case scenario flooded my mind. I won't lie, I was grateful for the chaplain requirements that required him to finish school first. I agreed that if he still wanted to do it in a year, I would be supportive.

A year and a half later, he still knew this was what he was built for. He needed the sense of purpose that the military offered like he needed air. Even then, it was a half-step in my heart as he signed on for the Reserves. I continued to work on my credentials as a mental health counselor, relieved that I still had control of my life.

By the time our second son was born, we were living close to family and friends. Matthew was working at a church and I was building my own practice. Life was good. We were building our young family and life, finally establishing our groove as adults. But something still wasn't right. There was a stirring in our hearts, a longing to do more and we felt held back. Not by anyone in particular, not by the circumstances around us, but we didn't feel like we fit in. Matt told me one night he had been thinking about us switching to active duty and I pushed back again.

Sometimes every decision in marriage feels like the biggest decision you will ever make. I'm not sure if that ever changes considering the stakes and consequences only increase over time. Yet in that moment, I felt like we were on the edge of a cliff about to dive into a vast dark hole and build a house there. I bet if you asked my husband, though, he would say that we were about to soar into the clouds and feel alive for the first time.

One night, we were asked to attend a dinner for those who were considering chaplaincy. I went somewhat reluctantly, but wanted to show Matt that I could be supportive. The room was filled with active duty chaplains and people like us that were also considering the leap. My husband, dressed handsomely in his Class A's, gently pulled me by the arm to introduce me to someone who had helped him prepare his paperwork. To be honest, I don't remember who I was introduced to, but this moment changed everything in our story. One statement. One strong, courageous statement shifted the course of my heart and cast vision all at once. Standing in front of another service member who clearly outranked him, Matt introduced me saying, "Sir ... This is my wife. You aren't just getting me, you are getting both of us. You are getting a team."

I was all in. I can't tell you why other than I had clearly been given a mission, too. I felt like I belonged in this room. People who were serving their country. People who wanted to serve those who served their country. I pulled Matt outside to make my own statement, "If we do this ... then we *really* do this." I said. "All in ... and we do it well."

I knew that jumping into active duty would mean that my career was going to get a whole lot more complicated. We were leaving the state I had a counseling license in. Moving to Colorado would mean I would have to work towards a Colorado license as well. I decided to volunteer my clinical skills to the squadron to which we were assigned while I figured it out. It gave me the opportunity to be a stay-at-home mom to my two young sons.

As a chaplain, Matt was offered opportunities to provide marriage and family retreats to the families we were serving. I remember the first time we attended one of those retreats, taught by a chaplain who was a priest. He was wonderful, funny, and a great teacher, but as I looked around the room the spouses looked like they felt forced to be there. There was no one up front speaking from a spouse perspective. No one that could validate what they were feeling considering we were a few short months away from a deployment to Afghanistan. Matt and I decided that I would also extend my volunteer time to teach with him at any marriage retreat we provided. After the first retreat together, we knew this was our first love. It was like magic when we taught together. We would tag team throughout the talk, share our own story of successes and failures, and provide hope to couples who were struggling with the weight of military service.

The more marriage retreats we did, the more we fell in love with it. We opened up other opportunities for couples to have date nights out. We knew that what couples really needed was a chance to get away from the kids, reconnect over dinner and conversation, and have someone acknowledge the tension of the military's call on a family. They needed hope and our Team Weathers mission was to bring it.

As we approached our first deployment, we were told that it would be a difficult one. I had never gone through a deployment before so I figured that is what everyone says. There was no way they could have truly prepared us. This "team" mindset that Matt and I shared was one we intended to keep even if we were apart. Considering Matt was the one soldiers would unload their burdens on, he explained to his command that he would need me to be that for him. We agreed that he would tell me anything he needed to decompress during his deployment. I also wanted family members to feel that if they were concerned about their soldier, they could talk with me and I could relay their concerns to Matt. It was a fantastic strategy that allowed soldiers who were struggling to get checked on by their chaplain "randomly" without making a scene. I also served as the Care Team Coordinator that would serve and lead out on caring for any family members that were notified of their soldier's death.

We lost 11 great men that year. Serving some of the spouses who received that life-shifting news has been one of my greatest honors. I cannot describe the feeling in your gut when you are walking up to a new widow's door and see the Blue Star Flag hanging in the window. They have just been notified, not even ten minutes earlier, that their soldier is dead. There are no words. No stories, no hugs or gifts that can take that pain away. Not in that moment. I have watched as some of these families transition out of the military community shortly thereafter. It was never forced, but some of these spouses realized that it was being married to a soldier that made them a military spouse in the first place. It was being a team in their marriage that gave them the strength to endure relocations, reinventing themselves every time, building new friendships, and facing their biggest fears. For them, their teammate was gone.

Perhaps it was all of this that made me want to fight for military marriages. I want them to thrive, not just survive. Matt and I began to put everything we had into our marriage retreats. It made us feel alive to teach marriage curriculum to other couples and say the things out loud they wished they could say. We watched as they connected to their spouse in face-to-face moments of tears and forgiveness. We started to take on every marriage retreat opportunity we could. Other chaplains even gave us their retreats if they felt more talented in another area.

Matt was right. We were soaring in the clouds. But something in me was growing weary. Every time we got relocation papers, a part of me panicked even though I was excited about the adventure. Moving brought the opportunity to reinvent yourself. Mistakes you have made (for the most part) can stay in the past. Remember the time you greeted a high ranking commander wrong? A new commander gives you a fresh start. There have been times when I even thought, "I could chop my hair into a cute bob and completely change my style and no one would know I was ever anything different." I didn't of course, but I thought I could leave all insecurity behind me and walk in with new confidence. Confidence I wished I'd had from the beginning. The panic, though, sets in soon after. Everything I had done in my career, the friendships I had built and struggled through, volunteer work I had invested in was all being left behind. Every time. Starting over also made me panic.

As my children got older, I returned to part-time counseling. Luckily, we were now in Georgia where I had a license to practice. Local military spouses found out that I was also a military spouse, and I suddenly had a 6-month wait list. Military spouses came into my counseling office and poured out their heart behind confidential doors. They loved their service member. They loved being a military spouse, but were growing weary from the never-ending cycle of training, deployment, and reintegration. So many of them were attempting careers but felt they weren't able to climb the ladder. They were faced with many of the same struggles I faced. Interviewing for a job you could be loyal to for only three years is extremely discouraging. Many spouses were seeing their service member come home different. Matt and I were not the exception. Although Matt did not come home from his deployments wounded, his soul was. He, like many others, witnessed the death of soldiers he deeply cared about and had to compartmentalize these intense feelings for the sake of the mission. When the service member comes home, it is not easy to pick up where you left off. Instead, military families describe it as "finding a new normal."

From my office view, I was surprised during that season with how much resentment was building within the spouse community. They were unsure of how to balance their internal sacrifice with being a loving teammate. When given the opportunity to talk to their service member, many of them felt that their feelings paled in comparison to the sacrifice their service member was making, so they kept it inside. I watched as this led to a quiet, stifled suffering. Marriages were not thriving, couples were hiding from each other. In fact, the spouses that did not have the coping skills to handle the stress, would implode into depression and anxiety or explode in rage, impulsive decisions, and divorce.

Of course this wasn't the only side of military spouses I saw. I witnessed amazing feats of strength, endurance, and service. I saw neighborhoods rise up to raise each other's kids in a soldier's absence. I experienced the soft mentoring of senior spouses that wanted me to succeed. In my heart, it seemed this community that I loved was hurting. They wanted their families to succeed more than anything, but were beginning to crumble.

I love counseling because I get to watch the power of someone processing their story out loud. It brings courage, confidence, clarity, and healing. I wanted to be an example of how to share your story and not stifle resentment. I wanted to start a community conversation. My goal was to keep at least one spouse from suicide or one marriage from imploding. The conversation would be about the power of marriage being a source of emotional safety and support. We were only military spouses because we were married to a service member. It was the one variable that brought us all together. Little did I know then, how much work there still was to do in my own heart.

Around this time, Matt saw a little Tweet roll past his feed that said "Nominate your Spouse for Military Spouse of the Year." He thought to himself, "Gee, Corie really could use a 'thank you' or a certificate for her hard work." We still laugh at the power that one little Tweet can hold. I went on to win 2015 Armed Forces Insurance Army Spouse of the Year and was later invited to Washington, DC, for the overall awards ceremony. There, in the presence of the highest ranking military leaders, Deanie Dempsey awarded me the 2015 Armed Forced Insurance Military Spouse of the Year Award. My opportunity to advocate for military spouses and encourage them to invest in their marriages took off. I traveled to installations and vowed to meet them where ever they were. I wanted them to feel heard, down to their core. Regardless of age, status, or position I wanted them to know that fighting for their marriage started with not neglecting themselves while holding down the home front.

The biggest test of all came in December of that year. I was invited by the Secretary of Defense's office to travel with Ash Carter overseas on his tour to thank the troops. They had realized that no military spouse (who was not a service or staff member) had ever traveled with them. Families have always been limited to using their imagination when it came to picturing deployment conditions. The SECDEF's office and I agreed that if I could find a way to communicate what it was like to go overseas as a spouse, perhaps it would encourage families. It didn't seem fair to me that I was getting to go overseas and so many others weren't. My mind immediately went to the Gold Star Widows I had served, the mothers, the children. So many that needed to see what I was going to see – for closure, for clarity, for understanding.

One of the biggest obstacles that military couples have in their marriage is the long gaps of life they experience apart. Especially when it's during a deployment. Significant life-changing moments can happen without the other person there to experience it with you. People change, both the service member and the spouse. Reintegration proves to be our biggest challenge. In preparation for my trip, I thought about how many deployment stories my husband had shared over the years. I heard his stories; I even tried to envision them. Without realizing it, I created an imaginary world of his deployment, to the point that I believed that what I saw in my mind was his actual experience. There were occasions where he would tell the same story he had told me to friends at a dinner party and extra details would emerge. The picture in my mind would burst like a bubble with the reminder that I had not been there and truly did not understand. This trip overseas would give me the opportunity to finally see with my own eyes, hear with my own ears, and feel in my body what deployment was like— at least as close as I could get.

They say that memories are made in our brain when our five senses engage during a significant moment. In a way, our senses play a key role in storing our biggest memories. I knew that post-traumatic stress disorder symptoms involved the sensory part of the brain lighting up causing someone to see (in their mind), feel, smell, and hear the traumatic experience again when triggered. Matt and I had both experienced life-changing moments while separate. Our reintegration had been difficult because no matter how much we detailed out the event, the other person was not there to experience it. Eventually, we started calling these significant moments "sacred spaces" because we needed to tread lightly in the spaces we could not understand. Without the ability to truly understand each other, we would need to learn to respect those spaces.

If this was how memories were created and stored, my plan was to engage my senses as much as possible during the trip, write, and do video journals each day. This was my way of bridging the gaps that had grown between Matt and I. This was my plan to understand the changes that had happened in him and this plan did not disappoint.

What I got from my trip was more than just my own new memories and sacred spaces. As I put myself in his shoes, I saw myself through his eyes. When I walked on endless gravel, I thought about the times he had told me that was his daily experience for a year. A tiny detail that I swept under the rug compared to my chaotic experience at home raising two small children. As I saw the mountains of Afghanistan up close, I felt the pain of the soldiers he lost and sadness gripped my heart more than it had during my own experience of it from the states. I saw through his eyes who he needed me to be as his team-mate and how I didn't know how to be that at the time.

I had the choice to feel shame, but knew that wouldn't be productive. We both needed to listen more. We both needed to practice more empathy. I was just getting to see my side of it first. He had been through some very traumatic experiences and I had grown too comfortable in just not understanding him or those sacred spaces. On a C-130 flying out of Afghanistan, I looked over the mountains.

Through the challenges and joys of our military life to that point, my mission had become more outward. I had given my all to everyone else and settled in my marriage. We were a team for everyone else, but were we a team for each other? I suppose that is what a lot of spouses do. You don't know what you don't know. As my son says, "You get what you get and you don't pitch a fit." But I had. My resentment surrounding the difficulty that military had brought into our family and into my career had grown over the years. I realized in that moment, that my teammate needed me more than the world did.

I left my resentment there in the mountains of Afghanistan, just like he left the bliss of not intimately knowing things like loss and death. I realized that we were not just called to be a team for others, we are first and foremost a team for each other. For the first time, I truly understood my role as a military spouse and I couldn't wait to get back and be more intentional in my marriage. I forgave myself for not knowing differently, and vowed to be more purposeful.

When I look back on my marriage of 18 years, there are markers, moments in time that changed the trajectory of our story. When we were dating, Matt came into my apartment while I was studying and simply made the statement, "Let's make this work, okay?" implying that we had had each gone through enough past relationships that he was ready to move forward. I simply said, "Okay," and we have. The second one was that day Matt introduced us as a team. Team Weathers. Two kids that started out with a mission to serve those who sacrifice everything.

God never promised life would be easy. In fact, Jesus said, "*In this world you will have trouble.*" (John 16:33). The mission isn't easy, but it is fulfilling. In the moments where I am faced with the challenges, I am reminded that sometimes you just decide to "make it work" and then you do. Time and time again, when life and marriage seems too difficult to push through another second, I remember his words, "Let's make this work, okay?" Then, I take a step toward my teammate emotionally and physically and remember there is no one else I would want to share this adventure with. My mission is to be the teammate he needs me to be.

Today, Matt and I aim to be more intentional about creating more *shared* sacred spaces while we are together knowing the military could call him away. Shared sacred spaces are significant. Hopefully they are marriage-changing moments that change your story. The most significant shared sacred spaces we have experienced are the moments that we have allowed God to shape our hearts for one another. Realizing we are the best tool that God can use to heal and grow the other person. Our higher calling is to care for each other.

We aren't alone in this. The rest of John 16:33 is Jesus, who reminds us, "*I have told you these things, so that in me you may have peace. In this world you will have trouble. But take heart! I have overcome the world.*" It is impossible for Matt and I to be perfect team players every time. This entire journey has shown me that I will fail every day if I depend on my own strength and wisdom. I will also fail if I expect Matt to get it right every time. We are human, and perfectly imperfect.

Our faith in Jesus who has shown himself to be perfect every time, is the one we turn to for direction and forgiveness. He has been the ultimate team player, our coach even, that can see the outcome of the game if we would just trust Him. He gives us compassion for those we serve, grace when we fail each other, and a heart of forgiveness that brings healing when we need it. Without Him, our team would have crumbled, too. With Him, there is a path through the black hole that sends us soaring into the clouds.

Corie Weathers, licensed professional counselor (LPC), is a sought-after speaker, consultant and author of Scared Spaces: My Journey to the Heart of a Military Marriage. In 2015, Corie was named the 2015 Armed Forces Insurance Military Spouse of the Year® where she advocated for mental health issues and served as a media correspondent writing online and print publications and consulting for command teams. As a consultant, Corie works with organizations and nonprofits like the Chris Kyle Frog Foundation to bring lasting change in the loves of military and first responder families.

Looking Beyond

Michelle Aikman

Just before I cracked my laptop open to start writing this, I grabbed a pack of my favorite licorice as a reward for the small victory of surviving yet another emotionally draining saga that unfolded over the weekend, all while continuing on with my personal and professional commitments and obligations. I imagine it is much like juggling, having to catch a football and throw it back, all without dropping any of the juggling balls or falling over in the process. If you are thinking, "Hey, that is me … every day!" then pull up a chair because I will share my licorice with you.

I have learned that real happiness and success is about celebrating the small wins on the route to achieving the big wins because life just seems to get crazier the farther along we all venture on our paths.

As far as celebrating, although my mouth waters for red licorice, I actually prefer an intense cardio workout or a small adventure that gets my adrenaline rushing whenever I need to relieve stress or reward myself for small victories. As life gets busier, it is difficult to cut out time for this type of stress relief so, just as military spouses do so skillfully, I adapt. I seek out ways to integrate those release elements into my life. I embrace every chance to move and find fresh ways to motivate myself to move more – especially when it is not my idea of a fantastic time – because I know how great it makes me feel. I know that the benefits are worth it and without it, I am unable to juggle anything.

Keeping those balls in the air is important to me. The swings of military life have caused me to put down balls, but it has also given me the opportunity to pick up balls I never thought were within my grasp and to juggle way more balls then I thought was humanly possible. As a result, almost 15 years after embarking upon this military spouse journey, I find myself in an interesting position, able to contribute to our world in a very unique way through a rare array of skills and experiences. I see many balls within reach, or within eyesight that could be within grasp with concerted effort, but I must make the difficult decision to choose. Although I recognize the importance of the short game, I believe I can make the most impact on the strategic level in the long game so my gaze is from the bird's eye and into the distant future. I am very proud of the balls I choose to juggle and am delighted to talk about two of them that have a fantastic long-term purpose: STEM and Cerno.

STEM
Science, Technology, Engineering and Mathematics

I think like an engineer because I am an engineer. I may not have a paid engineering position at the moment but that doesn't stop me from solving problems, considering alternate perspectives, evaluating risks, seeking efficiencies, integrating ethics, taking social responsibility, and viewing the world as an engineer. Although I would love to continue working in the STEM arena, my path has veered in another direction but that doesn't lessen my passion and commitment.

I wholeheartedly believe that STEM education is vital to the health and longevity of our planet and the human race. It is not imperative though, or even wise, for everyone to receive a STEM education because diversity in thought and education is just as important. However, it is critical that we foster STEM education across all lines of diversity. This includes gender and military spouses, two diversity groups with tremendous imbalance in STEM careers.

Women are significantly underrepresented in STEM. In engineering alone, women account for less than 13 percent of engineering jobs according to a 2016 source citing data collected by the reputable Society of Women Engineers. It is important to me to see the gender gap in STEM eliminated so I take the time to raise awareness of this issue and give my time and energy to mentor, share my passion for STEM, expose others to the vast possibilities, and act as a positive role model to the best of my ability. I am just one person though. It takes all of us to get involved if we want to see a change. Women need male allies and STEM exposure can't just come from STEM professionals, it needs to come from everyone. In the same way that we celebrate and support music, the arts, and culture, we should all celebrate and support STEM.

With upwards of 95 percent of military spouses being female, it is not surprising that the representation of military spouses in STEM professions is so small that it has yet to be measured. The lack of proportional representation is a lost opportunity for everyone! Military spouses are high-value talent in the professional scene and could collectively contribute even more if there were more spouses with STEM backgrounds. In order to support the educational draw though, there needs to be additional advancements in the employment and career sphere because military spouses with career interests are still under-supported and underserved resulting in an alarming unemployment and underemployment rate.

According to the 2016 Social Cost Analysis of the Unemployment and Underemployment of Military Spouses report prepared by Blue Star Families, 35-40 percent of military spouses are underemployed compared to 6 percent for civilian spouses. Also, 12.04 percent of military spouses are unemployed compared to 7.74 percent of civilian spouses. This dim situation amounts to an estimated $710 million to $1.07 billion negative impact on society. This is an issue that affects everybody.

There has been tremendous progress made in the past five years regarding military spouse employment support. The U.S. Chamber of Commerce and the Department of Defense have made concerted efforts to improve the situation along with a number of nonprofit organizations. However, there is still a great deal of work that needs to be done and I am not one to stay silent when my voice is needed to continue to highlight the areas that require more attention. Unlike the civilian world, expressing dissatisfaction as a military family member is not always warmly received, and often times even prompts stern defensiveness by federal contractors and employees, and the message falls into a silent abyss. In recent years, we have seen an uprising of nonprofits attempting to fill the gaps but the ongoing tug-of-war between military families, politicians, military leadership, front-line service members, federal contractors and employees, and nonprofits, and even between nonprofits themselves, results in the inefficient use of precious tax dollars and many claims of "success" that leave military families frustrated and underserved.

After years of being a single voice and setting aside my career ambitions to dedicate my energy to improving this issue for future generations, I am proud to unite with others through the Society of Military Spouses in STEM, a 501(c)3 member-run nonprofit organization. I co-founded this organization with another military spouse engineer and assembled a team of ten military spouse STEM professionals for the inaugural leadership team. The team is spread across the globe and working tirelessly to lay the groundwork for long-term sustainable success for future members and those that the organization will advocate for and serve.

If you are a military spouse in or interested in STEM, or an organization interested in partnering or sponsoring, please contact us at www.smsSTEM.org. Together, we can support and strengthen the individuals, communities, and organizations that will benefit from STEM contributions.

Cerno

Another important aspect of my life that I direct a great deal of energy towards is with Cerno, an adventure learning company focused on helping those who aspire to reach their potential. I am the director of adventure learning and co-founded this company after many transformative life experiences, and unexpected moments of enlightenment, which opened my eyes to the need to help people self-activate their growth and success. Transformative life experiences ... moments of enlightenment ... those are heavy statements. I will walk you through a couple examples because these are the reason my fire burns bright for Cerno.

As a military spouse, my life is full of change. So much change, I would categorize it as constant change. It doesn't seem to get easier but I seem to resist less, accept the uncertainty more, and capture the benefits even more. I have learned how to roll with it and make the most out of the situations in which I find myself and my family. It is not an easy life because change and uncertainty are difficult, but with every change, the next one seems more palatable. Outside of the military community, change is not as common but is still very difficult. Possibly even more difficult because without the developed tolerance, initiating change in the face of the unknown seems to be so scary that most people just avoid it altogether. Over the years, I popped in and out of many workplaces, social groups, and organizations and I repeatedly noticed people who were living and working below their potential because they were simply scared to make a change. They gave up on their dreams – settled for the status quo. I could see what they were missing out on all because they didn't want to make their lives more difficult and gave into their fears. Their employers, their families, our world – everyone was missing out because they weren't living out their potential. These moments helped me to see that it is vital to help people overcome their fears and make difficult changes that will lead them to a better life.

When I think about life experiences that transformed me, one in particular always comes to mind first. Losing my mother. I was 25, cranking away at my professional goals, living in sunny Florida with my handsome husband. I had lived away from my parents for seven years and was just starting to fully appreciate them and want them near. One day, my mother started acting strange so my sister took her into the emergency room. It wasn't long before they diagnosed her with Stage IV brain cancer. My mother was physically with us and could respond to questions but was otherwise mentally incapacitated. We never had the chance to really talk with her after her diagnosis so she was sitting with us but we had already lost her. She died four months later. Losing her changed my life. Everything I had in motion no longer mattered. All the tasks and to-dos instantly became less important. All of the frustrations and anger I previously had melted away. All that mattered was the people I loved. The precious years, days, seconds we spend on this planet. Living as we should live our life because we only get one and we never know when it could end. This centered my compass and helped me to see that we shouldn't get lost in the distractions and give in to the pressures that keep us from maintaining our energy on what is most important in life.

We picked the name Cerno because it means, "to separate, sift, distinguish, decide, resolve, determine; to see." We want to help people figure out what they are missing and really want to do, understand what is standing in their way and what they need to change and build to be successful, conquer their fears, and communicate how their journey will benefit their employers and the world around them. People want to live happy lives, employers want happy and engaged employees, and our world needs all of the talented individuals on our planet contributing to the best of their ability. We are helping the world achieve its potential through Cerno!

I recognize that I would not have developed Cerno had I not been a military spouse. I am grateful for the challenges and hardships because they have led me to this wonderful place. Looking back, my entire journey has contributed and enabled me to identify and serve this need so even though my journey has not always been smooth or pleasant, it has brought me to this rare and amazing opportunity.

I also recognize that this venture would not be possible without my business partner. We each bring unique skill sets and interests that make creating and running a business manageable and enjoyable. I had a business that I ran solo before Cerno and it is night-and-day difference. I realized early on in that business that I needed a business partner so I searched and extended a few invitations. Thankfully, I am now teamed up with a remarkable professional that shares my dedication to making our dream a reality.

We originally met while we were both working in an entirely different profession. Once we decided to team up, we threw all of our work in motion out the window and sat down at the same table, grabbed a drink, and opened up our minds to the vast possibilities. We tapped into our collective knowledge, diversified skills, and innovative energy and out of that came Cerno. At the time, we were geographically separated by ... the entire country! My family lived in Washington State and his was in Connecticut preparing to move to North Carolina. Our business model entailed situating ourselves in a physical location so we picked North Carolina as our hub and celebrated when our market research showed very favorable conditions for our new company. We are now several paces down the path of building a new business. I am living on the same coast so in-person meetings are much easier and my work schedule is synced with our team and our community. We have stretched ourselves to the edge of our comfort zone then stretched a bit more. We have taken calculated risks and not always succeeded and yet have continued to build and gain attention and support from the community we serve because we are doing it all for the right reasons – our passion to help people live out their potential continues to drive us forward. We did not escape the pains that come with entrepreneurship but we have overcome and continue to *Keep Climbing!* in the same fashion in which we help others.

2017 is a pivotal year for Cerno. We are focused on delivering three key programs this year: 1-Day Retreats, Team Adventures, and Give A Squat™ fitness challenges.

1-Day Retreats are single-day experiences that individuals can sign up for or companies can elect to send a handful of people. Retreat participants spend a day away from the office to disconnect from the chaos of life and reconnect with themselves during a day of learning and adventure. Each retreat has a specific topic so participants can pick topics that resonate with them.

Our Team Adventures are a fantastic replacement for traditional team building. Forget the boring classrooms and don't waste precious dollars on fun activities that don't deliver any other benefits. Our Team Adventures provide an exceptional experience through "Day in the Life of ..." immersion experiences designed to bring people together through shared challenges. New this year is the Survival Challenge Team Adventure, which is one of the "Day in the Life of a HERO: Military Edition" theme options. The Survival Challenge is perfect for groups of five to 54. We can come to your team or you can come to us.

Finally, Give a Squat™ is a monthly fitness challenge aimed at encouraging people to adopt healthy and fit lifestyles by challenging them to move their bodies more and push themselves physically to support a good cause! Every month the challenge sponsor commits to make a financial donation to the benefiting nonprofit after the challenge is complete. The amount that they donate is tied to the squat goals so the more squats performed by challenge participants, the more money the nonprofit will receive. All you have to do is donate squats! It is free to participate so share with your friends and together we will reach the challenge goals faster! Each month there is a new theme, a new set of goals, a new sponsor, and a new benefiting nonprofit. By May 2017, six challenges were completed, over 50,000 squats donated, and six 501(c)3 nonprofits were supported through Give a Squat™.

Beyond

This year, just like most years, I put down many balls because life happened: we moved across the country, purchased a home, lost a pet to cancer, filed and battled out a lawsuit in court, struggled with sickness affecting my respiratory system and mental processing for six long weeks while my spouse was gone for training, and are trying to figure out how to support an immediate family member who is facing a very serious medical situation.

Despite the changes and unexpected events, I try not to drop the major balls I am juggling and always even manage to pick up a few new ones because that is what military spouses do. We survive. We overcome. We find a way to thrive.

Thank you to my support system because without my family, friends, neighbors, teammates, mentors, champions, colleagues, and community, I would not thrive. Military family life is a team effort. Thank you for being on my team!

Michelle Aikman is Military Spouse magazine's 2016 Armed Forces Insurance Air Force Spouse of the Year. She co-founded and acts as the Director of Adventure Learning for Cerno, a Charlotte-based company committed to helping those who aspire to Keep Climbing! She is a recognized thought leader in the field of career management and speaks nationwide about attracting, retaining and engaging top talent and a diversified workforce.

Leave Your Imprint

Marcia Hutson

We all have opportunities to connect with people and make a measurable impact in our everyday lives. More times than not, this opportunity comes in the guise of uncomfortable effort in uncomfortable situations for the benefit of people who we might be uncomfortable with. Whether it be everyday situations or special situations, making a positive impact, does not happen by accident. It will always start with a decision to give of your highest self, fully and selflessly regardless of your comfort or circumstances.

If you know anything about being a military spouse you know there are generally three types – those who hate their base, life in general and complain bitterly; those who live for the military paydays and care very little about anything else that is unrelated to the pay cycle; and finally, those who try to make the best of it and look for ways to pursue their interests despite the often spirit-crushing burden of being lonely in a new place. The third group are, most often, the people who change their corner of the world for the better.

I'd like to think that I made a different at our first duty station fand in the community outside the wire where we spent just under two years. I remember being new to the PCS game, where you leave your life and career and go somewhere you have idea about. My sole concern was, "What will I do in North Carolina?" I had to leave my career in southern California and I was consumed with worry about how I would navigate the job market in rural eastern North Carolina. I was clueless, and no amount of internet searching helped. Fast forward to the actual move. Little did I know that I would then spend long, very frustrating months looking for opportunities. I took pains to remind myself that we wouldn't be there if it wasn't for his job and that is a good thing and that the right thing would eventually come along. You can say I wrestled with my attitude. Take note of that because you absolutely will go crazy if you do not do an internal, and external (for the sake of your loved ones), attitude adjustment as often as necessary. Let me be careful to say that it is completely okay if adjusting your attitude takes time.

Now, everyone will tell you, with the right amount of enthusiasm: "Use the installation resources to find jobs." Only a handful of those people will admit that the installation's resources did not work for them. I did my due diligence and checked out the

189

installation's resources, around month two. I went to the library and asked what the resources were. I was directed to a website. I checked the website; it hadn't been updated since 2003, and every single link was a dead link. The website referenced a partnership with the county off base and the family readiness center on base. I reached out to the family readiness center. They referred me to the link. I shared that the link was dead and that the contacts were all outdated and dead ends. It dawned on me during the conversation that every single newcomer since 2003 may have had this same conversation and yet here we were. So I made the decision then and there to offer to help, not just myself, but every other spouse or dependent who would be attempting to utilize those poor resources. I gave my name, my contact information, and said I was available to volunteer my time and skill to work through the website and update it and the relationships with partner agencies in the community.

I was told that every summer the Family Readiness Center utilized high school interns who would be updating the site but if they needed me someone would be in touch. I found it frustratingly odd that high school teens had more insight to the military spouse employment issue but decided to follow up the conversation with an email memorializing my offer to volunteer on this critical project. I waited another five months until someone contacted me and paid attention to the need for this update. (The family readiness centers are organized in a way wherein staff members are rotated often so they become jacks-of-all-trades and masters of none, add that to PCSes and retirement, and my offer fell through the cracks. I spent those five months stretching my liberties in the community, networking, speaking on behalf of spouses on my installation; it was amazing how little it took. I was automatically treated as though I had an official capacity as soon as I announced that I was a military spouse, although I made it clear that I did not. At this point I stopped looking for a job. It became a full-time effort to network on the installation and in the community.

I needed more information. To fully feel like you have a handle on the new location, you need to be there, present, showing up, seeking out, asking questions and listening, and that takes time. I had to get around people, get to know people – people have information, the more people, the more information. But getting to know people meant spending time outside of the house, time that I wouldn't be paid for, so it had to be purposeful and it had to be something I liked doing and had a natural knack for.

The volunteer bug hit me and I didn't even know it. I talked my husband into volunteering his free time as well so that I'd have a ride to my networking events. By setting out to serve a need greater than the sum of my own I had found my niche. I didn't know it yet but I was a volunteer job developer. One year and two months after we PCSed in, I got a paid job with this title with the city to work with the underserved communities in the local area, to do the same thing I was doing for military spouse, except now for the most vulnerable members of the city – the long term unemployed; a job that someone who knew of my volunteerism, notably, a fellow military spouse, recommended me for.

I went around the community, I opened my mouth and engaged business and regional partners in the conversation about connecting mostly highly-qualified, certainly hardworking military spouses with local employers, and I found surprisingly that everyone was interested in aligning their business with the military community. I didn't have convening power, but I engaged and shared the job information gleaned with those who did.

I actively listened online on the spouse's pages and started the conversation with, "Why not?" Enough people shared their experiences and unbeknown to me someone else was listening, someone who did have convening power and power to make the changes that were necessary at the installation level to get spouse employment on the family readiness agenda, not in the manner it was, cursory, but actively. That person was the commander's wife and the rest is history. She was more of a mover and shaker than I was and she supported and pushed through every initiative that benefitted spouses. It was the honor of my life to have someone with that kind of clout and convening power and access, taking the time to recognize the movement I was starting and voilà, add ten levels of "done."

Fast forward to today, there has since been installation-wide, command-sponsored, base agencies and county organizations involved; the first-ever, live online (Facebook) spouse employment forum. Vacancies and openings were announced, hiring managers shared their contact information, and details about how to apply and what may prevent applicants from being successful. Job offers were made, eligibility requirements explained, hiring policies shared, questions answered, and hope returned to the job-seeking spouse population.

Stemming from the success of that live forum, I was consulted to help the Family Readiness Center create a Facebook page which now serves as a central forum to share with community employers, both on and off base and military job seekers alike. Opportunities are posted directly by employers and also by a designated person at the Family Readiness Center. There is now a culture of wide-spread sharing of job information at squadron levels via spouse advocacy organizations.

The clamor around the issue of high unemployment of military spouses inspired the city along with the base to commission a survey which will be used to inform a new partnership program with the installation and city-wide employer partners to understand needs, qualifications, flexibilities, and accommodations required in the military spouse/dependents talent pool. Through my own employment with the city I was able to network with state officials and connected the installation with an existing statewide apprenticeship program to help with job training needs in the area for transitioning service members, military kids graduating from high school and military spouses.

I reached out to a military spouse entrepreneur group and started a chapter of the Milspo Project at the installation with ties to the local chamber of commerce and business ecosystem. This caters to the needs of military spouses who decide that self-employment is their best option and strongest desire. Due to advocacy with the city's downtown development corporation, military makers and small business owners are now widely invited to participate as vendors in city-sponsored vendor events.

Due to volunteerism and networking on a national scale, more national military spouse advocacy groups now have a presence in the form of chapters at the installation so spouses are more plugged in than ever. For a small base that was previously overlooked, the wider conversations on those critical issues are affecting the spouse community.

The real difference is seen in what has changed. For example more spouses have become employed and this is from being specifically recruited. Local employers now know who to contact at the installation whenever they have a recruitment campaign to share or are looking for specific talent. For years they had claimed that it was difficult to pin down a POC or that they'd be given the run around with calls to the Family Readiness Center. Now that there is a dedicated desk and channel of communication this is no longer an issue. Local employers are more tuned in to this new channel and now have increased access to a talented pipeline through revitalized job fairs attended by well-prepared job seekers. Local employers have a free forum via the Facebook page to get their openings in front of active and qualified talent. Military spouses and dependents now have more relevant and up-to-date job market information at their disposal to make informed choices prior to arrival at the duty station.

There's a marked improvement in the "job info sharing culture" in the online space and for those spouses who have joined the local chapters of these global spouse organizations, they have found suitable mentors in the spaces they occupy (career, business and entrepreneurship, etc.), and now have a local forum from which to communicate across the world with others in the same space.

For my part I feel like all I did was I become the change I wanted to see. I wanted to see someone doing more to help spouses like myself navigate the local job market which was new to them, so why not be that person? I wanted the tiny installation and its community to be more aware of what was happening in other places as it relates to the military spouse community and I wanted them to have access to the same beneficial events so why not try to figure out how to make it happen? Remember, I came from a larger city and I have to admit to being less than satisfied with the way the small installation felt "cut-off" or "passed-over" in the grand scheme of decisions and events that affected and impacted military spouses.

We are two hours in either direction away from the mammoth Fort Bragg and the equally large Camp Lejeune, and everything happens in either of those two places from large hiring events to milspouse festivals. Accessibility of the installation was not the problem, more than 5000 dependents and spouses live there; the problem was lack of action. No one knew who or how many people cared enough about what to organize and get them mobilized and attending, so unless an event was local and specific to the base itself, it just didn't happen. I might have written to every single major military sponsor and organization in that year to talk about our base and how perfect a time it was for them to add our base as a location for their programs.

To be clear, I didn't create resources that did not exist. I just wouldn't shut up about "why not at this base" and I reached out to regional and national partners to speak on behalf of the installation. I saw an opportunity to do what I was sitting around hoping someone would do for me and it made sense to become that someone. My choice to act wasn't an accidental one. I do believe that we as military spouses are privileged to experience the life we do, the access we're given because of what our spouses do and even though for some it is a lifelong career, in my mind it is but a fleeting opportunity to pay that privilege forward. Nothing you will ever do for yourself will ever be as impactful as what you do for others.

I also realized early on, before I got a handle on my frustrations, the effect my feelings of utter uselessness for not having a reason to leave the house every morning like my husband did, was having on my family. We were not a brand new couple, we'd been together for years but this first relocation was threatening to undo us because of my attitude to it. I listened to all the briefings about resiliency and readiness for the mission, and I knew I couldn't be the only one feeling like the lack of knowledge about my prospects in this new community was hopeless. On top of that all I had to do was connect online to see the state of morale in the spouse community. So when I made the decision to put my own job search on hold I did so thinking that if one less family would stop having arguments because the job-seeking spouse was frustrated, if one more spouse finds a job and is happier contributing to the family's financial security, if one more spouse discovers the ways to monetize her craft and is introduced to a network of customers and business mentors shifting the attitude of that family, there's more security and with security comes hope. Family finances is the biggest readiness issue for families, military or not, add in the extra stresses of military life (\the costs of relocations, childcare, deployments) and the way it all connects to mental, physical and emotional wellness of family members, other huge readiness issues for our nations service members and you understand the need for more to be done to engage the spouse and dependent community in these critical areas at their installation level.

If someone were to ask me how did I, someone with no official title from the base, make a difference, I'd start by saying that making a difference does not require a title. A title certainly helps and actually mandates you to make a difference, but I just decided to be the change I wanted to see. We as military spouses are part of the most inspiring community of individuals. The people who we love and care for have answered the nation's call to stand in defense of our values and freedoms. We have no further to look to be inspired to make a difference in whatever way we can. We don't have to seek out opportunities. The military life places us in circumstances where those opportunities abound. Start where you're at, offer your time, your talent, or your treasure in an area that you have an interest in supporting. Yes, you will learn that people who started out wanting to help may have gotten complacent or comfortable and still think that they are actually helping when they're not. This will frustrate you but stay enthused.

To make a difference you have to be agile, learning, adapting, pivoting and most of all accommodating to others. You cannot make a difference by yourself; you can get a lot of attention, but for impact, at some point you have to be part of this human chain. If I get a message from someone thanking me because they got hired, or their business is now growing, I know that I didn't actually create the job, or the opportunity, I may have simply connected some dots or physically helped with the application package, an introduction, or maybe I simply remembered that *Sarah* (not a real person) was interested in working at a health facility and tagged her under a new opportunity.

Your efforts can be very simple or more involved, what really affects the impact you make is the selflessness with which you do it. Giving of your highest self, regardless of the lack of personal benefit to you.

Marcia Hutson co-hosts a popular military podcast with a cultural perspective. (Mocha Milspouse Podcast). Although she and her husband have recently PCSed overseas she continues her advocacy efforts for military spouses.

Someday Is Today

Bianca M. Strzalkowski

I was so full of optimism when I loaded that moving truck and headed to a place foreign to me at just 19 years old. So awake. So 'my glass is half full,' and I was going to have it all: the Marine, the family, the goals, and the accomplishments. It was 2000 when I made the decision to leave everything I knew to live with my then-boyfriend, now husband. At the time, I didn't know a single thing about the military outside some understanding of Desert Storm when I was a young teenager. In fact, no one in my family had ever heard of Jacksonville, N.C. - the other Jacksonville (with the Florida city being more prominent), so beginning a new chapter near Marine Corps Air Station New River gave me a blank canvas to be whoever I wanted to become. This move meant I was saying goodbye to my comfort zone, which encompassed the small radius of the town I lived in in New Jersey, and also that I would be abandoning a very comfortable setup at Rider University where I was a freshman studying business. Then, the unthinkable happened and what military life should have looked like, never was, leaving me with a quick introduction to the lonely nights and eluded goals of a post 9/11 military wife.

The towers in New York fell just two months after I said "I do" in a courtroom ceremony. I was still just getting acclimated to living with someone and learning the ropes of being in a military town. Soon, I would learn, this unfamiliar place would wrap itself around people like me who instantly became alone in the wake of ongoing deployments. There wasn't much time to get to know this new world, one I really wished would have stayed a stranger. On that Tuesday in September 2001, I saw how quickly things change and that the rumor mill will frequently place military families on high alert over the unknowns. From that point on, any sense of normalcy escaped our lives, just like everyone else in communities around installations. What I thought I could do or how I would do it, needed to be adapted - including family life, college, work, and my own marriage.

When I moved to North Carolina, the belief was that I would transfer to school full-time so that I could finish the degree I started back home. Instead, I didn't qualify for in-state tuition because I wasn't a dependent yet, and so I had to work full-time to afford any classes. Employment became the priority and the school idea fell to the side. At each and every duty station, I took some notches off my degree

196

requirements and the four-year degree turned into the length of a PhD. A variety of life circumstances seemed to always get in the way of that finish line, including self-inflicted ones. We would get PCS orders to a new place, I would transfer schools, and in turn, I lost credits that were not transferable. It was a maddening cycle. Once I would have to re-take those already completed courses, time and money would be the issue. At times, it was defeating and at many points I considered quitting.

In the midst of the moves, we were growing our household. We already had one son and when we reached the desert of Yuma, Arizona, two more baby boys were added to our family. This would also be the point in my life where I faced the hardest challenges of being married to someone with a job that took us far from the people we loved. During the three years in the southwest, my husband left often to train aircrews in Hawaii, California, North Carolina, and Iraq. I was so isolated. As a young enlisted wife, I was in the minority at our unit. I didn't have a single friend or person to lean on, outside my midwife who was responsible for my maternity care. When I look back on pictures from that point, I see a sad emptiness in my eyes that I can easily recall today. On top of the loneliness was a host of stressful financial struggles that are often not talking points in our community for fear of judgment and even trouble at work. The relocation from North Carolina to Arizona meant I was leaving a management job, and the two salaries of bills we had established. The spousal unemployment issue is a very real thing.

The mix of isolation, financial problems, and solo parenting erupted into very real feelings of postpartum depression. Although, I didn't know that was what was happening. The once outgoing person I had been was now paranoid all the time about the safety of my kids. I wouldn't even leave them with their dad so that I could get a haircut. My round-the-clock paranoia took a real toll on my ambition and self-worth. I was disinterested in life. I was not a participant in anything around me, rather I just existed. I have no idea how I got through those times with my whole-self intact, and it is one of the many reasons I have tried to reach out to people like that girl I once was. Military life is full of pride and a sense of belonging, but it also challenges every fiber in you to overcome over and over and over. Luckily, the highest points in my life came after the lowest ones leaving me with the wholehearted belief that anyone can fight their monster as long as they find a way back to themselves.

I left that desert in 2008 and that girl stayed there, thankfully. Upon returning to the east coast, Ron would start an even more demanding job as a recruiter (who knew a non-deploying billet could ask for so much). There I stood at a crossroad, either I was going to make this life work for me with all of its imperfections, or my marriage would most likely crumble. A few months after all the PCS boxes were unpacked, I called up our unit's sergeant major and asked this unknown man to give me a shot at revamping the family readiness program so that it could make a tangible difference. I wasn't a fan of check-in-the-box programs that only sought to say it was doing something out of an obligation. He said yes, and just like that I was on deck for the game of life again.

Since my second year of marriage I was a big advocate of that program. I can only speak to how things are done in the Marine Corps, but it was the link that really helped me to find my own connection to the military, our unit, and other families. It gave me a sense of purpose outside of just being 'his Marine wife' by carving out my own role in completing the mission. Upon being appointed as the Family Readiness Advisor for this new unit, I decided to treat it like a paid job and went all in. Because we were a recruiting unit, our Marines and families were spread over the roughly 41,000 square miles that is the state of North Carolina. This required creativity in planning get togethers, but the real challenge came in getting spouses to give things a try. Moreover, I have always believed that when military spouses find a sense of their own purpose, something all of their own, that their outlook on military life is more optimistic. Thus, it also greatly benefits the state of the marriage. And so that was the challenge – get people who were probably feeling like me in Yuma to show up to our events, while building trust over geographic obstacles.

My entire life changed at that duty station. I made friends, I was working, the kids had activities, and the alterations we made to family readiness for independent duty assignments (those away from a base) were gaining traction throughout the entire branch. It is an amazing thing when you adapt a program to the needs of people, rather than expecting them to make a circle work in a square peg. We started doing regional meetups so that the distance to travel accommodated everyone. The sergeant major allowed me to do presentations at the all-hands briefs to educate the unit personnel on how they could benefit from getting their families involved in what we were doing. Then, we created a meals delivery system that rallied the spouses to make home-cooked meals for other military families who were going through hard times - new babies, deaths, or medical situations. This achieved two things: first, it made our spouses feel the support of their military family even though we were all scattered. And, it helped people connect in person who may not have originally gotten to meet. In the end, the overall changes made to that recruiting station in North Carolina grabbed the attention of all of Marine Corps Recruiting.

I was asked to travel to different states to try to duplicate these successes. In turn, I also made some lifelong friends out of these unexpected trips. By May 2011, the 35th Commandant of the Marine Corps, General James Amos, awarded me a Certificate of Commendation for my volunteerism. It was an eye opening moment to see how a new attitude and believing in change rather than letting things take their course, led me to the brightest chapter in my life. From here, life continued to get busy with unexpected opportunities. The work I did on the local level for my unit transformed into a national platform on spouse education. Remember that degree I started? It still sat left unfinished by the time 2012 rolled around. During my visits to different parts of the country, I learned many of my peers were experiencing the same obstacles when trying to complete their education. The frequent moves and demands on their spouse's career caused them to take the same road I was on, or quit altogether. It was disheartening to know that with all of the programs and services that existed, the quality-of-life issues were still front and center on the table with no resolution.

The reality is that there are just some components of military life that are not flexible. We have to move, they have to deploy, and the paycheck never keeps up with inflation. So, it is a confusing conundrum when all of the organizations and the government departments do not make policies that work with the characteristics of this lifestyle in order to ease some burdens. For example, I met with the Department of Education about an idea to make colleges more flexible in accepting transfer credits as long as the student's prior school had proper accreditation. Those conversations first occurred five years ago and nothing has changed. Why? Because most likely education is really about profits, not getting students a diploma in hand. (Yes, I am bitter on the subject). Second, tuition costs and childcare costs continue to rise. Why not offer more childcare grants to nontraditional students? Instead, we expect already strapped military spouses to take from the small budget that is the military paycheck and pay for both. Not to mention, the extreme limitations on financial aid that exist. We yell at spouses that they shouldn't wear their husband's (or wife's) rank, yet we create scholarships based on rank. (I'm looking at you, MyCAA program.)

Sadly, little has changed in any of those hurdles, but what has changed is the drive of the roughly 1.1 million men and women married to the U.S. Armed Forces. We are different. I am different. What we want is different from our predecessors of decades ago who mostly stayed home and filled volunteer positions. We still do those things, but we also do more. We hold elected office, like Christine Gilbreath, who is married to a member of the Texas National Guard.

We start nonprofit organizations to help others, like Bonnie Carroll who created TAPS - Tragedy Assistance Program for Survivors, after losing her own husband in a training crash. We write books (Kristine Schellhaas), star in films (Kerry Ann Ellington), fight on Capitol Hill for change, and so much more. Military spouses are simply amazing, and it is why quitting on yourself is no longer an option. We have too many role models that show us it can be done. And that, my friends, is how I finally did it. This girl got her graduation day.

Last year, I decided it was time to fully commit to getting my college degree completed. After all, not only was my own pride hanging in the balance, but my three boys had a front row seat as spectators to this thing. A friend, Army wife Janet McIntosh, told me many years ago that if I do not make my goal a priority, no one else will either. What did that mean? I had to stop spreading myself so thin with commitments and put this at the top of my to-do list. I could no longer feel entitled to taking a break or putting homework on the backburner for some other activity. I had to dive all in. It worked. Eighteen years after first stepping foot in that university in New Jersey, I finally walked across the stage to hear my name called. My family and friends watched from the stands as my tassel was moved from right to left, symbolizing the end of a very long journey. It definitely was not straight, there were so many detours, and it was not pretty, but it is done. I can easily say I am so damn proud of myself. I earned this all on my own with a little encouragement from different cheerleaders.

Military life can easily make you feel defeated, frustrated, and like everything that can go wrong, does. I will not preach lessons learned because I believe each of us have to stumble and fall before we triumph. However, I am fortunate to have gotten to know so many diverse groups of people over the close to two decades. They have endured challenges that would make some people shatter, but they still pressed on. I believe in you because they believed in me. Whatever your version of a graduation day is, you can achieve it. Rely on the people in this community and when life gives you a crossroad, take the harder path because the biggest rewards are at the end of it.

Bianca M. Strzalkowski is a communications specialist focused on creating content that engages readers. A proud Marine wife of 16 years, she encourages her other military spouses to find something they are passionate about to pursue. Bianca is a graduate of University of Maryland University College with a Bachelor's Degree in Business Administration and Journalism. She resides in Jacksonville, North Carolina with her husband and three children.

The Intersections of Military Spouse Life: Common Experiences

Suzie Schwartz

I married my husband when he was a captain. I thought I knew what to expect as I had grown up as an Air Force brat and had moved around the country and had also lived overseas.

Boy, was I wrong. I never realized how much of a built-in system kids have when they go to school. Yes, you leave friends behind, but within a month of arriving at new locations, just being in school gives you a ready-made friend-making machine.

I arrived at Hurlburt Field in Florida, having left my job, my friends, and my apartment, and I did not know a soul. I thought it would be easy to find a job, but it wasn't at all. I was a special education teacher and I knew my specialty was in demand at this particular time. I never even dreamed that being a military spouse was a negative for employers in the area. This was not the way I wanted my military spouse life to begin. I would stand at the picture window of the home that my husband bought and cry my eyes out, but then dry them and act happy when he arrived home from work.

I couldn't stay home all day and do nothing, so I joined a weight lifting gym and I accepted an invitation to attend the Officers' Wives' Club luncheon. I could not believe that I would belong to a wives' club, as that was what my mother did, not me. But I was truly lonely and another spouse agreed to pick me up and take me to the luncheon. I honestly don't remember a lot about the event, but the spouse that picked me up that day is my very good friend to this day. We have remained close, no matter where I have moved, and when we get together it is as if we were never apart. In this world of phone numbers stored in our phones, her number is the one number that I have never forgotten. Good friends make military life great.

The purpose of this introductory story is that senior spouses are you. The end of our military experiences may be very different from others, but we all start out the same. NO ONE ever dreams that their future will include being the spouse of a general/flag officer. That is never in anyone's mind as they go about just making the best of the opportunities and challenged presented to them in this crazy world of marrying a person in the military.

My husband and I continued moving and he continued to be offered wonderful opportunities of command. We had a squadron at McChord Air Force Base in Tacoma, Washington, and a Group Command at Hurlburt Field, Florida. I managed to work on and off during this time, to find my way to make an impact as a military spouse and also to pursue work and career opportunities for myself.

One day, while working at the Hyatt Regency Reston in Virginia, I received a phone call from my husband. This was unusual, as we had never called each other at work. I think both of us had workaholic tendencies, and both were proud of that reputation. He called to tell me that he had come out on the newest Air Force one-star promotion list. This is a really momentous occasion, and it honestly was not something that either of us had expected. I was so happy for my sweet husband, but I also knew I had to get off the phone quickly as I was about to cry and I did not want to spoil this fabulous day for him. I knew what this meant. I knew my life was about to go in a different direction. We were not headed toward retirement and maybe time for my career to flourish, but instead, it was going to be a time of greater responsibility and expectations of me.

It took me time to process this incredible change in our lives, but I did. I honestly just decided to make the very best of this new situation. In all honesty, what else was there to do? I wasn't sure how to do this, as I had always resisted being the "traditional" military spouse. But if we were going to continue in the Air Force, I was going to do the best that I could in my new role. I was not going to lose myself, but somehow I was going to figure out how to be positive and make a difference. I had never had any role models that inspired me. The only "senior spouses" I knew at the time were quiet and reserved, and I often wondered if they were naturally introverted or if the Air Force had instructed them to be quietly supportive but to not make waves.

Norty and I arrived in Florida for our third assignment at Hurlburt Field. This time he was to be the wing commander, in charge of the base and about 8,000 active duty airmen and their families. I did not know what to expect, but early on my husband told me something that stayed with me the rest of our Air Force life. He said, "You can do whatever you want on this base. You don't have to ask me to do it for you, as long as it is NEVER for us or yourself." This one comment would become my guide as I slowly figured out what was important to me and how I could stay "me" and also make a difference for Air Force families.

I ran almost every day and as I ran through the base I saw and met many wonderful people. I also saw and recognized many things that my husband never did. This became part of my mission and this may have been how lots of leadership couples managed their roles; seeing things and reporting them either to my husband or directly to the commanders responsible for those areas. I also learned from my husband to give people the opportunity to succeed. Sometimes, showing up somewhere unannounced is not the best way to accomplish your mission. Give people notice and they can prepare and may have the answer you are looking for when you arrive. It is also amazing what you can see and hear when you are discrete and unrecognizable. It is a powerful thing.

The military also sends leadership couples to various leadership training courses. Some courses are conducted by your service and some are joint courses run by the Department of Defense. At first I resisted these courses, telling my husband that if I had wanted to join the military ... I would have. But over time I came to value and even look forward to attending these sessions. They gave me a global perspective on world affairs and also kept me current in the family programs run by the services. Another aspect of attending these classes is that you meet people who you will run into again and again as you continue in your military journey. This was an unexpected gift, as many of these people would become our friends and joint teammates as we continued to move through our career.

Our Air Force life continued and my husband's final assignment was as the 19th Chief of Staff of the United States Air Force. This was definitely a huge surprise for us and we enjoyed every single minute of these four wonderful years. For me, all that I had learned in the past led to this. All the spouses I had learned from and watched through the years ... both the ones I wanted to emulate and the ones I wanted to make sure I did not.

I knew I wanted to support our families. I knew I wanted to support the Air Force and all of our airmen. I focused on improving Air Force family support programs. You also have to work within the framework of your Air Force programs and budget. I realized I could work on the Key Spouse Program that the Air Force had started several years before (modeled on the Navy's Ombudsman Program) but had never really been focused on by Air Force leadership. This required no additional funding, just lots of persuasion on my part. Persuasion is easy for me to do. I had NO problem talking about and pushing forward to help make this a program that would endure and benefit communication within the Air Force.

My focus came together pretty quickly. People were surprised and happy because they did not have to guess what it was that I was interested in and it helped shape our visits to Air Force bases throughout the country and around the world.

So now that I have laid out many of the events and situations, and even the wonderful and not so wonderful individuals who had shaped my development as a military spouse, let me share some of my thoughts on the role of a "senior spouse."

Make a difference.

You are finally in a powerful place, that just by showing interest and caring deeply, you can make a difference. You have access to the people making hard choices, so help them make those decisions by sharing the knowledge you have gained over time and the information you receive from other spouses.

Represent well.

As you travel the country and the world, you are representing your service and your country. The beautiful blue and white airplane emblazoned with "The United States of America" makes a powerful statement when it arrives on any tarmac. With that privilege comes responsibility. Represent well. You are there to learn about what spouses in that country are concerned about. You are also there to share as much information as you can with them and honestly, to make them feel respected and loved. You are also there to listen to their concerns and bring them back to leadership … and that leadership is your spouse, so you are fortunate to have direct access.

Thank everyone.

Thanking people is more important than you can ever imagine. After base visits, I sometimes had dozens and dozens of thank you notes to write, but I knew they were important. Every other form of communication can be done electronically, but handwritten thank you notes are universally appreciated. I had active duty airmen come up to me to tell me that their spouse kept few pamphlets or information received through the mail, but they kept my thank you note as a special memory.

Entertain beautifully.

For many people, a dinner or event at a senior leader's home is a once-in-a-lifetime treat. Make it special and memorable. You live in a home that is made for entertaining and I believe in using that home to make others feel acknowledged and special. People often remark that they finally live in the "big house" and they no longer have the need for so much space. Wrong. That space is meant to be shared with your service and maybe even more importantly, with people outside your service. In an ever-challenged military, inviting people into your home is more valuable than ever.

I would not change one minute of the incredible life I have lived. It is not the life I imagined when I married my husband many years ago. It has been an honor and a privilege to serve my country, even if I never wore a uniform. Remember, I am you. I am a military spouse who just happened to be able to serve alongside my husband and make a difference. You can, too.

Suzie Schwartz is the President of Military Spouse Programs for Victory Media Inc. As the wife of recently retired Air Force Chief of Staff, General Norton Schwartz, she has long been a champion for military spouses and families. Suzie actively serves on various boards of military related charities, including the Fisher House Foundation.

A SPECIAL THANK YOU

Bianca Strzalkowski, I don't know where to begin to thank you. You have helped me, listened to me, given me great ideas, were straight with me, and never ever let me down or let me fail since we have met. I can't thank you enough for our friendship. Your support has helped me through some tough times putting this project together.

Sheila Rupp, thank you for giving your time freely editing this project and letting me bounce ideas off of you and continuing to work on future projects together. Your support and friendship means everything to me.

Lori Simmons, thank you for believing in this project from the very beginning and helping make it possible. Thank you for your friendship and support not only for me, but for all military spouses. You will always hold a special place in my heart.

Emilee Rehling, thank you for answering all of my calls without fail for the past six months and helping me work through my ideas. I value our new friendship and working relationship.

Thank you to all of the writers that agreed to tell their story so others will know how incredible you are and what a big difference you are making. I am honored and humbled you said yes.

But mostly, thank you to my husband John Loken for putting up with my crazy ideas and helping me bring them to reality. Thank you for always loving me unconditionally and supporting everything I do. I wouldn't be able to do any of this without you by my side. I love you more than words can ever express. Thank you Tyler and Conner for supporting your mom and keeping me grounded. I love you both always. A special thank you to my beautiful granddaughter Harper for all your hugs and kisses, I love you!
—Cara

Thank you to my husband Michael – thank you for sharing this incredible journey with me, and for all of your support in everything I do, and loving me always, especially on my worst days. I love you!

To my wonderful daughter Emily – thank you for making me smile and laugh when I need it most. I love you, Little Bear!

To my parents and family members – thank you for supporting us even when it's difficult being away or not understanding the military way of life. I love you!

Thank you to Cara for inviting me to be a part of this amazing project! I am grateful for your friendship and this experience. To my military spouse brothers and sisters – without all of you, this military life wouldn't be the amazing adventure it is. The bonds we share are tight and everlasting, and I am grateful for your love and friendship.
—Sheila

Resources for Military Families

Armed Forces Insurance
    www.afi.org
CG Suprt
    www.cgsuprt.com/
Career One Stop
    www.careeronestop.org
Cerno
    http://gocerno.com/
Coast Guard Foundation
    http://www.coastguardfoundation.org/
Combined Arms
    www.combinedarms.us/
Corie B. Weathers: Breathing Life Into Marriages That Serve
    corieweathers.com
Disabled American Veterans
    www.dav.org
Fisher House Foundation
    www.fisherhouse.org/
Homefront United Network
    homefrontunited.com/
Lifeline for Vets
    https://nvf.org/
LightBridge International
    www.lightbridgeonline.org/
Love House Ministries
    www.lovehouseministries.org/
MCCS Forward L.I.N.K.S.
    www.usmc-mccs.org/services/family/l-i-n-k-s/
Military Family Advisory Network
    https://militaryfamilyadvisorynetwork.org/
Military Family Alliance Mediation Services
    www.milfams.com/
Military One Click
    militaryoneclick.com/
Military One Source
    www.militaryonesource.mil/
Military Spouse Advocacy Network
    https://www.milspouseadvocacynetwork.org/
Military Spouse Behavioral Health Clinicians
    www.msbhc.org/
Military Spouse Corporate Career Network
    www.msccn.org/

Milspousepreneur
milspousepreneur.com/
National Military Family Association
www.militaryfamily.org
Navy-Marine Corps Relief Society
www.nmcrs.org/
Nebraska Arts for Vets and Caregivers
http://nebraskaartsforvets.wixsite.com/veterans
Our Military Kids
ourmilitarykids.org/
PTSD Resources
www.afi.org/Resources-And-Tools/PTSD
PTSD: National Center for PTSD
https://www.ptsd.va.gov/
Resilient Endeavors
https://www.resilientendeavors.com/
Semper Fi Fund
https://semperfifund.org/
Society of Military Spouses in STEM
www.smsstem.org/
SpouseWorld 1to1
spouseworld.libsyn.com/
The American Legion
https://www.legion.org/
The American Military Partner Association
militarypartners.org/
The Veteran Spouse Network
https://www.texvet.com/vsn
The Yes Process
www.theyesprocess.com/
Tricare for Kids Coalition
www.tricareforkids.org/
U.S. Chamber of Commerce Foundation, In Gear Career
https://www.uschamberfoundation.org/in-gear-career
USAF Services Spouse Support
https://www.usafservices.com/Home/SpouseSupport.aspx
VALOR
www.valorclinic.org/
Veterans of Foreign Wars
https://www.vfw.org/

Official Resources

U.S. Army
www.army.mil

U.S. Army National Guard
https://www.army.mil/nationalguard

U.S. Army Reserve
www.usar.army.mil

U.S. Air Force
www.af.mil

Air National Guard
https://goang.com/

Air Force Reserve
www.afrc.af.mil

U.S. Marine Corps
www.usmc.mil

U.S. Marine Corps Forces Reserve
www.marforres.marines.mil/

U.S. Navy
www.navy.mil

U.S. Navy Reserve
https://www.navy.com/about/about-reserve

U.S. Coast Guard
www.uscg.mil

U.S. Coast Guard Reserve
www.reserve.uscg.mil/

U.S. Department of Veterans Affairs
https://www.va.gov/

A Word from Victory Media.

Military Spouse is the leading destination for the nation's 1.1 million military spouses, who contribute to their communities, the military, and each other every day. A division of Victory Media, Military Spouse publishes online and print resources for military families on PCS, careers, education opportunities and family life. It also recognizes the outstanding achievements of individuals through its annual Military Spouse of the Year® award and Town Hall programs.

Founded in 2001, Victory Media is a service-disabled, veteran-owned small business that connects the military community to civilian employment, entrepreneurial and education opportunities through its Military Friendly® G.I. Jobs®, Military Spouse, Vetrepreneur®, and STEM Jobs^{SM} brands.

Made in the USA
Columbia, SC
18 March 2018